RURAL SETTLEMENT IN ROMAN BRITAIN

To my mother, who
introduced me to
archaeology

RURAL SETTLEMENT IN ROMAN BRITAIN

Richard Hingley

Seaby
London

© Richard Hingley
First published 1989

Typeset by DMD, 52 St Clements, Oxford
and printed and bound in Great Britain
by Biddles Ltd., Guildford, Surrey
for the publishers
B.A. Seaby Ltd.
8, Cavendish Square
London W1M 0AJ

Distributed by
B.T. Batsford Ltd.
P.O. Box 4, Braintree, Essex CM7 7QY

All rights reserved. No part of this publication may be reproduced, stored in a retrieval system or transmitted in any form or by any means, electronic, mechanical, photocopying, recording or otherwise, without the prior permission of the publishers.

ISBN 1 85264 017 0

British Library Cataloguing in Publication Data

Hingley, Richard
   Rural settlement in Roman Britain.
   1. Great Britain. Rural regions. Human settlements, 43–410
   I. Title
   936.104

ISBN 1-85264-017-0

Contents

	Acknowledgements	viii
1	**Studying the countryside**	1
	What is wrong with Romano-British studies?	1
	The past	1
	New directions	3
	Theme one: Family and community	6
	Nuclear and extended families	6
	Community	8
	Theme two: Wealth and poverty	9
	New ideas – economic growth	9
	Indications of wealth	11
	Poverty	11
	The organization of this book	12
2	**The evidence**	13
	Collecting evidence	13
	Excavation	13
	Aerial photography	14
	Field survey	14
	Types of settlement	20
	Villas and villa buildings	20
	Non-villa settlements	23
	Local centres	25
3	**Houses**	30
	Defining house types	30
	Plan	30
	Building materials	31
	Architectural features	31
	Round houses	31
	One to three-roomed rectangular houses	35
	One-roomed houses	35
	Two to three-roomed houses	35
	'Cottage houses'	37

	Aisled houses	39
	The aisled house as a barn/farm worker's residence	41
	The aisled house as the residence of an extended family	41
	Corridor houses	45
	Winged corridor houses	47
	L-shaped houses and courtyard houses	51
4	Compounds – family farms	55
	What is a compound?	55
	Enclosed compounds and open compounds	55
	Houses, outbuildings and compounds	59
	Compounds on non-villa and villa settlements	59
	Compounds at local centres	71
	Summary	74
5	The settlement	75
	What is a settlement?	75
	The size of rural settlements	75
	Single farms	76
	Hamlets and small villages	76
	Large villages and towns	78
	The layout of villa and non-villa settlements	80
	The layout of local centres	86
	Variations in wealth	86
	Zoning of activities	87
	Summary	93
6	Local groupings of settlement	95
	Groups of non-villa settlements	95
	Villas, non-villa settlements and estates	100
	Close associations between villas and non-villa settlements	102
	Evidence for localized estates	102
	The estates of large landowners	105
	Summary	109
7	The network of local markets	111
	Market networks	111
	The villa and the market	116
	Summary	120
8	Regions of the south and east	121
	Villa regions	121

	Regions of non-villa settlements	123
	Imperial estates	127
	Physical constraints and social organization	128
	Summary	132
9	**The north-south divide**	133
	Settlement patterns in the south and east	133
	An intermediate zone	138
	Settlement patterns in the north and west	139
	Reasons for the north-south divide	144
	Economic poverty and stagnation	144
	The reasons for poverty	145
	Possible evidence for wealth distinction on settlement sites	147
	Summary	148
10	**Some themes in the archaeology of rural settlement**	149
	The family and the community	149
	Extended families	149
	Communities	152
	Status distinctions within the family and community	153
	Regions and economic growth	156
	New directions for study	157
	Was the villa a 'normal' development?	157
	Was the villa the only way to indicate status?	159
	Summary	161
	Notes	162
	Abbreviations	197
	Index of sites	199
	Bibliography	207
	Index	226

Acknowledgements

My greatest debt is to Christina Unwin who discussed the ideas behind this book, kept me on target, edited my text and drew the illustrations. I am also grateful to my parents for enabling me to spend leave from work reading in the Ashmolean Library. Thanks to various friends for reading and commenting on the text, particularly to Steve Dickinson. I would also like to thank David Miles, Richard Bradley and Simon Palmer for general discussion of the themes and ideas behind this book. Photographs were provided by the Royal Commission on Historic Monuments (England), the Cambridge Committee for Aerial Photography and Professor D Harding of Edinburgh University. Finally, my thanks to Rosemary Bradley and Struan Reid for their help during the production of the book.

Chapter 1
Studying the countryside

The archaeologist of Roman Britain is unusually lucky in terms of the material available to be studied. This is particularly apparent when this information is compared to that available for prehistoric or early medieval Britain. The advantage is two-fold. First, the evidence for the Roman occupation of Britain includes literary sources which are particularly useful if an attempt is to be made to understand how people lived. Second, Roman Britain has produced a great wealth of archaeological evidence and is considered by many to be the best researched province of the empire.

The quality and quantity of evidence for Roman Britain should result in an interesting debate on the nature of the Roman occupation and the indigenous contribution to the archaeology of the province. Why then have a number of authors recently stressed their dissatisfaction with the lack of advance and general academic stagnation in Romano-British studies? This is a consequence of the history of the development of the subject and the nature of current research. At present too much emphasis is placed on historical sources and the attempted historical reconstruction of the archaeology of the province.

A new perspective is required. The approach taken in this book underlines the importance of archaeological evidence and its vital role in the understanding of Romano-British society. It is also argued that knowledge of the poor and lowly is equal in importance to research that concentrates on the rich, influential and powerful.

WHAT IS WRONG WITH ROMANO-BRITISH STUDIES?

The past[1]

In the eighteenth and nineteenth centuries the Roman interlude provided an antiquarian field of study for rich, landed country gentlemen. In the nineteenth century a clear division was drawn between the 'native' and the 'Roman' population, the latter being considered to be widely dispersed in isolated stations among hoards of uncivilized, underclad natives. This model is ultimately derived from Britain's own empire and the relationship between the British rulers and the rural peasantry of nineteenth-century India.[2] The study of 'Roman' sites in Britain appealed to the landed gentry and to academics because they were seen as the homes of the military and cultural élite, individuals with whom the wealthy and educated of the British Empire felt a common identity.

At this time villas – particularly extensive, wealthy villas with large areas of substantial walled buildings and interesting figured mosaics – were thought to be of particular significance and were excavated in fairly large numbers.[3] In contrast to this the homes of the less wealthy and the poor were largely ignored.

Early in the twentieth century the frontiers of the study began to be advanced. The first work of importance was Haverfield's *The Romanization of Roman Britain*.[4] This book contained many basic concepts which have been widely adopted and have undergone continuous development over the eighty years since they were proposed. Haverfield's idea was that many of the apparent 'Roman' sites in the province, the rich villas and walled towns, were actually the homes of romanized Britons rather than socially and politically dominant immigrant Mediterraneans. Haverfield's work provided a major intellectual boost to the study of Roman Britain and also coincided with an improvement in archaeological field techniques.[5]

During the 1920s an important new figure appeared on the academic scene. The philosopher and historian RG Collingwood was the first to attempt a full summary of the historical and archaeological evidence for the Roman province. Collingwood's two studies also established a precedent for large-scale historical synthesis of the archaeology and history of Roman Britain and have been updated successively by a number of authors over the past fifty five years.[6] A consideration of these works indicates that one set of concepts has long been dominant in Romano-British studies.[7] This approach is characterized by an attempt at an historical analysis of the archaeological evidence and utilizes the works of classical authors, classical documentary sources and inscriptions to provide a chronological, political and social framework on which to hang the archaeological evidence.[8]

The value of the historical perspective in the reconstruction of the military, administrative, urban and rural organization and history of Britain appears to have been demonstrated and the historical approach has produced a useful framework into which the archaeological evidence has been fitted. An outline chronology for the development of the province has been established and the existence of *coloniae*, *civitas* capitals, *vicus* settlements and villas, all of which are also attested in the better-known provinces of the Roman Empire, has been demonstrated.[9]

The success of the approach provides an explanation for the similarity of accounts of the province over the last thirty or forty years. Each new synthesis on the history and archaeology of Roman Britain or on the archaeology of one aspect of the province represents, in effect, a new edition of the work that it replaces. A great deal of old and some new data are fitted into the same analytical framework, which in the main had been established by the 1940s. Why then has dissatisfaction with and criticism of the historical approach recently developed?[10]

Criticism of the 'historical perspective'
There can be no doubt that the new directions introduced by Haverfield and others resulted in an improved understanding of Roman Britain. There is still, however, a clear bias among all the accounts discussed above; the emphasis on 'Roman' attributes of the province with a relative disregard of the native.[11] Attention is focused on the rich and wealthy and little effort is directed to the study of the poor.[12] The quantity of attention lavished on the excavation of villas, walled towns and forts and the relative absence of detailed study of non-villa settlements and unwalled small towns demonstrates the bias,[13] as does the use of over-simplistic explanations for the significance of villas, non-villa settlements and unwalled small towns.[14] The approach does not give a true picture of Romano-British society or of the history of the province. Historical models are often distorted simplifications of the real situation,[15] as it is necessary to distort the archaeological evidence in order to fit it into the historical framework. The lack of advance in methods and theory of study over the past forty years is at least in part a result of a continuous process of distortion.

In this book it is argued that the archaeological evidence should not be forced into an over-simplistic historical framework. Roman Britain was a unique province; the major interest lies not in attempting to force the evidence into an irrelevant and pre-conceived framework of assumptions derived from a limited and biased sample of historical sources, but in understanding how the province differed from other areas of the empire.

New directions

Archaeological work during the last twenty five years has produced a considerable increase in the number of known settlement sites. This appears to indicate that the population of Roman Britain was far greater than had previously been considered and that the landscape was intensively exploited. Archaeological research indicates a very great density of settlement in many areas of Roman Britain.[16] This evidence may suggest that the population of Roman Britain was as high as four to six million (*see* Figure 1).[17] This is far higher than earlier estimates,[18] and in fact can be compared with those for the population of England

4 *Rural Settlement in Roman Britain*

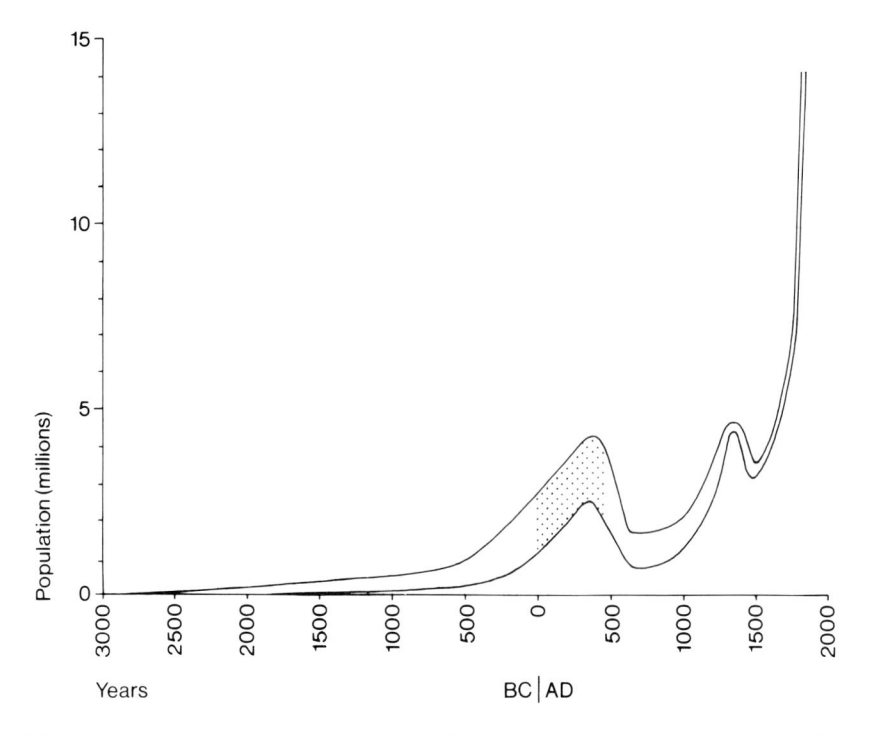

Figure 1 *A possible population curve for Britain from 3000 BC to AD 1801. The band of 'possibility' indicates the maximum and minimum population figures. (After Fowler 1978b, figure 1).*

during the fourteenth century at a time shortly before the Black Death of 1349.[19]

In addition to a general increase in the quantity of information during the 1970s and 1980s, greater attention has been directed to the study of non-villa settlements[20] and the less impressive small towns[21] of Roman Britain (*see* Figure 2). There is no doubt that this represents a more even-handed approach to the archaeology of the province. It is evident that, even in southern Britain, villas did not form more than 15 per cent of the total number of settlements.[22] Consequently there continues to be bias towards the selection for excavation of villas at the expense of non-villa settlements.[23] The new types of evidence which have been collected suggest, however, that new orientations are required to explain the existing evidence. If the evidence for the social élite in the villas and *civitas* capitals of Roman Britain is not fully compatible with the models of the historical approach, as will be shown below,[24] then it is highly unlikely that Britons lower in the social order would immediately have adopted, or have been forced to adopt, a complete set of Roman standards.

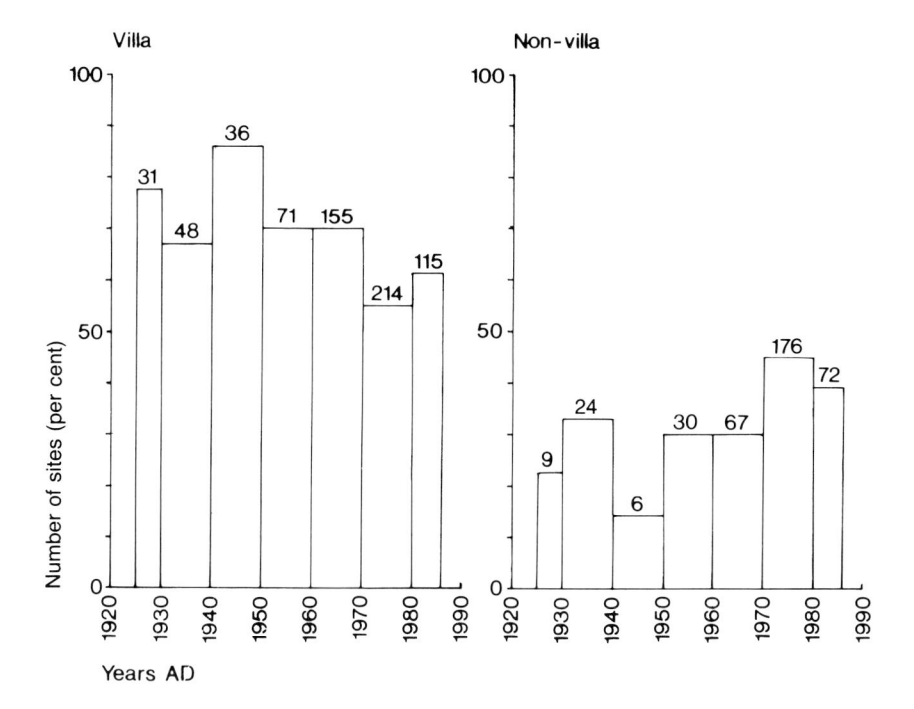

Figure 2 *Proportion of villa in relation to non-villa excavations. Figures denote actual numbers of sites excavated.*

In recent years a number of authors have considered approaches that differ from the traditional historical perspective.[25] The studies tend to be rather disjointed and deal with only one type of site, or one aspect of its function, rather than with the significance of whole landscapes of settlement.[26] The problem of developing a coherent account of the province from these approaches remains to be faced.

An integrated study will be attempted in this work. Particular emphasis is given to the use of the archaeological evidence for rural settlement as a source for the production and assessment of ideas about the organization of the Romano-British family and community. Two themes will be used to demonstrate this. First, the idea that the basis of family, and perhaps even community, organization in Roman Britain was characteristically 'Celtic' rather than 'Roman'. The second theme focuses on evidence for economic growth and the spread of wealth across much of the province, and the contrasting pattern of poverty in other areas. It is argued that this process was affected by the nature of relations within and between family and community groups in different areas of the province.

THEME ONE: FAMILY AND COMMUNITY

Excavation and survey work on rural settlements have produced a wealth of evidence for the character of buildings, the form of settlements and the distribution of settlement. There has been, however, little discussion of the value of this evidence as a source for an understanding of the Romano-British family and community. It will be proposed in this work that archaeological evidence provides a useful picture of certain aspects of family life in the province.

J Smith has suggested that over much of Germany, Gaul and Britain villas are found that were built largely in the classical architectural mode, but that these villas violate the basic standards of classical architecture in order to express the needs of a social order which was based on joint occupancy of settlements and probably on joint ownership of land. This joint occupancy may, according to Smith, reflect the 'kindreds' or extended families which were the basis of the Romano-British community.[27] In other words, the basic outward form of the building – the materials used and elements of the plan – were Roman, but the nature of the family groups who lived in these houses remained unaltered by the influence of Rome. This suggests a basic underlying continuity of family structure which contradicts the argument for change in many accounts of the archaeology of the province.

The definitions of the terms 'family' and 'community' are not totally straightforward and there is some difficulty in tying them down to the evidence provided by archaeological studies of settlement.

Nuclear and extended families

The household, or resident group occupying a single house, in modern Britain usually represents the family, but this is not true of all societies. It will be argued that the evidence indicates that families in Roman Britain often consisted of more than a single household. On many Romano-British settlement sites 'compounds' of related buildings can be defined and these often appear to include two or more dwellings. The terms 'nuclear' and 'extended' are often used in the discussion of family groups and are relevant to the discussion of the Romano-British evidence. The nuclear family is the group of mother, father and dependent children. The extended family is a larger group of which there are many varieties. No attempt will be made to discuss extended families in detail as the evidence is very complex.[28] A few points will, however, be made.

First, many societies are 'polygamous', each man having a number of wives. In other societies 'polyandry' occurs, where a group of men share a wife, or wives, in common. In some societies basic family groups consist of two or more generations of men or women related through a common father or mother and descended from a common ancestor (*see* Figure 3). In these extended families each component nuclear family often forms a distinct family group and is a sub-unit of a larger extended family. The actual size of the family group, or number of generations represented, and the rules that define its membership differ between societies.

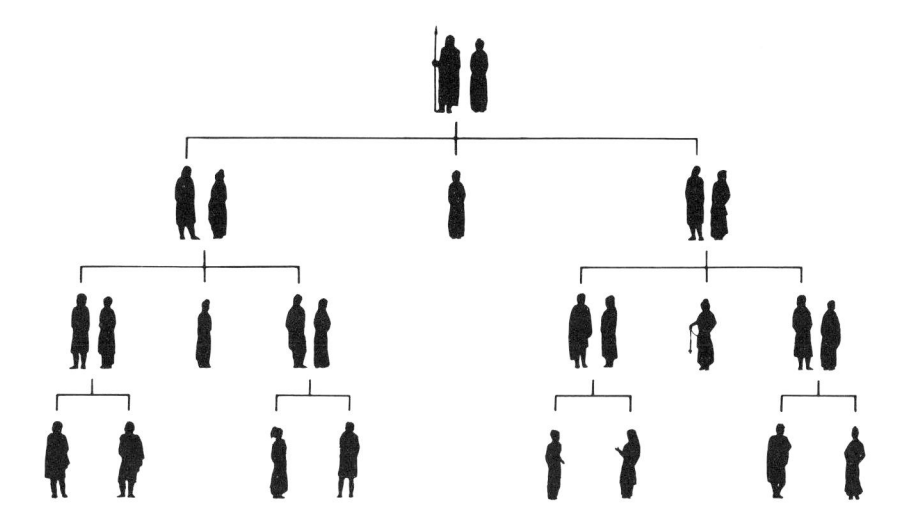

Figure 3 *A model for a three-generation family. (After Charles-Edwards 1972, figure p 15).*

Literary evidence indicates that Roman marriages in the imperial period involved a single man and wife. In other words the family group in Italy at this time was a nuclear group consisting of father, mother and dependent, unmarried children. The Roman term *familia*, however, did not have the same meaning as the modern 'family' and included everybody and everything under the control of the household head. Wealthy Roman families often included numbers of slaves and the *familia* could be very large, containing scores or even hundreds of members. In contrast to this the households of those too poor to afford slaves would have been nuclear.[29]

Unlike the Romans, the typical Celtic family outside the bounds of the Roman Empire appears from the limited literary evidence to have been extended. The area where the evidence is most complete is early historic Ireland. The Irish customary laws appear to indicate that the most effective local social unit comprised the descendants of a common great-grandfather. In other words, for the purposes of inheritance and

8 *Rural Settlement in Roman Britain*

for most forms of obligation an effective extended family of three generations existed (*see* Figure 3). This extended family would consist of all the male descendants of a common great-grandfather, including the wives and unmarried children of the sons.[30] It also appears that in Celtic society rich individuals were able to have more than one wife and that the number of wives depended on the wealth of the individual household head.[31] The average male would clearly have had only a single wife, otherwise there would have been many unmarried males. Celtic families may therefore have varied in size from area to area, with the wealthiest having the largest family group.[32]

The concept that extended families of this 'Celtic' type existed in pre-Roman Gaul and Britain has been discussed by a number of authors.[33] Archaeological evidence to support the existence of the extended family in the Iron Age has been obtained from a re-analysis of the evidence from the Glastonbury lake village (Somer). At this site a repeated 'module' occurs, comprising a range of houses and structures including two large round houses occupied by males and a single hut occupied by females, with associated storage and working areas. Seven of these modules or compounds have been identified and each one housed a kin group of around twenty persons. An important aspect which may be of relevance to the study of Romano-British settlement is the apparent distinction between the areas of the settlement reserved for the women of the family and those occupied by the men. At Glastonbury this may relate to a type of social structure in which men held groups of women in common.[34]

A number of authors have proposed that the pre-Roman extended type of family survived among Romano-British communities.[35] Of particular interest is the concept introduced above that the ground plan of many Romano-British villas demonstrate the existence of extended families based on two or more houses.[36] This has been called the 'unit system' theory. The unit system on villa sites is characterized in two ways. First, on some sites two suites of rooms can be identified within a single building and this probably indicates two families living within the single house. Second, on other sites two distinct buildings exist alongside one another within the same villa compound and again an extended family is indicated. Studies considered in this work indicate that the unit system also occurs on non-villa settlements.

Community

The extended family may occasionally have comprised a fairly large-scale social group, possibly up to three generations. The community, however, was larger in size and consisted of a group of families. As with the nuclear and extended family, the community may have been defined through descent from a common ancestor. It is possible that the Celtic or Irish extended family, after growing to a maximum size of three or four generations, could split but that the members of the two new extended families retained some ties. These may have been practical, for instance common ownership of certain resources such as arable land, pasture and woodland.[37] Alternatively, the ties that bound the community together could have been rather more ephemeral; some human communities are united by nothing more concrete than a sense of common descent and kinship, or connections with a particular god or ancestor, or vague common rights to areas of land.

Very little work has been undertaken on the Romano-British community. A number of case studies discussed here may indicate, however, that communities had an important significance in determining patterns of settlement and the response to Roman contact in the province.

THEME TWO: WEALTH AND POVERTY

Differing areas of wealth and poverty can be identified within the Roman province of Britain. It is usually suggested that the wealthy areas are characterized by the occurrence of villas and towns, while in the poor areas non-villa settlements predominate to the virtual exclusion of villas. This theme involves discussion of the reasons for differing patterns of wealth and poverty across the province.

New ideas – economic growth

Although the evidence for the density of settlement has multiplied, and population estimates have been adjusted upwards, the explanations for this evidence have not been changed by new information. A population of the order discussed above raises questions about Romano-British society and economy. For instance, how did such a densely populated and exploited countryside relate to the towns? How large were agricultural surplusses? Who consumed them, and through what means of marketing and distribution?[38] Of equal importance is an understanding of the forms of land tenure and social organization which enabled such intensive exploitation of the landscape.

The evidence for dense population provides partial support for a body of theory, outlined by Hopkins, for economic growth in the Roman Empire during the late first millennium BC and first two centuries AD.[39] This growth involved increased production, trade and consumption throughout much of the empire. Agricultural production became more intensive and there was an associated increase in population. The general requirements of the inhabitants of the empire for industrially produced goods increased and at the same time a higher proportion of the population became involved in activities other than agriculture, especially in administration and industrial production. Those involved in administration and industry no longer produced all their own food and had to be provided for by others within the empire. Thus a greater demand existed for surplus agricultural produce.

What were the factors that led to economic growth in Roman Britain? Iron Age societies in Britain generally appear to have been fairly small-scale and to have been in a continuous state of warfare and conflict.[40] The production of surplus agricultural and industrial goods in Iron Age Britain was constrained by the decentralized and warring nature of society. The Romans introduced several innovations of which the following are important.

Peace, order and security
The Roman Empire imposed a new order on the people of Britain. Rural communities were integrated into tribal groupings, each based on a single *civitas* (tribal) capital, and a number of *civitates* (tribes) occurred across the province. Peace was enforced within the territory[41] and peaceful conditions persisted throughout much of the Roman period.[42] Peace and stability were important because they created the conditions in which the production of a regular agricultural surplus was possible.

Coinage and monetary supply
A second innovation was the regular supply of coinage. Although coins were produced by a number of tribes in Late Iron Age Britain, Rome introduced a standardized coinage that could be used for exchange purposes all over the province and indeed the empire. In Britain taxes appear to have been collected in cash during the first and second centuries. This may have stimulated the production of surplus agricultural goods and industrial goods for sale on the market.[43] The importance of coinage is that in addition to paying taxes it could be used for a range of other purposes, such as purchasing luxury goods in the market.[44]

Market exchange and industrial production
Rome also encouraged the development of market exchange. Exchange and trade occurred in Iron Age Britain and may have been responsible for the distribution of some goods across Britain, particularly in the Late Iron Age. The large-scale movement of goods within and between provinces, however, was a new factor and a hallmark of the early Roman Empire.[45]

The growth in the quantity of long-distance trade was also associated with an increased desire for luxury and manufactured goods by the rural and urban populations of the empire.[46] The evidence for increased consumption in Britain is demonstrated, for instance, by the occurrence of industrially-produced pottery and other goods on even the poorest settlements. The material requirements of the average Briton had increased and new goods were desired.[47] The rural peasant landowner therefore became incorporated into the economy of the empire through the need to produce a surplus to be exchanged for money to pay taxes. Further surplus wealth was often produced and could be invested in industrially-produced pottery and other goods. In addition, new types of buildings which indicated the status of their builders could be constructed.

Indications of wealth

The important indicators of economic growth and prosperity are usually thought to be the villas and local market centres of the province. Rivet has suggested that villas and small towns were interdependent. The villas were based on the creation of an economic surplus and were material symbols of its investment as indicators of status. The agricultural surplus necessary for the process of development was created through ownership and exploitation of an estate, which was often worked by tenants or slaves.[48] Surplus agricultural goods produced on the estate were marketed to create what Collingwood has termed 'capital'.[49] The local market centres were the markets through which the agricultural goods could be sold and the surplus cash accumulated which enabled the construction of villas.[50] The local centres of the province originated and developed through their function as markets. In other words, villas and local market centres appear to have formed part of an integrated economic system in some areas of the province. This would suggest that regions in which villas and local market centres occur are those in which surplus wealth was being created.

It is necessary to keep an open mind when considering the evidence, however, as it will be suggested below that some wealthy settlements did not have villa-type buildings. It may be simplistic in some cases to interpret non-villa settlements as the homes of the poor, as the occupants of some of these settlements may actually have been relatively wealthy.

Poverty

If it is argued that villas and local market centres are indicative of wealth, then it appears that economic growth was a regional phenomenon. Some areas of the province developed a fairly lively market economy soon after the conquest, but in other areas villas do not appear until the third

12 *Rural Settlement in Roman Britain*

century or later. In other words, the spread of surplus wealth into the southern British countryside occurred at different rates in different areas. Indeed, in some areas a villa economy does not develop at all during the Roman period.

The economies of the societies in these 'stagnant' areas form a contrast to the developed regions of southern Britain. The stagnant areas include most of the north and west of the province. In addition, economic stagnation appears to have characterized some areas of southern Britain, for instance the Fenland and some of the chalk upland areas and river valleys of southern Britain.[51] Why did these areas fail to develop a villa economy? Explanations that focus on physical factors (soil, climate), tenurial factors (the presence of large estates) and social factors (social organization) will be explored.

THE ORGANIZATION OF THIS BOOK

The two themes introduced above are discussed in this book through a study of the evidence for Romano-British rural settlement. Chapter 2 is concerned with the ways in which the evidence for rural settlement is collected and also with the definition of differing types of rural settlement. The following chapters discuss the evidence for rural settlement at various levels of scale. Analysis begins with the evidence for houses and this is followed by the evidence for compounds. Information for the settlement is discussed in Chapter 5 and then varying types of settlement pattern at a regional scale are analyzed. The final chapter summarizes the evidence for Romano-British rural settlement.

Chapter 2
The evidence

COLLECTING EVIDENCE

Three methods of obtaining evidence for Roman settlement exist. These are excavation, aerial photography and field survey.

Excavation

Excavation has a lengthy history, but methods and standards have changed dramatically over the past hundred years. The quality of information from many of the early excavations is not high enough for much use to be made of the results. The majority of archaeologists prior to the beginning of this century appear only to have been interested in the plans of stone-walled buildings and possibly to a lesser degree in the artefacts from these buildings. This is particularly clear in the case of the early excavation of large wealthy villas in many parts of Britain.[1]

In the twentieth century the methods of excavation have become far more scientific but all too often, even in comparatively recent times, the recovery of the plans of stone-walled buildings appears to have been the overriding aim of excavation. Buildings of timber, daub and cob appear to be far more common on rural sites than buildings of stone, but it is only in recent years that archaeologists have started to pay serious attention to timber and cob buildings.

In addition to an interest in studying stone-walled villa houses excavators often appear to have felt no need to explore beyond the bounds of the single building. The additional dwelling houses, outbuildings and field systems on the settlement have often been ignored. This type of approach can result in a misunderstanding of the significance and context of buildings on a site. At Catsgore (Somer) the area of the settlement excavated in the 1950s has been referred to as a villa;[2] subsequent excavation, however, has indicated that the site is actually an extensive non-villa settlement with about twelve separate farm compounds.

Webster remarked in 1969 that only seven or eight villa excavations could provide answers to the basic questions that he wished to ask.[3] Only recently have attempts been made to excavate complexes of contemporary and related buildings on a large scale. Archaeologists now appreciate that it is necessary to excavate sites on a far larger scale if useful information is to be gained on the family structure and economy of their inhabitants. Without this type of work the vital evidence for farm compounds and settlement organization discussed in later chapters cannot be collected. In addition to the excavation of related groups of buildings, detailed stratigraphic work is necessary to reconstruct the detailed structural sequence of stone and timber buildings and to reveal the chronology of the development of individual settlements.

During the 1970s and 1980s large-scale, professional excavations have become fairly common.[4] It is true, however, that the number of well-excavated settlements remains fairly small. In addition, some of the sites that have been excavated have been so badly damaged by later occupation, also in many cases by the plough, that they yield little information of interest for the study of the family groups which occupied the sites. Although it is possible to begin to ask interesting questions from the available evidence, many of them cannot yet be fully answered and further research will be necessary.

Aerial photography

Excavation is the most important way of examining the individual site, but aerial photography and field survey are of greater use for the investigation of settlement patterning across the landscape. Aerial photography can produce a useful record of sites that survive as earthworks (*see* Figure 4). In addition, many sites that have been flattened by cultivation show crop marks or soil marks at certain times of the year (*see* Figure 5). Diagrams can be produced to illustrate the layout of earthwork and crop mark sites (*see* Figure 6). The details of how these marks are produced are discussed by a number of authors and will not be considered in this book.[5]

Aerial photography provides information about the layout of the individual site and also the distribution of sites across the landscape. Aerial photography does not, however, provide direct evidence on the dating of crop mark sites. Some attempt can be made to date such sites through morphological characteristics, but this can be a dubious procedure.[6] Excavation or field survey is necessary if crop mark evidence is to be used as anything more than an indicator of potential areas of settlement.

Field survey

Two types of field survey exist: earthwork survey and surface collection. Many sites of Roman date survive in the uplands of northern and western Britain (*see* Figure 4). Until recently sites of this form survived

The evidence 15

Figure 4 *Aerial photograph of a non-villa settlement at Crosby Garrett (Cumbr). Copyright Cambridge University Committee for Air Photography.*

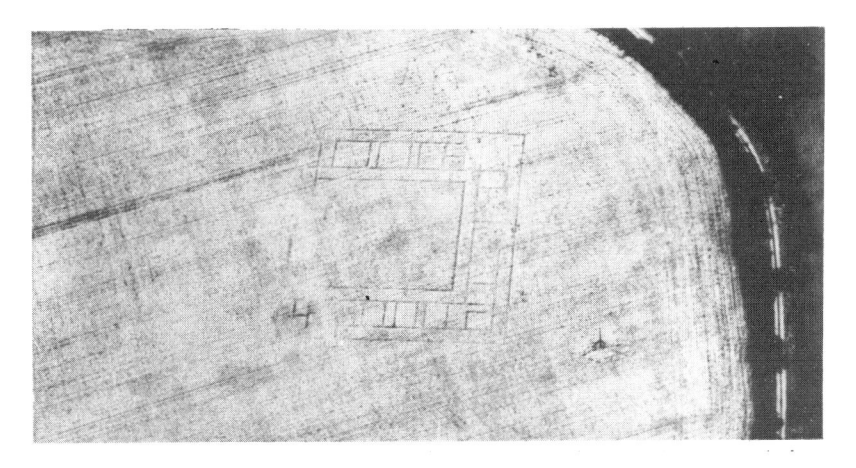

Figure 5 *Aerial photograph of the villa at Chignall St James (Essex). Copyright Cambridge Committee for Air Photography.*

in marginal agricultural areas of southern Britain – for instance on the chalk downlands of Wessex and the Fenland of Cambridgeshire and Norfolk – although many of these sites have subsequently been flattened by cultivation. The field survey of archaeological sites that have been ploughed flat is also a valuable technique, as the plough often disturbs

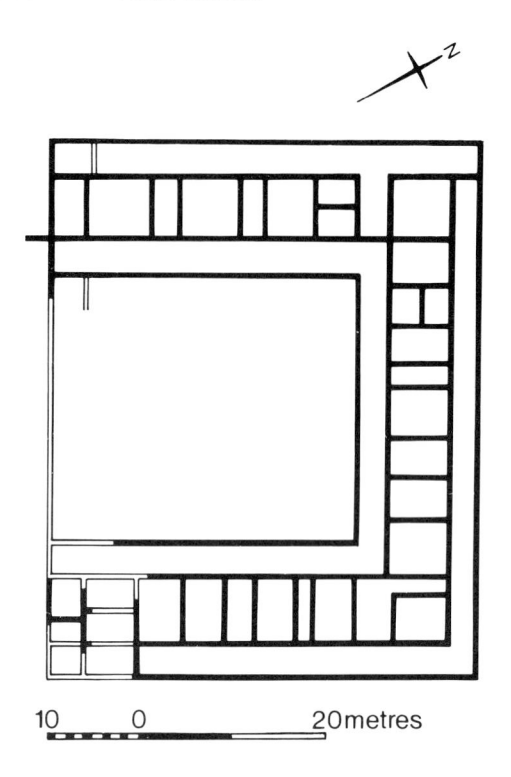

Figure 6 *Plot of the crop marks of the villa at Chignall St James (Essex).*

artefactual material providing information on the chronology and extent of the site. Field survey combined with aerial photography can cover larger areas than excavation and it is possible using these techniques to reconstruct the distribution of settlements across the landscape. Field survey and aerial photography are therefore useful as complementary techniques to excavation.

Hallam's survey of the dense concentration of Romano-British sites in the Fenland of Cambridgeshire, Lincolnshire and Norfolk was the first effective, large-scale field survey project on Roman sites in this country.[7] The soils of the Fens are particularly susceptible to the development of crop marks and the area was flown over frequently for many years. This susceptibility, combined with the absence of large-scale prehistoric and medieval settlement of the Fens, has resulted in the definition of large and almost complete Roman settlement landscapes (*see* Figure 7). Hallam, and a number of other archaeologists, visited most of the occupation sites revealed by aerial photography and collected dating evidence from the surface of the ploughed fields. The resulting reconstruction of the social and economic geography of the Fens

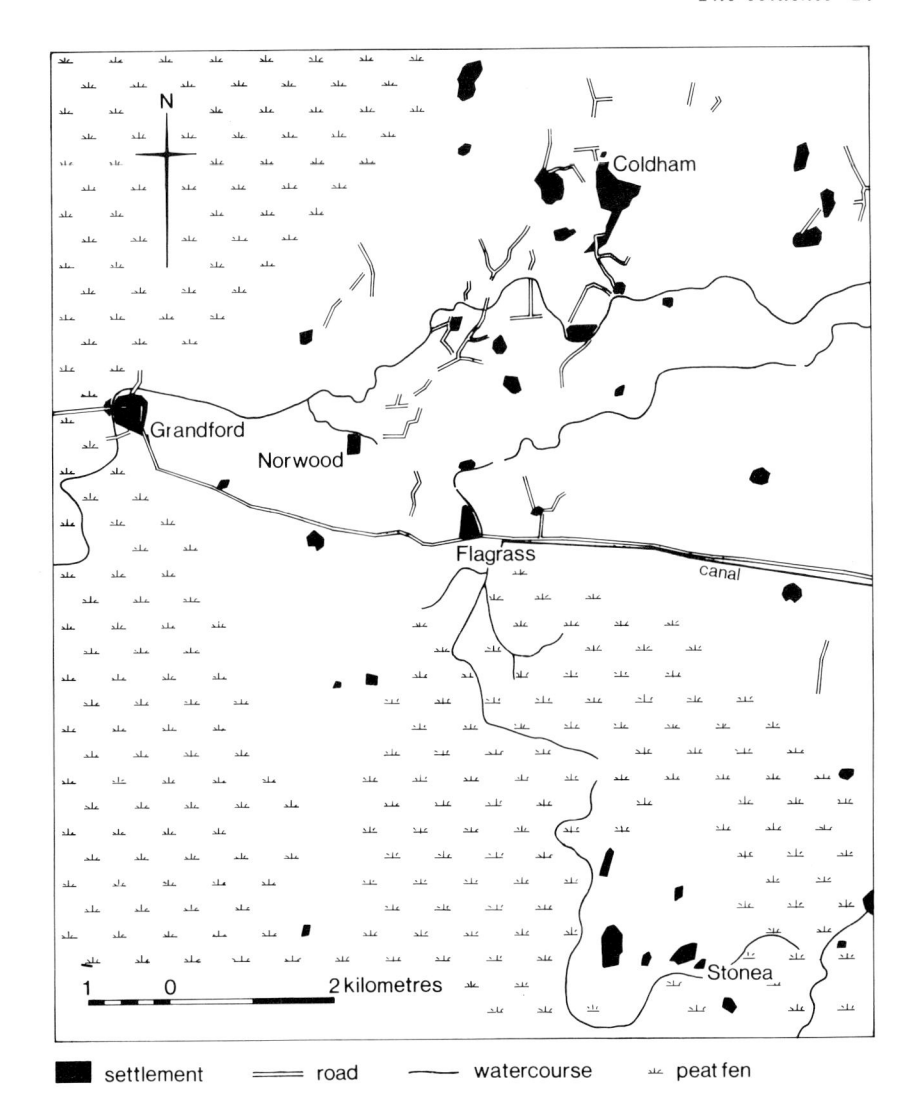

Figure 7 *A Fenland landscape. The area around Grandford and Stonea. (After Potter 1981, figure 3).*

remains the most useful published survey of a large area of landscape in the Roman province.

Field survey is now a very popular activity and is being conducted in some form in most of the counties of Britain. Methods and aims vary, however, with each project. At Lockington (Leic) a single settlement site has been investigated (*see* Figure 8), while at Maddle Farm (Berks) the lands of one villa farm have been revealed by manuring scatters. At

18 Rural Settlement in Roman Britain

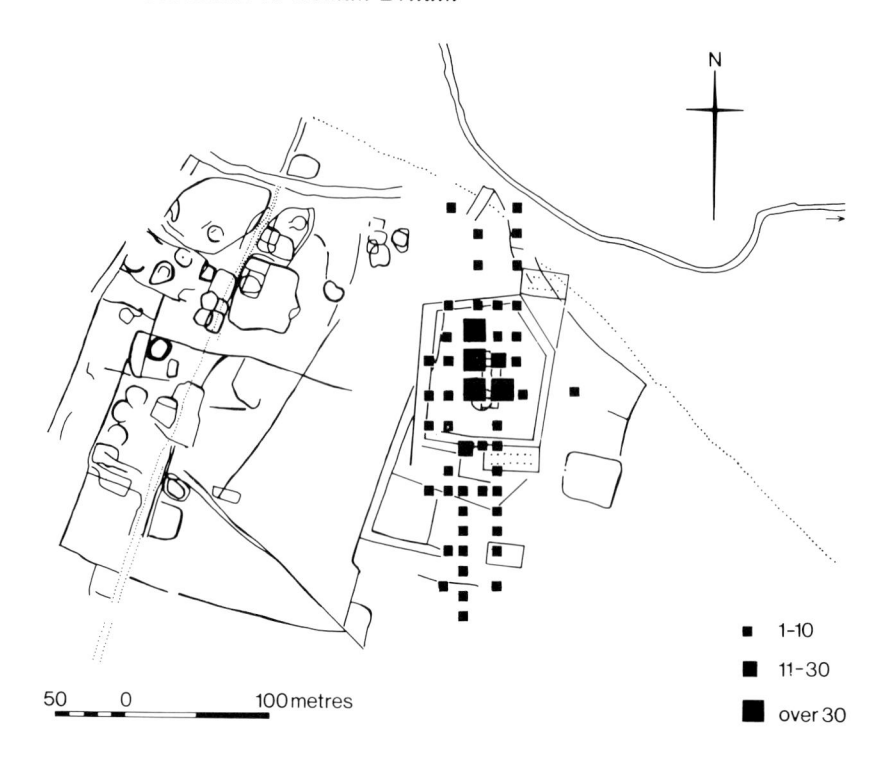

Figure 8 *The distribution of* tesserae *in relation to the villa and non-villa settlement at Lockington (Leic). (After Clay 1984, figure 6).*

Littlebury Green (Essex) a region including a number of settlement sites has been investigated (*see* Figure 9), while at Wharram (N Yorks) a number of Roman sites spread over the area of six medieval townships have been examined. The high standards of these surveys are not, however, shared by all projects. It has recently been argued that Britain lags behind areas of the Mediterranean in the scale and organization of field survey projects. It is possible that this is a consequence of the pressures of rescue archaeology which have resulted in each regional unit and institution pursuing its own individual methods and objectives. Comparison of work undertaken in different areas of the province can therefore be difficult.[8]

The progress of field survey in the past twenty years is demonstrated graphically by comparing the information on two maps of rural settlement in northern England, one compiled in the mid-1960s and one in the mid-1980s (*see* Figure 10). Large numbers of new sites have been located through aerial photography and ground survey and the knowledge of the distribution of sites in England transformed. It is

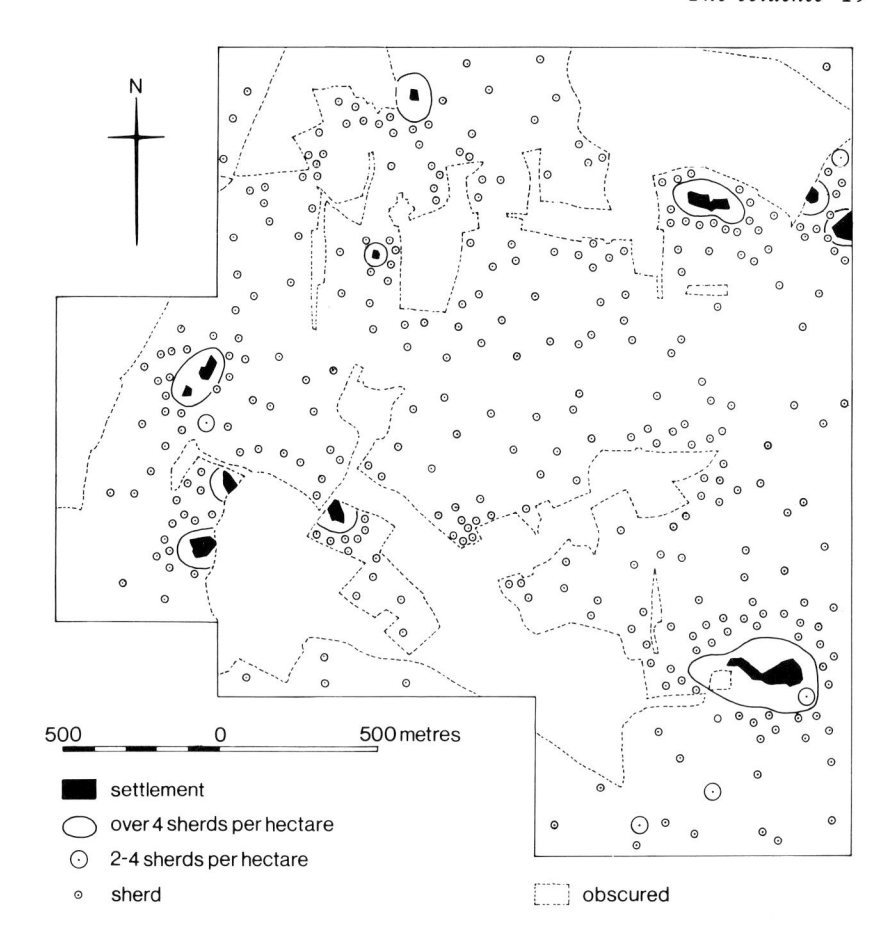

Figure 9 *The distribution of Roman settlements and pottery at Littlebury Green (Essex). (After Williamson 1984, figure 2).*

important to stress, however, that although a large quantity of information exists for Roman rural sites this represents only a minute fragment of what once existed. Many sites have been totally destroyed by activities such as quarrying and house construction – evidence now lost for ever. Nevertheless, many additional sites remain to be located in the British countryside.

Intensive survey work indicates that only fragments of the true picture of rural settlement in Roman Britain are available to the contemporary archaeologist. The available evidence may impose incorrect interpretations on the researcher and there is an evident need to be open-minded and critical in assessing the models that are put forward in this book or elsewhere.

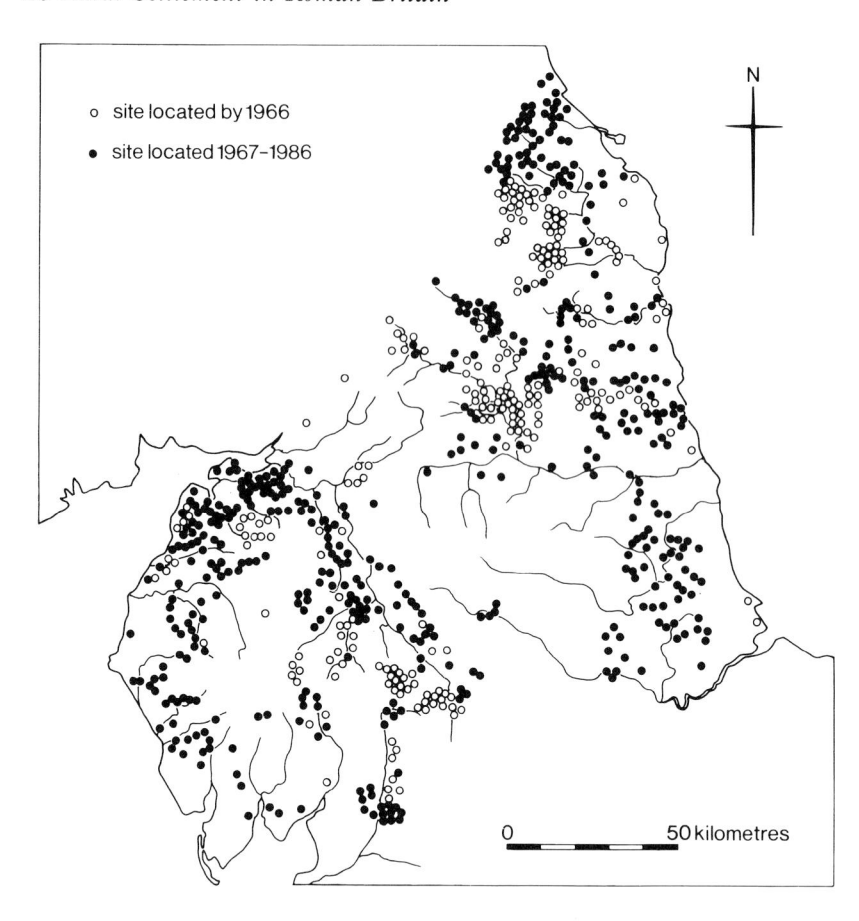

Figure 10 *Progress of settlement research in northern England and southern Scotland. (After G Jobey 1966, figure 1 and Higham 1986, figure 5:1).*

TYPES OF SETTLEMENT

In archaeological studies sites are usually placed into one of three 'types': villas, non-villa settlements/'native settlements' and small towns of the province.

Villas and villa buildings

At least two types of definition of the villa exist in the literature on Roman Britain, an archaeological and an historical definition.[9] A number of researchers have recently proposed the abandonment of the term 'villa'. This is a consequence of the fact that the historical model proposed for the villa is inadequate in the context of the province of

Britain; in short, the archaeological evidence for the province does not fit the model. The term is, however, firmly entrenched and it is proposed in this book that its abandonment is not a practical proposition.

The term 'villa' is widely used by Romano-British specialists when studying the countryside of Britain to the south and east of a line from the River Tees at Middlesbrough via the Bristol Channel to the River Exe at Exeter.[10] The villa, in archaeological terms, is a domestic building with evidence for the investment of a considerable level of surplus wealth in its construction. Characteristics that indicate this wealth include elements of building structure that can be recognized as distinctly 'Roman', a trend resulting from the desire of individuals with surplus wealth to appear more 'Roman'.[11] The relevant building techniques and forms adopted were probably derived mainly from the Roman army, foreign settlers in the province and urban administrative buildings.

Elements that indicate the investment of wealth include building plan and elevation, the use of stone and tile or slate in construction, and often the occurrence of additional features which point to a high level of romanization such as mosaic, tessellated floors, hypocausts and bath-houses.

The use of stone rather than timber and daub combined with the replacement of round indigenous buildings with rectangular forms is often taken to indicate the adoption of Roman norms on native sites.[12] It is argued below, however, that cottage houses and other simple rectangular buildings should not be defined as villa buildings unless some other indicators of surplus are present.[13] The same is true of aisled houses, which also occur in a variety of contexts, in some cases as the homes of fairly poor families, in others as villa buildings.[14]

Two particular building types, winged corridor houses and courtyard houses, represent an attempt to attain or indicate status through the adoption of fashionable new Roman building forms. There are Mediterranean and Gallic parallels for both types of building and they were presumably adopted in Britain through the process of emulation.[15] The construction of mosaics, heated rooms and Roman-style baths were clearly also ways to emulate 'Romans', as all three elements also occur in Mediterranean and continental villas.

Archaeologists often attempt to forge a link between the archaeological definition of a villa and the historical sources. Thus it is usually suggested that the discovery of a villa building in a ploughed field or on a construction site indicates the existence of an estate centre belonging to an individual villa owner.[16] To many archaeologists this initial assumption results in further suppositions, for instance that a private estate could be bought or sold on the land market.[17]

No direct evidence exists for the significance of the Romano-British villa. Among all the classical sources there is only one reference to a Roman villa in Britain and this does not appear to relate to a villa-type building.[18] Rivet has argued that, as there is no directly relevant evidence, it is easier to understand the Romano-British villa in terms of the evidence for the social and economic history of the Roman Empire as a whole than to attempt to develop a model purely from the scattered scraps of archaeological evidence. Rivet's model for the villa as the country estate of the town-dweller is primarily derived from the writings of Varro, Virgil and Columella.[19] The relevance of Rivet's model has been questioned by the archaeological evidence for the province. It would now appear that during the first century of Roman rule the development of elaborate, wealthy dwellings was more advanced in the countryside than in the towns. This would suggest that the tribal élite, traditionally country-dwellers, retained their rural homes after the conquest rather than becoming town-dwellers with country estates. Although these wealthy individuals presumably visited the town to attend the tribal capital their houses, or at least their main residences, were located elsewhere.[20]

There is no specific reason why a definition derived from the Mediterranean provinces should be of relevance to Roman Britain.[21] The idea has already been introduced that villa buildings were owned and occupied by extended families, or perhaps even by groups of families.[22] This would suggest that villa lands were usually the property of a group of related kin rather than that of a single individual. In addition this presumably indicates that the lands could not, as the historical sources suggest, always have been bought and sold in a land market, as this would presumably have necessitated the agreement of all concerned. The proposal that villas were owned by groups of families does not necessarily indicate that they were not the centres of estates, or that landowners and subservient estate workers did not exist.[23] It does, however, suggest that the estates centred on villas were not necessarily owned and controlled by a single individual with full rights over his lands.[24]

The archaeological definition of a villa is a rural domestic building which was constructed in such a way as to indicate the status of an individual or family group. This archaeological definition tells the archaeologist nothing about the way in which surplus wealth was created – whether this method was agricultural, industrial, related to commerce, or a combination of all three. It also gives no insight into the family structure of those who lived in villas.

If the term 'villa' is to be more useful than merely a description of building form, a great deal more must be discovered concerning the origin and nature of the settlements on which these buildings are found.

In addition, it will be necessary to study the relationship of these settlements to other neighbouring settlements and to the resources exploited by the villa. Until this type of information is available for a site the term should be used purely for building form. The alternative – forcing inadequate evidence into a predetermined and over-simplistic historical framework – will not create a true picture of the economic and social background and lifestyle of the rural élite of Roman Britain.

Non-villa settlements

Non-villa settlements[25] have generally been neglected in the past and the sites have usually been considered in negative terms. Non-villa settlements are the homes of those who, for one reason or another, failed to become highly romanized. In other words, these are the sites on which villa buidings do not occur. A wide and varied range of non-villa settlements occur across the whole of the province of Roman Britain and vary from extensive village-type communities to the single upland farmstead. Non-villa settlements clearly formed the most common settlement type in the province and therefore constitute an important theme for research.

These settlements are characterized by the absence of buildings that show any high degree of surplus or wealth investment and also an actual or implied absence of material items of wealth. When they are excavated or fieldwalked non-villa settlements usually produce a poor range of pottery, few coins and little metalwork. Therefore it would appear that these settlements were usually poor. A brief review of the evidence indicates, however, that sites of this type were certainly not standardized in form. The non-villa settlements of Roman Britain varied both in physical form and, it will be suggested, in social and economic significance. The variety in the evidence makes these sites a rewarding theme for research.

Variation in size amongst non-villa settlements will be discussed below. The majority of the settlements of the north and west appear to consist of only a single ditched or walled enclosure surrounding one or more round buildings, presumably the homes of single families. A few farmsteads of this type are also known in southern Britain. Many non-villa settlements, however, appear to be larger in size than the single farmstead and a wide range of sizes of sites seems to occur. The non-villa settlement at Chysauster (Corn), for example, has at least eight houses and presumably represented a nucleated village community.[26]

Non-villa settlements also vary in the level of material wealth available to their inhabitants. In the upland areas of northern and western England the non-villa settlements were often very poor and on excavation they produce only very limited quantities of wheel-made pottery, an occasional Roman coin or bronze artefact. In the lowlands the settlements usually appear to have been more fully integrated into the Roman economy and items of Romano-British material culture are consequently more common. It appears, however, that these sites were often relatively poor in comparison to villa sites. Local items predominate while non-local items are very scarce. It is, therefore, surprising to discover that a number of non-villa settlements that have been investigated seem to have been richer than would be expected. On these sites it is possible that the inhabitants were fairly prosperous, although elaborate stone-built villa houses were not constructed.[27] It would seem that the level of wealth on non-villa settlements was not standardized.

Non-villa settlements differ in their relationship to other settlements. A characteristic that will be stressed in this book is the location of non-villa settlements in two distinctive types of situation. First, many non-villa settlements occur in close proximity to villa settlements. In these cases it is usually supposed that the occupants of the non-villa settlement were tenants or slaves of the villa owner.[28] In other areas, however, broad landscapes are defined by the occurrence of non-villa settlements and the absence of villas. In these cases the status of the inhabitants of the non-villa settlements is less clear.

Many non-villa settlements will therefore have represented the homes of estate workers, whether these workers were tenants or slaves. The scale and significance of the estates of which these sites formed a dependent part will have varied. For instance, the Emperor owned numerous estates of varying size throughout the empire.[29] Other large and small estates evidently existed all over the province. Some of these estates were owned by landlords from other provinces.[30] At the bottom end of the scale a small landowner or small land-owning family might own a modest estate centred on a humble villa, perhaps with a single community of estate workers resident in a non-villa settlement nearby.

An even poorer type of estate-owner probably existed over the area of the province. In northern, western and possibly also in southern Britain estates of this type may be indicated by some isolated non-villa settlements. Although it is difficult in individual cases to be certain that non-villa settlements did not belong to an estate based on another settlement it is probable, at least in the north and west, that small-scale individual estates existed based on the multitude of isolated and enclosed non-villa settlements.

It will be argued that an understanding of non-villa settlements is vital if a reconstruction of the social structure of communities in the Romano-British countryside is to be attempted. Any approach that ignores the homes of the poor, or of those who appear to be poor, will not create a realistic understanding of the province. The detailed attention paid to these settlements represents an attempt to correct the bias that exists in other accounts of rural settlement in Roman Britain.

Local centres

Definitions of local centres vary, as do the terms that are used for the sites. The term *vicus* is used by some authors and 'roadside settlement' by others, but 'small town' appears to have the highest incidence.[31] The term 'small town', however, suggests that any site which is referred to had a certain basic level of urbanization. As many of these sites do not appear to be urban in any real sense the term 'local centre' has been adopted in this study. It is considered that the term 'small town' should be reserved for the larger local centres, many of which appear to have been urban in character.[32]

Two models that can be fitted to the archaeological evidence will be discussed. A traditional approach exists which attempts to define local centres through administrative characteristics. This approach identifies a narrow range of sites, the majority of which have walled defensive circuits. The narrow definition of the local centre fits into the perspective of Roman Britain which views Roman settlements as islands of civilization set among the uncivilized native population.[33] The range of factors that characterize local centres within this narrow definition has not, however, been clearly distinguished.

An alternative approach stresses economic factors and in effect characterizes a broader range of sites. This broader model suggests that local centres were the local markets of Roman Britain. The model is in keeping with the ideas of economic growth which were outlined in the first chapter.

Historical factors and a narrow definition
There has been a certain amount of discussion over the potential administrative function of the small town within the *civitas* and the term *vicus* has been used in discussing some of the local centres of Britain.[34] How is the term defined? It has been suggested that the *vicus* was the lowest class of town which was granted powers of government.[35] The idea is that individual *civitates* (tribes) may have had a number of *vici* in their territory and have retained overall control of these settlements while delegating an element of local government to them.[36] Unfortunately reality was not this simple. It is actually clear that the term *vicus*, like the term *villa*, had a range of meanings that changed through time[37] and it is not possible to adopt any simplistic model based on historical sources.

Attempts have, however, been made to characterize other aspects of these sites. In traditional studies the military origin and certain aspects of the administrative function of small towns are often stressed.

26 Rural Settlement in Roman Britain

Particular attention is placed upon official actions that led to their establishment. For instance, the military origins:[38] many of the small towns of Britain and other north-western provinces of the Roman Empire appear to have originated as market settlements exploiting the trade created by soldiers' pay.[39] When the army moved on into the west and north of Britain, some of these trading communities survived as exchange and administrative centres for the rural populations of their local hinterland. In northern Britain and Wales many forts were more permanent and the sites which developed outside their gates were occupied into the third and fourth centuries.[40]

Additional military and administrative factors may have been behind the development of small towns. The Imperial Post (*cursus publicus*) was the method by which messages were conveyed around the Roman Empire. These messages were transferred by means of a series of staging posts along the main roads of the province. The posts would have contained *mansiones*, guest houses for official travellers. The presence of an official post could have encouraged the growth of a local centre, as a demand for food and raw materials may have existed on these sites.[41] Examples of *mansiones* are known in a number of the local centres of Britain.[42]

A third factor that could have promoted the development of the small town was the setting up of centres for the collection of the *annona*, the tax in kind which took over from taxation in cash during the third century AD. It has been suggested that at this time some roadside settlements might have been used as collection points for the *annona*.[43] The presence of administrative officials who implemented the collection might have acted as a stimulus to trade.

How are the small towns which are considered in these studies identified? The important point is that a sample of sites is being used for analysis. How is this sample selected? Past studies have defined between seventy nine and ninety seven small towns (*see* Figure 11).[44] Some studies have considered only walled small towns, while others have considered a range of walled and unwalled sites.[45] At least half of the ninety seven sites have banked and ditched or walled circuits. The occurrence of such a circuit is taken to indicate the location of a small town even when little evidence exists for associated settlement.[46] In addition, a number of sites are included in traditional studies that have produced no evidence, or only unconvincing evidence, for defensive circuits.[47] Sites without walls appear to have been included when they have two particular characteristics. First, it is often argued that small towns would have been located on the major roads of the province.[48] The location of small towns on major roads is related to the function of these sites as centres for the Imperial Post and possibly as centres of taxation. Second, the area covered by these sites appears to be

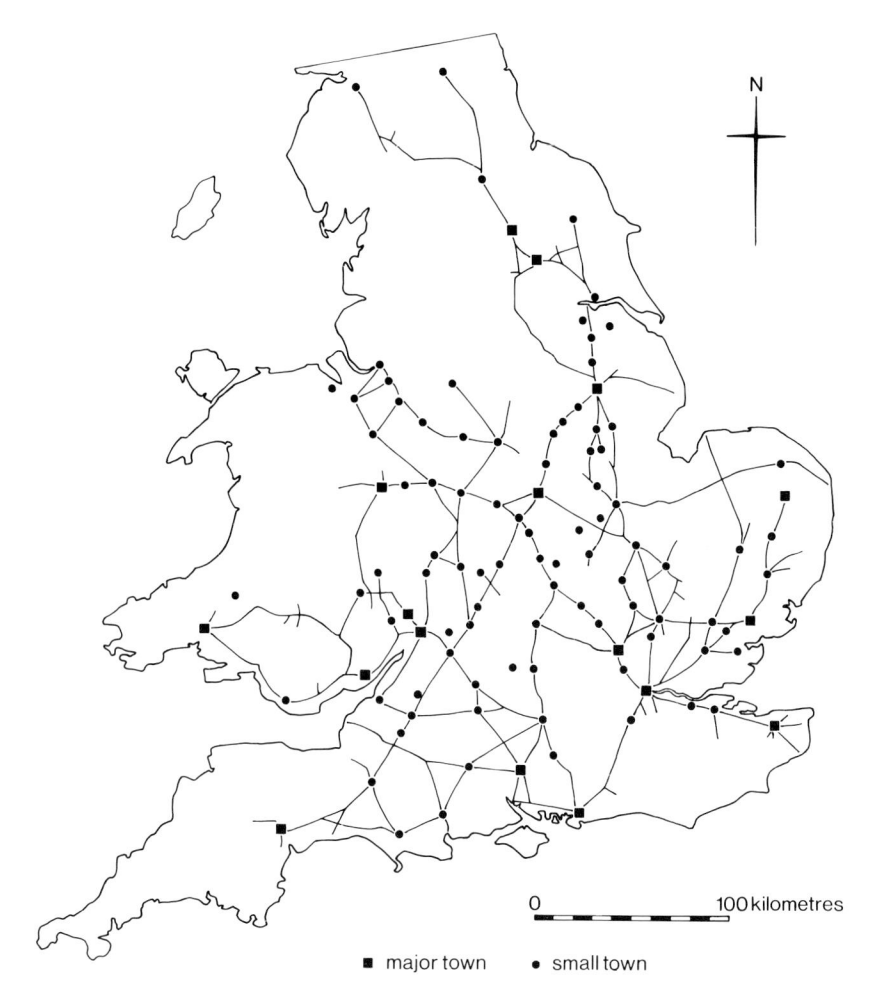

Figure 11 *The restricted distribution of small towns in Roman Britain. (After Burnham 1986, figure 1).*

significant, with small towns covering at least ten hectares.[49] In addition, evidence for a system of paved or metalled roads is sometimes used as a defining characteristic. Thus, the unwalled sites are included because of their comparative extent and location on the Roman road system.

Possible justification for a broader local market centre model
A further factor is probably relevant to the classification of local centres, the function of these sites as local market centres. As mentioned above, many local centres originated as markets serving Roman soldiers. It seems likely, therefore, that these sites retained a trading function once

the army had moved on. If this economic function is stressed the argument for their location on major roads is of less obvious significance. Location on a major road relates to an administrative factor, the running of the Imperial Post and the collection of tax, and there is no reason why important trading settlements in the Roman countryside should not have been served by networks of minor roads. The economic function of a local centre was not necessarily directly dependent on its administrative function, although the two may have been related on some sites.

The market function of the Romano-British local centre may provide a way of distinguishing these sites from non-villa farming settlements. Non-villa settlements will have had a largely agricultural function, while each local centre will have contained a market. There is a difficulty, however, because many of those resident within local market centres involved in production and trade would also have cultivated the land around the settlement, and the markets of some local centres could have been of relatively minor significance. It is clear that caution is required in identifying local centres; location in relation to the Roman road system and relative extent of settlement may not always prove sufficient to distinguish the sites.[50] Without conducting large-scale excavation, evidence for the function of a site as a local trading centre may be difficult to identify. Generally, however, the location of sites on major or minor roads and the size attained by these settlements often indicate the significance of trade in their development.

If local centres are defined as settlements of over ten hectares located in roadside situations, it is evident that the seventy nine to ninety seven sites defined by past studies constitute a small percentage of the total. The unwalled sites that have been considered in the traditional approach are merely the best excavated and best known examples of a very common type of settlement. A large number of other sites in southern Britain feature the characteristics that have been used to define local centres. The problem with studying the evidence is that these sites are very poorly known.

A broader definition of the local centre has been adopted in studies of the area occupied by the Trinovantes and that of the south-eastern Dobunni. Over much of these two areas local centres occur at about ten-kilometre intervals and it will be argued that this distribution supports the idea that the sites functioned as local market centres.[51] It is clear that comparable evidence does not exist for the rest of the province. However, evidence of this sort may be produced by future work in areas where local centres do not at present appear to have been very common.

It is clearly correct to keep in mind the models provided by the historical sources and the more traditional approaches when studying local centres. A consideration of the archaeological evidence does appear to indicate, however, that the historical perspective gives only a partial picture of the origins, general density and function of local centres. In addition, it would appear that this picture is biased towards administrative and military factors and biased against economic factors. It will be argued in greater detail later in this work that an alternative economic model that views local centres as local market centres has much to recommend it.

Chapter 3
Houses

Domestic buildings are the subject matter of this chapter and agricultural buildings will not be discussed in detail.[1] It is not intended to provide a full review of all the evidence for the variation in house structure as the quantity of information is considerable and many of the sites that have been excavated have not been fully published. The variety of evidence will be discussed and some possible explanations for this variation considered, with an emphasis on the nature of the household and the family.

DEFINING HOUSE TYPES

The analysis of the plan-form of Romano-British houses is at an elementary stage.[2] In order to analyze houses it is necessary to construct a typology of plan-form. This typology must necessarily be based on the shape, disposition and function of rooms within a dwelling. Roman specialists commonly distinguish a range of house types from the ground plans of the buildings.

Plan

Leech has considered the occurrence of buildings of oval/polygonal plan at Catsgore (Somer) and on some other sites in southern Britain.[2] These buildings are very common on rural sites during the first century and continue at many sites into the second century. In north Wales, Cornwall, Northumberland and on some sites in southern Britain round houses continue to be built into the third and fourth centuries. At Catsgore and on the majority of other sites in southern Britain, and also possibly in south-west Wales and Cumbria, oval buildings are replaced during the second or third centuries by simple rectangular buildings of one to three rooms.[3]

Richmond's discussion of villa plans provides a basis for the discussion of buildings of more complex form. Richmond distinguished 'cottage houses' – the simpler versions of which differ little from Leech's group of simple rectangular dwellings – and also 'winged corridor houses', 'courtyard houses' and 'aisled houses'.[4]

Building materials

An additional factor which is of importance in understanding the significance of house form is the material in which the house was built. It is usually argued that villas should have been built at least partly of stone and have had tile or slate roofs. This is in contrast to buildings in non-villa settlements which were often of timber and wattle-and-daub with thatched roofs. The use of stone, tile and slate need not always indicate wealth and status, neither for that matter need timber and thatch always indicate low status and poverty. It is probably generally true, however, that the materials in which the building was constructed and the form and complexity of the building indicate something of the wealth, status and cultural aspirations of the inhabitants.

Architectural features

Certain elements of villa form – such as the façade of the winged corridor villa and the elaboration and complexity of the courtyard villa – indicate wealth and social standing. The construction of mosaics, tessellated pavements, heated rooms, bath-houses and the use of painted plaster are all additional indications of the adoption of Roman standards which also indicate wealth and high status.

The information for Romano-British houses will now be considered and a range of house types will be defined.

ROUND HOUSES (*see* Figure 12)

The circular house – usually of timber, daub and thatch – typifies the Iron Age settlement record in Britain.[5] Round houses were very common throughout lowland Britain during the first and second centuries AD, so common in fact that they may have been the predominant building type over much of the province. These buildings also continued to be used in northern England, Wales and Cornwall and also on a number of sites in southern Britain throughout the third and fourth centuries. The comparative absence of discussion of this type of building appears to be a consequence of the fact that round houses are seen by many archaeologists as outmoded, the homes of the poor and so of little importance in understanding the history of Roman Britain.

Round buildings had a range of functions, including habitation, storage and industry.[6] Circular buildings form one of the most common types of temple building in Britain.[7] Storage, industrial and temple buildings will not be discussed in this work. A domestic function may be indicated by the location of a hearth within the house,[8] or by the occurrence of large quantities of domestic rubbish.

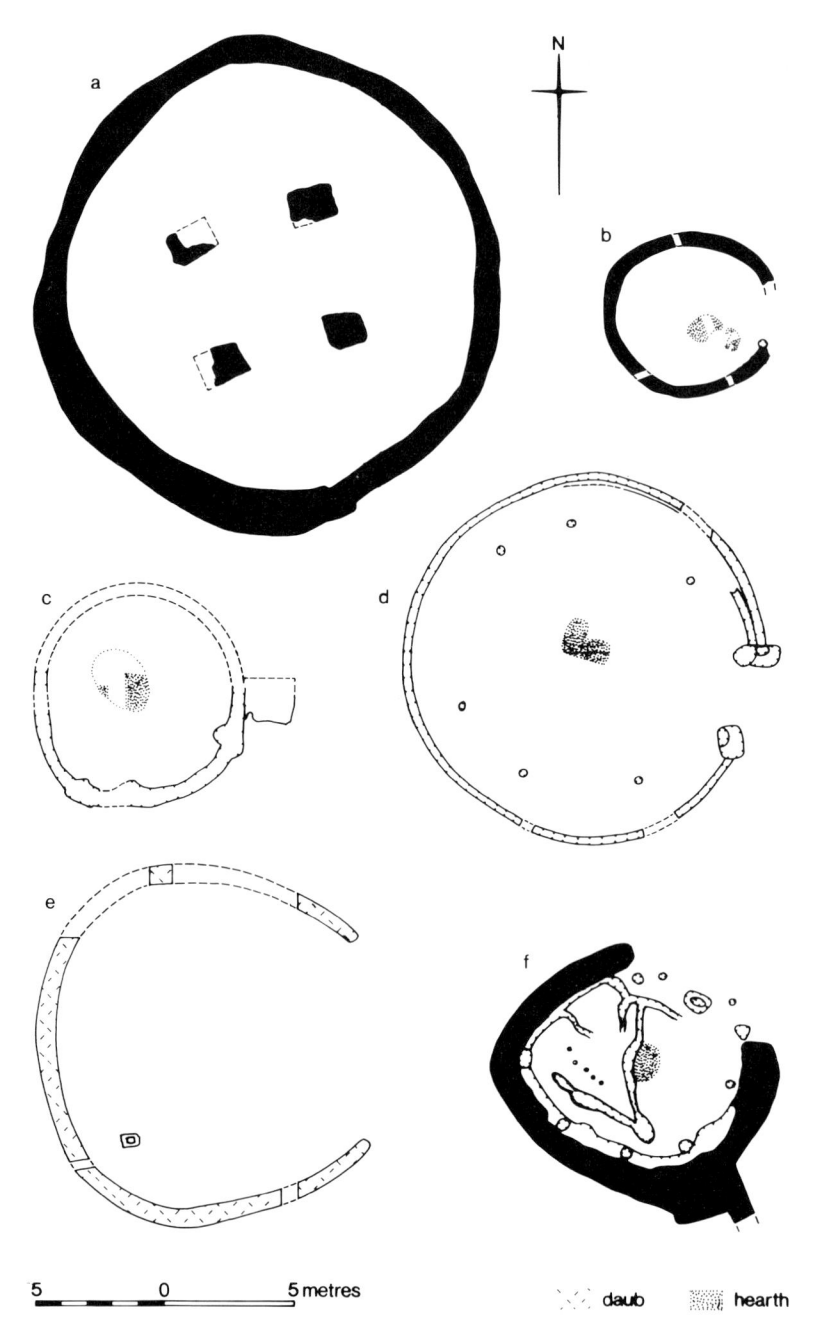

Figure 12 *Round houses: a. Winterton (Humbs); b. Thorplands (Northants); c. Gorhambury (Herts); d. Whitton (S Glam); e. Penrith (Cumbr); f. Trethurgy (Corn).*

Figure 13 *Reconstruction of a round house at Whitton (S Glam).*

The shape of round and oval houses varies from site to site. Some houses are round, others are elongated and oval. The boat-shaped examples at Grambla (Corn) are half-way between oval and rectangular in form. Constructional techniques for Romano-British round houses vary from site to site. In the lowlands timber round huts appear most common; these are often surrounded by a drainage gully and there is very little to distinguish houses of this type from Iron Age examples in southern Britain (*see* Figure 13). Stone-built round houses also occur (*see* Figure 14). Overstone (Northants) began as a timber round house, but in the third century was replaced by a circular house with stone foundations. Other sites in northern England, north Wales and Cornwall have produced stone and timber-built round houses.[9]

Round houses occur on a variety of types of site. Examples are known at local centres, on non-villa settlements, on sites that were later to have villa-type buildings, and as outbuildings or houses secondary to villa buildings.[10] There appear to be two distinct types of situation. On the majority of southern British sites the round buildings are of first or second-century date and were replaced during the second to third centuries by rectangular houses of the types which are discussed below. Secondly, the circular house form remains predominant throughout the Roman period. At Odell (Beds) small circular huts were in use into the third and fourth centuries, and only in the fourth century were they

Figure 14 *Photograph of a round house under excavation at Holme House (N Yorks). Copyright Professor D Harding.*

replaced by a rectangular design of several rooms. The same trend occurred on other non-villa sites in southern Britain.[11] Round houses were common over much of northern and western Britain during the third and fourth centuries, although rectangular buildings replaced them on some sites in south-west Wales and Cumbria.[12]

Where round houses were replaced by rectangular buildings, it is often argued that the transition was a consequence of Roman influence on British society. The desire of individuals or families to acquire symbols of wealth and civilization, combined with the influence of military and urban architecture, could have created the stimulus for change from round to rectangular form.

At sites on which round houses continued to be built into the third century, or even throughout the entire Roman period, it is usually suggested that the people concerned were socially backward or lacking in romanization and were thus presumably of low social status. At Dinorben (Clwyd), however, it has been argued that a large round hut which produced a rich collection of finds was probably the home of a landowner, with tenants living nearby.[13] The type of social structure found here could have been very similar to that of the villa-owner with tenants. Although Dinorben is distant from areas of Roman civilian influence this is a reminder that not all the residents of round huts in the north and west need have been poor and backward.

ONE TO THREE-ROOMED RECTANGULAR HOUSES
(*see* Figure 15)

One-roomed houses

Although round buildings appear to form the predominant type in Iron Age southern Britain rectangular houses are also known. In the south-east of Britain, for example, there is a great increase in continental contact and consequent social change in the hundred years before the Roman conquest. In this area the rectangular house form appears to be fairly common by the end of the Iron Age.[14]

Simple rectangular houses consisted of rectangular blocks of rooms, without additional corridors or annexes. Rectangular houses with only a single room occur on a number of sites in southern, northern and western Britain (*see* Figure 15a, b, k). The one-roomed rectangular house may represent the conversion of a single-roomed round dwelling to a rectangular form. These buildings were usually fairly insubstantial timber and daub structures and it is often impossible to be certain that the buildings were not divided into rooms by partitions that have not survived.

Houses of this type are common on a variety of sites, such as non-villa settlements in the south, north and west of the province and at local centres in the south.[15]

Two to three-roomed houses

Leech has identified a type of rectangular house that is common on the extensively excavated site at Catsgore (Somer) and on a range of other Roman sites in southern Britain (*see* Figure 15, c-j). These houses have two or three rooms and one of the rooms is always larger than the others and usually contains a hearth.[16] Two to three-roomed rectangular dwellings were constructed in a variety of ways. Some houses were built of timber and daub with thatched roofs, others had stone foundations and timber walls, and further examples were built almost entirely of stone.[17]

Houses of the simple rectangular type are known on a variety of sites. They occur at local centres as outbuildings to villa buildings and on

36 *Rural Settlement in Roman Britain*

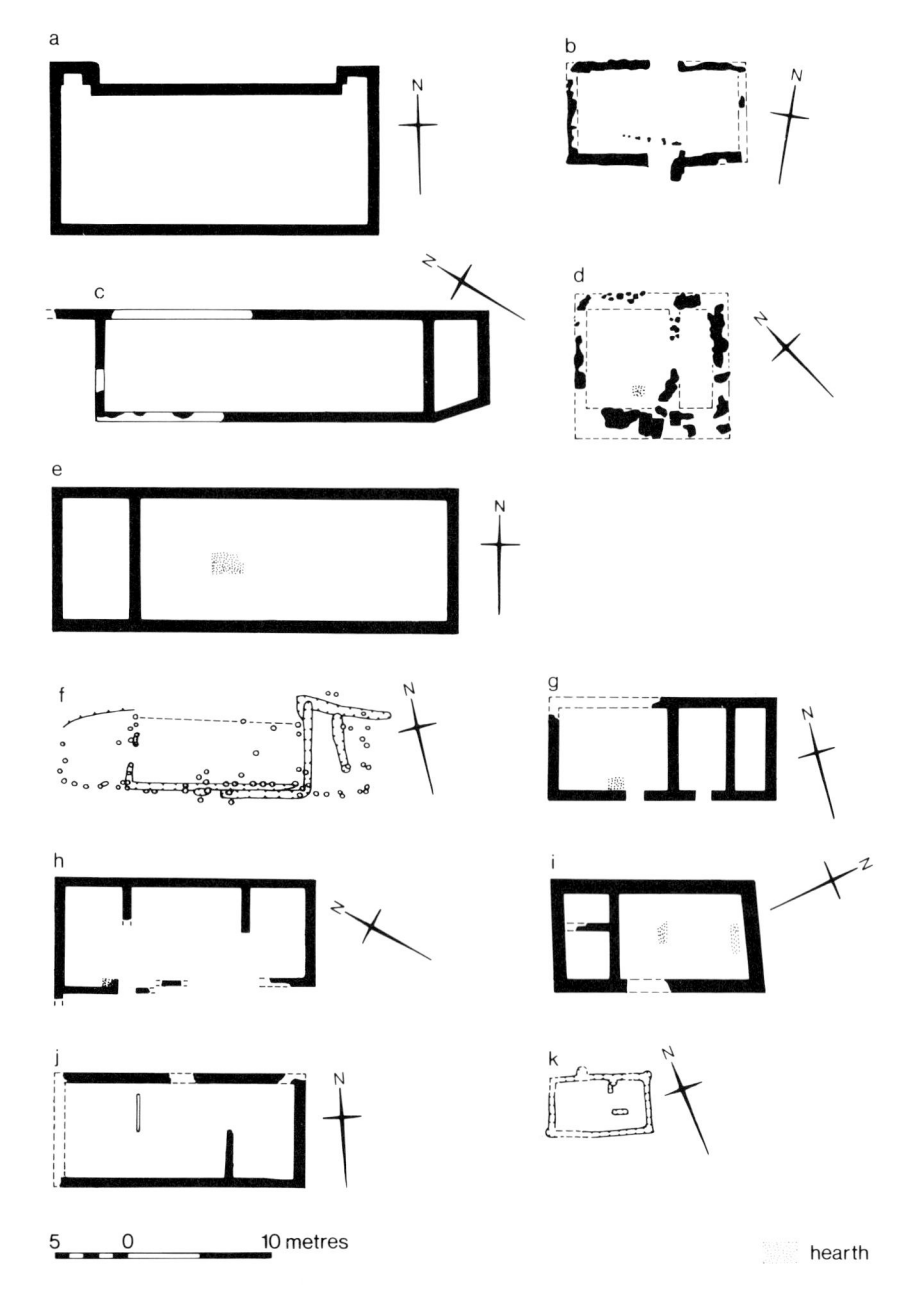

Figure 15 *Simple rectangular buildings: a. Weeting (Norf); b. Studland (Dorset); c. Cwmbrwyn (Dyfed); d. Overton Down (Wilts); e. Clear Cupboard (Glos); f. Dunston's Clump (Notts); g. Bradley Hill (Somer); h. Trelissey (Dyfed); i. Catsgore (Somer); j. Wymbush (Bucks); k. Chelmsford (Essex).*

non-villa settlements in southern Britain.[18] This type of building occasionally appears to form the first phase in the development of winged corridor villa buildings,[19] which will be discussed further below.[20] Leech has suggested that the main room in this type of building was used for living, eating and sleeping and that the annex rooms were possibly private rooms for sleeping. The buildings probably represent the conversion of simple round and rectangular one-roomed houses into a slightly more complex form with the addition of one or two small annex rooms.

At Bradley Hill, Leech has attempted to estimate the potential population of two houses of this type using the evidence provided by a contemporary associated cemetery. The excavation report stresses that the estimate is hypothetical and rests on a number of untested assumptions. It is suggested that each house contained a nuclear family of two adults – a mother and a father – and six children, four of whom died at birth or in infancy and two of whom lived to adulthood.[21] Two to three-roomed buildings may therefore in many cases have housed nuclear families of one generation.

'COTTAGE HOUSES' (see Figure 16)

Richmond has named other more complex rectangular houses with a larger number of rooms 'cottage houses'.[22] According to Richmond the cottage house comprised rooms ranged each side of a passageway running from the front to the back of the building (see Figure 16a, b). Not all cottage houses fit Richmond's model, as some consisted of rectangular blocks of rooms without a passageway and differ from the simpler rectangular houses discussed above only in the number of rooms (see Figure 16, c-f).

A simple addition often made to the cottage house is a timber or stone corridor constructed at the front of the building (see Figure 16a). Such a corridor converted the building into a 'corridor house' and this type is discussed below.

Examples of cottage houses are fairly common and most if not all were stone-built. Few free-standing cottage houses are known, as the majority appear to represent the first stage of villa development.[23] Cottage houses are not found in large numbers on non-villa settlements or at local centres, where the simpler round and rectangular house types are more common.

It is of interest that Richmond's structural description of the Roman cottage house is almost identical to that of the medieval cross-passage house. The cross-passage was a predominant feature in all late medieval houses with more than one room. The passage ran transversely across the building, providing access to the house from both front and rear and

38 *Rural Settlement in Roman Britain*

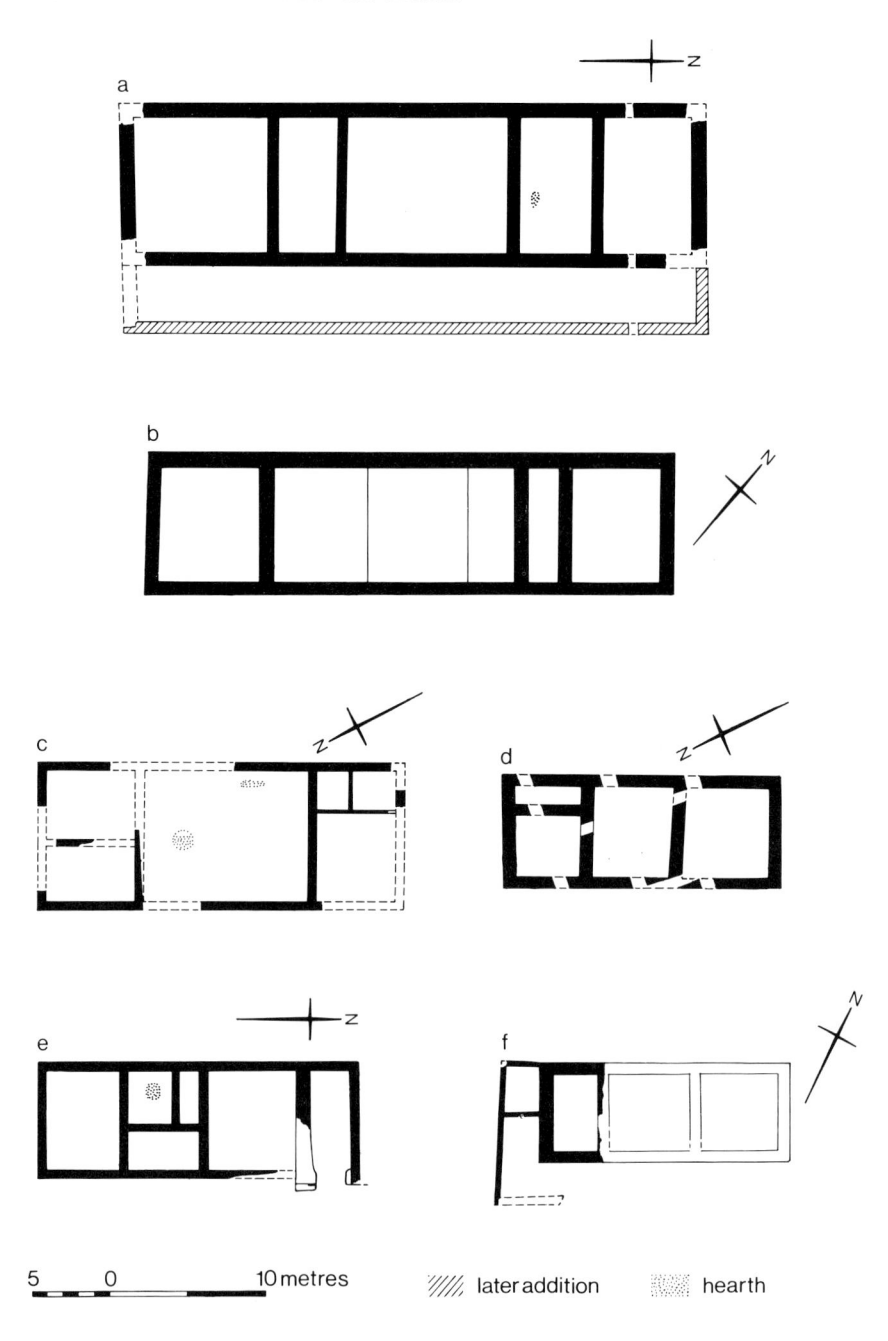

Figure 16 *'Cottage houses': a. Feltwell (Norf); b. Frocester Court (Glos); c. Carsington (Derby); d. Holme House (N Yorks); e. Park Street (Herts); f. Rockbourne (Hants).*

dividing the living quarters from the service rooms.[24] Richmond has suggested that the additional rooms of the Roman cottage house could indicate an increasing desire for privacy and the development of separate roles in family life.[25] In other words, the development of the cottage house with cross-passage could indicate the separation of the rooms of the head of the household from those of his kin, or the division of the rooms of a kin group from those of their servants. It does not appear possible from the available evidence to assess which of these two models is correct. Todd has proposed a third possible explanation in the case of Whitwell (Leic), that the passage divided the living-room from the work space of the community.[26] The passage is also a common feature with many corridor and winged corridor villa buildings.

Little is known of the size of family groups resident within cottage houses. While some of these houses have a fairly small living area and were probably the residences of nuclear families, other cottage houses are more extensive and could have housed larger extended family groups.

AISLED HOUSES (see Figure 17)

It has been suggested that the origin of the aisled house is pre-Roman. A number of authors have noted the similarity of Romano-British aisled buildings to examples in pre-Roman Iron Age contexts in northern Europe.[27] Aisled buildings appear on present evidence, however, to be very rare in Iron Age Britain; only a single example has been excavated, at Gorhambury (Herts). According to Applebaum, aisled houses do not in fact become common in Roman Britain until the second half of the second century.[28] Although first/early second-century examples are now known,[29] aisled houses still seem to have been rare before the second century. It is possible, however, that future excavation of pre-Roman and early Roman sites in southern Britain will provide evidence that aisled buildings are in fact more common at this time than the existing evidence would appear to suggest.

The aisled house has a central room which runs the length of the building with aisles defined by posts or columns on either side. A range of functions can be defined for these buildings in the Romano-British countryside. Some aisled buildings were probably comparable to the medieval barn and were used solely for storage.[30] Other aisled buildings, particularly in the Nene Valley, clearly had industrial uses.[31]

The evidence appears, however, to indicate that the majority of aisled buildings had a domestic function[32] and it is the domestic examples that will be discussed in this book. They occur in a range of settlement contexts, as villa buildings, as outhouses associated with villa buildings, at local centres and in non-villa settlements.[33] It is impossible to review

40 *Rural Settlement in Roman Britain*

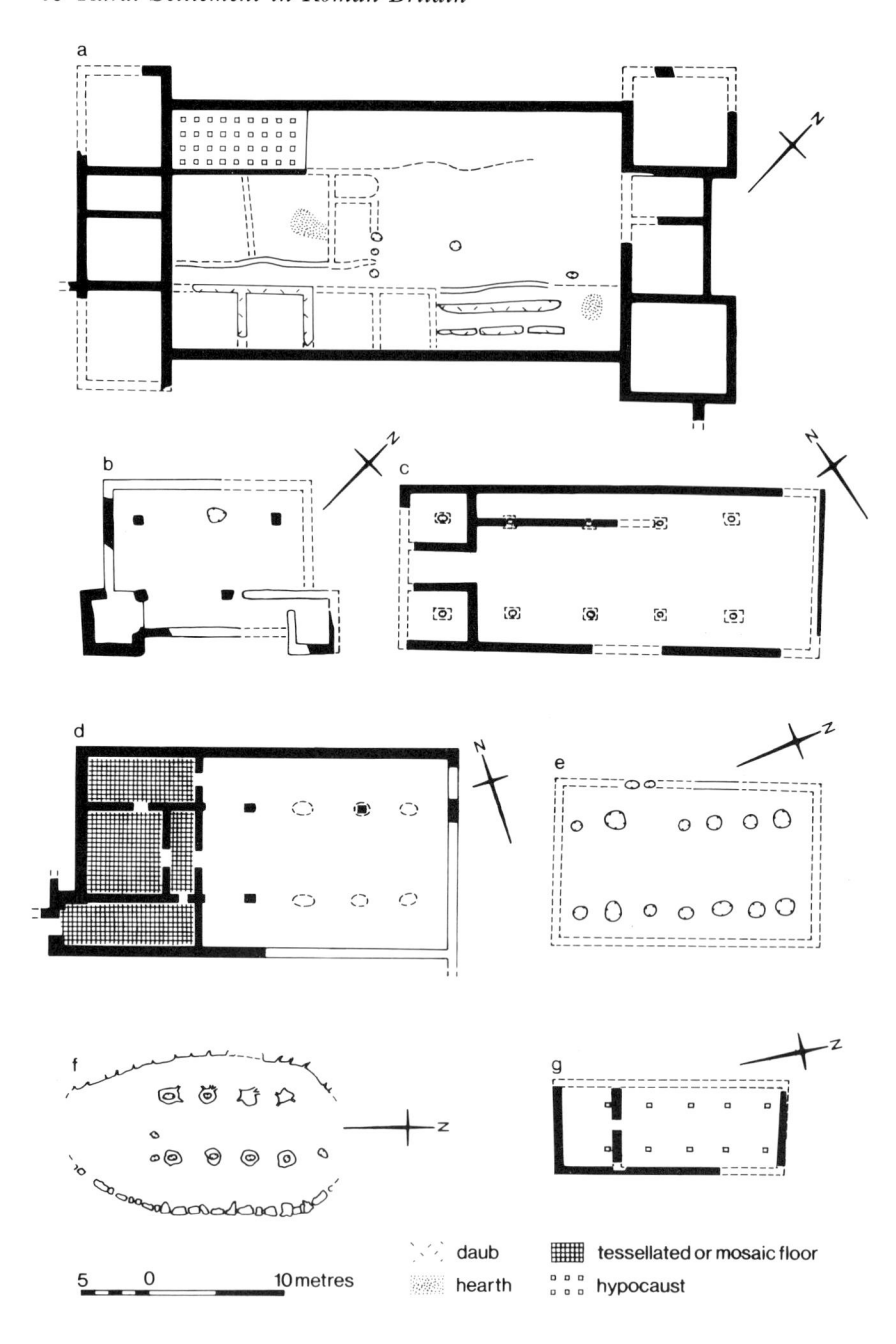

Figure 17 *Aisled houses: a. North Warnborough (Hants); b. Tiddington (Warw); c. Bancroft (Bucks); d. Combley (I of W); e. Claydon Pike (Glos); f. Roystone Grange (Derby); g. Holcombe (Devon).*

the structure and development of aisled houses in detail in this context, although it is of interest that on a number of sites a timber phase appears to pre-date a stone phase.[34]

Two general models have been proposed to explain the evidence for aisled houses. Richmond observed that aisled houses were often associated with winged corridor and courtyard villa buildings and suggested that the aisled building represented the home of estate workers associated with a wealthier house occupied by an estate owner. J Smith has proposed a completely different approach and has suggested that aisled houses were the homes of extended families, some of which may actually have owned estates.

The aisled house as a barn/farm worker's residence

Richmond observed that aisled houses are frequently associated with what he calls 'houses of more advanced pattern' in the guise of a barn, or *villa rustica*. There are a large number of cases in which aisled houses occur alongside winged corridor and courtyard villa buildings. In some instances these buildings produce little evidence of wealth, such as hypocausts, mosaics and bath suites and, as Richmond suggested, it appears that a staff of labourers, tenants and slaves belonging to an estate were resident within the aisled house.[35] The association of aisled houses with winged corridor and courtyard houses is considered in greater detail below.[36]

The aisled house as the residence of an extended family

An alternative model for the structure of the largest and most complex aisled houses helps to explain some of the patterning in the evidence. The idea is that there need have been no rigid separation of landowner from tenant or worker in the aisled house.[37] In Applebaum's words the aisled house was part of a Celtic/germanic tradition which pre and post-dated the Roman period, and the house type was not appropriate as a residential form for slaves and farmworkers on an estate.[38] In addition, a number of aisled houses occur in isolated contexts, away from other winged corridor and courtyard buildings. Indeed, some of these buildings have winged corridor façades and are therefore villa buildings.[39]

Two types of residential aisled houses have been defined: simple undivided aisled houses (*see* Figure 17, e-g) and developed aisled houses (*see* Figure 17a, d; Figure 21a). Simple undivided aisled buildings have a single open and undivided room, possibly representing the residence of some form of large-scale extended family group in which all members of the family lived in common and in which individuals had very little privacy.[40] In contrast to this, developed aisled buildings are those in which a distinct suite of rooms had been defined at one end of the building. This suite of rooms usually contained a hypocaust and/or a mosaic floor.[41]

The developed aisled houses have been compared to the medieval hall houses. An 'upper' and a 'lower' end can be recognized in many medieval manorial hall houses and the same is true of some Roman aisled houses.[42] In the Romano-British buildings the upper end containing the suite of rooms with hypocausts and/or mosaics could have represented the private apartments of the Roman equivalent of a medieval lord. The headman of the extended family may, in effect, have been appropriating a private suite of rooms for himself and his immediate nuclear family in one end of the communal building.

The second important part of the medieval hall house was the hall itself, which was always the largest room and was where the family, guests and servants lived and slept and where the manorial court was held.[43] It is possible that the lower end of the Romano-British developed aisled house had a similar range of functions to that of the medieval hall.[44] The Romano-British aisled house could have been comparable to the medieval hall house in having an upper suite of rooms for the lord or headman of the community and his immediate (?nuclear) family, and a lower end or hall used by the followers, kin or extended family of the headman.

At least some of the developed aisled houses appear to have evolved out of simple undivided aisled houses. This may indicate that the headman of an extended family group was evolving new rights within the family and was appropriating a private area within the house, which therefore no longer formed the undivided property of the extended family.

Other aisled houses cannot be interpreted so easily by this analogy. In the case of some of the aisled houses of south-eastern Britain it appears that multiple suites of rooms can be identified.[45] Stroud (Hants) in an early phase consisted of an aisled building constructed with wing rooms on its south face, but with an undivided hall (*see* Figure 21a). This can be interpreted by suggesting that the building started with a single, undivided extended family in effect living communally within a single large room. At a later stage at least two suites of rooms were incorporated within the aisled house. This may suggest that there were two smaller family groups, possibly nuclear families, who constructed separate suites of rooms within the aisled house. These two individual family groups may have been dominant here, although their subservient kin probably continued to live within the hall. There are a number of other examples of aisled houses which may have had similar multiple suites of rooms.[46]

Two other aisled houses provide detailed support for this model and additional evidence about the nature of the community resident within the aisled house. A probable aisled building at Thruxton (Hants) has produced a mosaic which may indicate a headman and his associated kinship group. A second aisled house at North Warnborough (Hants) has produced artefactual evidence for the organization of the extended family resident within the building. The mosaic from Thruxton, which is now in the British Museum, is of particular interest in connection with the suggestion that the developed aisled house represented the home of a headman and associated extended family group. The building that contained the mosaic was excavated in the nineteenth century and information on the site is unfortunately very limited. The mosaic appears to have been found within an aisled building and may actually have been located in a wing room projecting beyond the building. Two lines of lettering occur in the mosaic. The upper line reads QVINTVS NATALIVS NATALINVS ET BODENI, while the lower line has been largely destroyed. 'Natalinus' was evidently a Roman citizen and 'Bodeni' is a latinized plural of a Celtic name. The inscription may refer to the owner of the aisled villa and the extended kinship group which had Natalinus at its head.[47] If this interpretation is correct it would appear that the Bodeni retained enough importance to be mentioned alongside their headman, and this may suggest a fairly egalitarian type of social structure.

The information from North Warnborough is also of particular interest in a discussion of the social significance of aisled houses. At this site the excavator recognized evidence for differing activities in the form of the distribution of artefacts. It is unclear why, but it appears that large quantities of domestic rubbish were deposited within the living rooms at North Warnborough. The excavator noted that it was possible to identify distinct areas of male and female activity on the basis of artefact distribution – combs, shuttles and spindle-whorls were taken to indicate female occupation and spearheads, keys, padlocks, knives and ironmongery to indicate male activities. This information enables an attempt to be made at a structural and social reconstruction of the North Warnborough aisled house (*see* Figure 18).

It has recently been proposed that the two wing rooms at the north-east end of the house may have consisted of tower-like blocks of two stories flanking an entrance in the gable.[48] At the opposite end of the house there was a range of four rooms which Applebaum has argued acted as stalls for livestock.[49] The artefactual information indicates that the living rooms were in the aisles and hall of the building. There is no clear division between an upper and lower end in this building, but it does appear, however, that the buildings can be divided approximately into two.[50] The south-western living rooms include a room with a hypocaust and a possible kitchen area indicated by a hearth and quantities of animal bones and oyster shells constituting the female area of the house.

44 *Rural Settlement in Roman Britain*

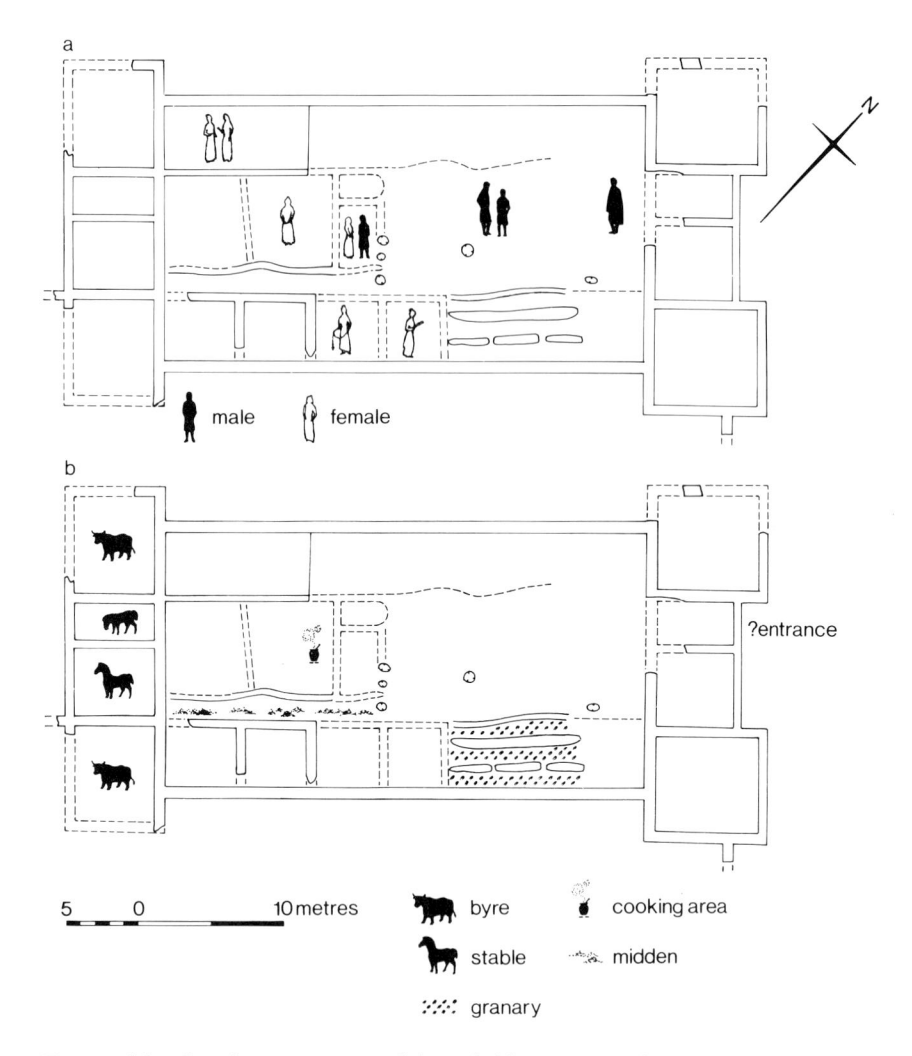

Figure 18 *Social reconstruction of the aisled house at North Warnborough: a. male and female; b. distribution of activities.*

The male area, in the north-eastern part of the house, included a structure identified by Applebaum as a granary and also the hall room of the building.

A close parallel appears to exist between the social model proposed for the North Warnborough villa and that distinguished by D Clarke for the family unit at the Iron Age settlement at Glastonbury.[51] In the case of both the Glastonbury farm compound and the North Warnborough aisled villa building a clear division occurs between male and female areas with the cooking area associated with the women. Although a number of distinct rooms occurred within both the male and female areas at North Warnborough, the building may have been home to a large extended family, probably of several generations and perhaps including as many as thirty to sixty individuals.[52]

The clear division of male and female activities is exactly the type of evidence that would be expected if aisled buildings represent the survival of the pre-Roman type kin group into the Roman period. The North Warnborough aisled house may represent the conversion of a Glastonbury-style family or kin unit into a single rectangular building, and the elaboration of the associated building through the addition of a hypocaust, wing rooms or tower rooms and an external bath-house. Rather than having been divided into two groups by status, as Smith's model would suggest, with the nuclear family of the headman resident in the upper end of the building and the rest of the extended family living in the lower hall end, the extended family at North Warnborough was allocated distinct areas of the building according to gender. This system of family organization appears very different from the type of historical model for the function of the aisled house that has been proposed by Richmond. There are, however, no obvious alternative explanations for the evidence from North Warnborough.[53]

CORRIDOR HOUSES (*see* Figure 19)

As stated above, timber or stone corridors were often constructed with or added to cottage houses without the addition of the wing rooms characteristic of the winged corridor façade.[54] Early examples of timber corridor houses occur in the Late Iron Age at Kelvedon (Essex) and in the mid-first century AD at Topsham (Devon). Some stone cottage houses had timber corridors, such as those at Brixworth (Northants) and Lockleys (Herts), but at the majority of sites both the building and the corridor appear to have been of stone.[55] The purpose of the corridor was presumably to provide access to a range of rooms without having to traverse others, as in the cottage house.

The addition of corridors without wing rooms indicates the development of new standards of privacy in family life. It is debatable, however, whether a corridor house should be defined as a villa unless other indicators of wealth and status are present on the site. It has occasionally been argued that buildings of this type represented villa buildings[56] and it is clear that some corridor houses developed into villa buildings, even if the corridor house itself is not accepted as a villa.[57] It is open to debate whether the other examples of corridor houses possessed a sufficient level of wealth and status to be considered as villas.[58]

46 *Rural Settlement in Roman Britain*

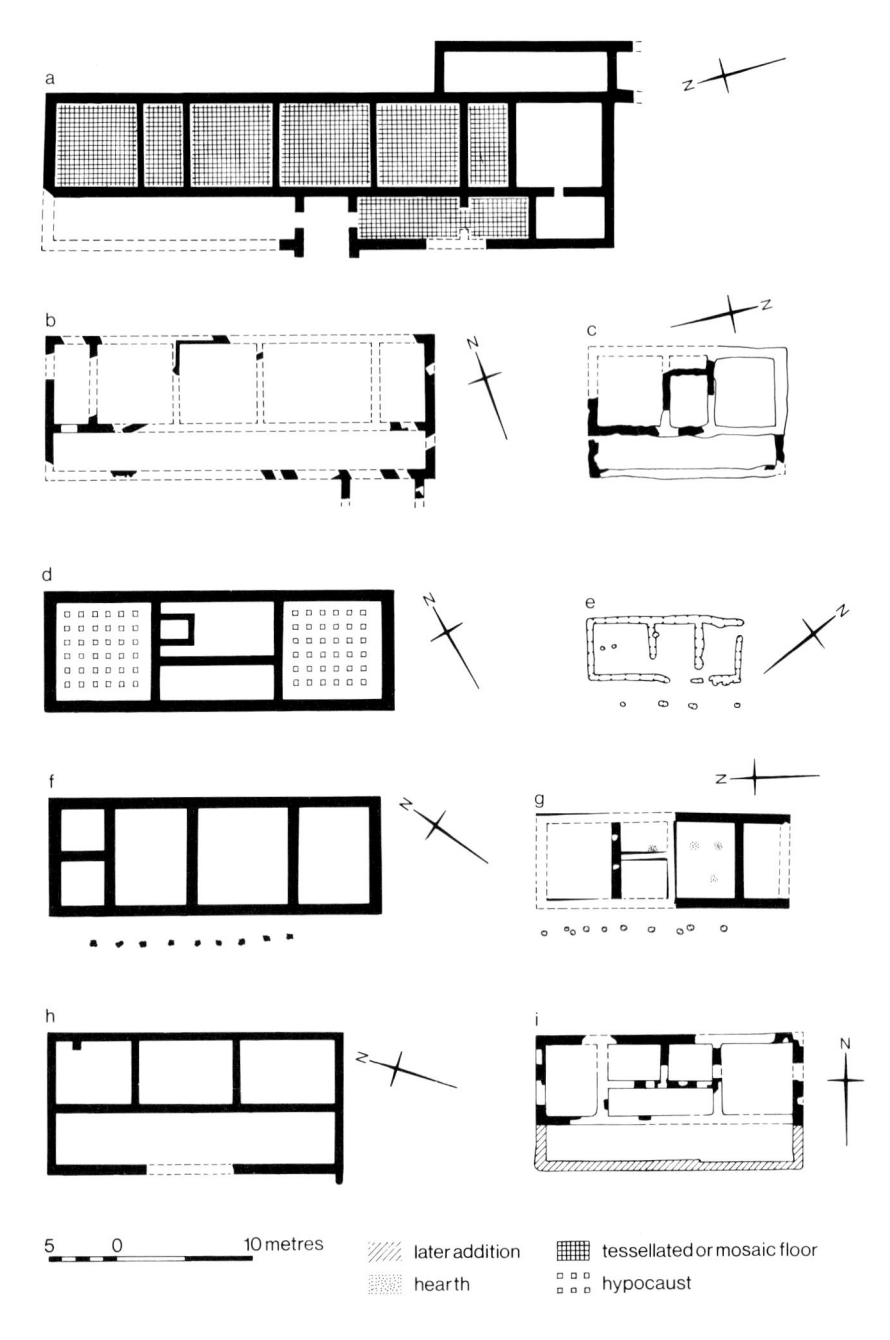

Figure 19 *Corridor houses: a. Downton (Wilts); b. Rock (I of W); c. Clay Lane (Northants); d. Langton (N Yorks); e. Topsham (Devon); f. Lockleys (Herts); g. Brixworth (Northants); h. Marshfield (Glos); i. Huntsham (Here & Worc).*

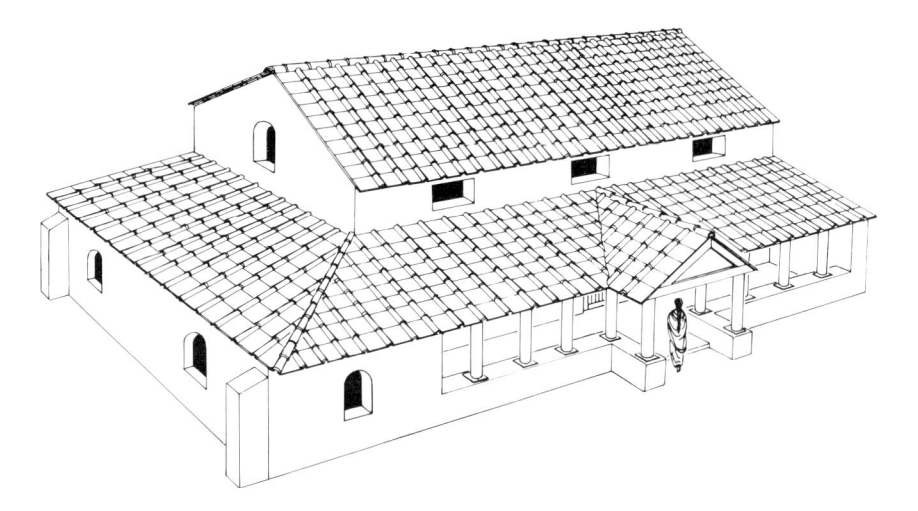

Figure 20 *Reconstruction of the corridor house at Wymbush (Bucks).*

WINGED CORRIDOR HOUSES (*see* Figure 21)

The addition of wings and a corridor to a house is taken to indicate the level of wealth and status of its inhabitants. Winged corridor villas represent the most common type of villa building in Roman Britain.[59] These buildings are nearly always at least partly stone-built, although an example at Boxmoor (Herts) which was built of timber and daub (*see* Figure 21f) is an exception. The winged corridor façade represents an elaborate symmetrical type indicating the investment of wealth as a symbol of status.[60]

Winged corridor buildings are usually identified as villa buildings, although there is some confusion between the archaeological and the historical definition.[61] Thus, while some winged corridor buildings clearly do represent the centres of agricultural estates, others possibly do not. A large number occur as isolated farms and there are too many to review here.[62] However, winged corridor buildings also occur in other contexts at local centres and *civitas* capitals.[63] The winged corridor building type was clearly indicative of wealth and status, but the construction of this type of house need not always have been associated with the ownership of an agricultural estate.[64]

Wings and corridors represent a standard package added to a range of building types throughout the northern provinces. Rather than focusing attention on the wing rooms and corridor it is of greater importance to understand the significance of the rooms behind the façade because, unlike the former, these rooms are not standardized.[65]

Aisled houses with wings and corridor occur on several sites[66] where the addition of wings to the aisled house probably indicates villa status (*see* Figure 17a, b; Figure 21a). It has been suggested above that winged corridor aisled houses were possibly the homes of extended families.

Hall villas represent the conversion of simple two or three-roomed rectangular houses of the type discussed above into winged corridor buildings (*see* Figure 21b, c). At a small number of sites the winged corridor house actually appears to develop out of a simple rectangular dwelling.[67] At other sites the simple rectangular dwelling unit lies at the core of the winged corridor building, although the entire building was probably constructed at one time.[68]

A parallel for this group of villa buildings has been observed in the 'hall villas' of Germany.[69] It has also been argued that the British hall villa indicates an influx of Gallic and germanic landowners to the comparative security of Britain during the Late Empire.[70] Both of these models can be disputed. Hall villas in Britain have proportionately narrower halls than the true germanic hall villa[71] and a parallel for the rooms at the core of the villa can be seen in the simple rectangular dwellings discussed above which presumably have an indigenous origin.

A number of authors have suggested that the hall villa relates to a particular type of social structure involving a kin group, perhaps of three or more generations, working a single tract of land.[72] This is a similar argument to that which has been considered in detail above for the aisled house,[73] that in the case of hall villa buildings the hall was used for communal functions by a kin group larger than a single generation. It has recently been suggested that at Barnsley Park (Glos) three families, resident within a group of round huts and holding land in some form of joint ownership, were converted into a single modified kin group living within a single hall villa.[74] This raises the question of whether some of the simple rectangular dwellings on non-villa settlements in Britain could also have contained an extended family of perhaps three generations. The evidence does not appear to exist to test this proposition and it seems equally likely that this building type indicates a single undivided or nuclear family, as has been suggested for the simple two to three-roomed dwellings at Bradley Hill.[75]

Cottage houses also occur with the addition of wings and corridors forming a range of small rooms behind the façade (*see* Figure 21, d-f). Richmond has suggested that this is the most common type of winged corridor villa in Britain.[76] It has also been argued that this represents a less patriarchal and more divided society in Britain than in areas of France and Germany where hall-type villas predominate. There may have been a division between landowners and tenants or slaves in Britain, as opposed to one between the head of the family and his kin on

Houses 49

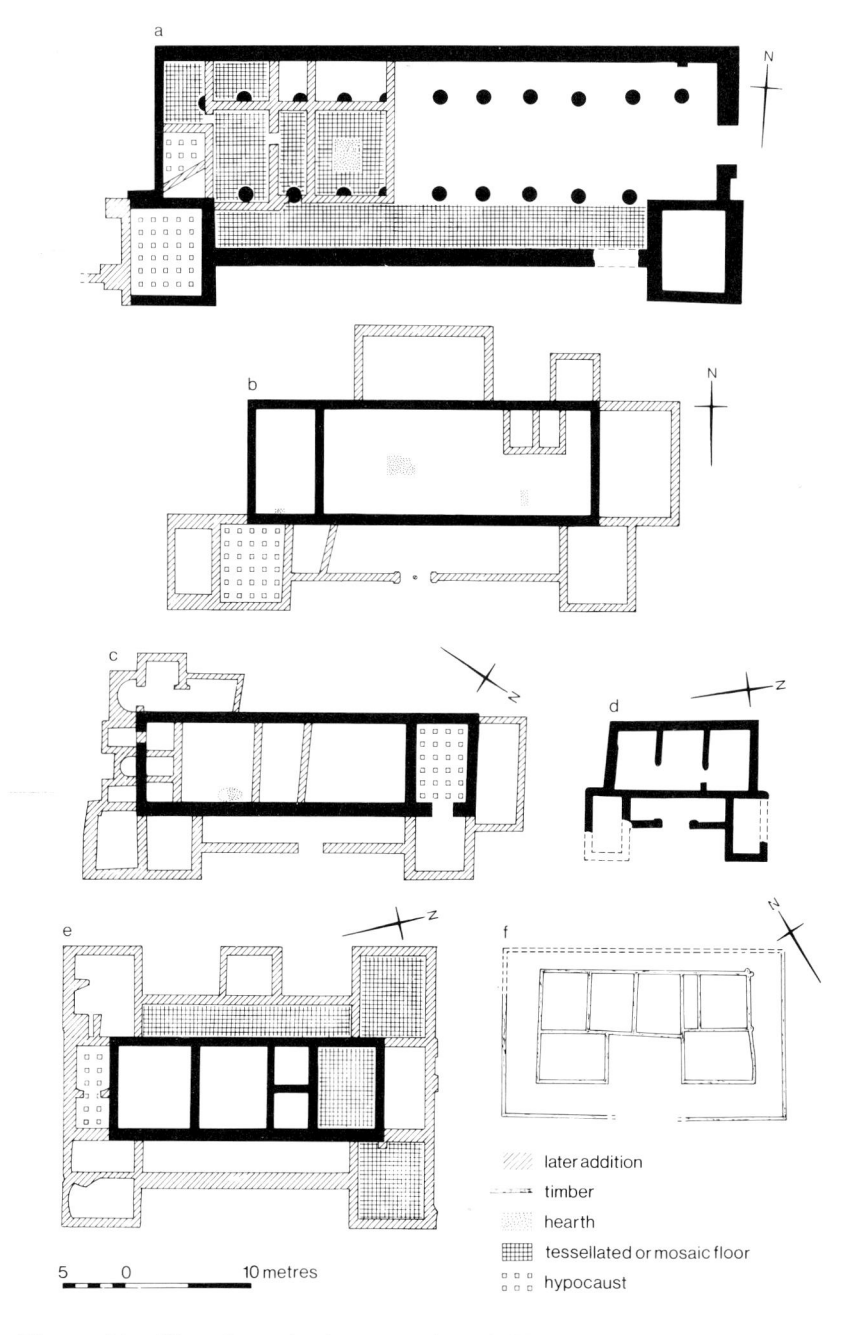

Figure 21 *Winged corridor houses: a. Stroud (Hants); b. Clear Cupboard (Glos); c. Cox Green (Berks); d. Hibaldstow (Humbs); e. Hambleden (Bucks); f. Boxmoor (Herts).*

50 Rural Settlement in Roman Britain

the Continent. It has been suggested that this is a consequence of the immigration of landowners from the Continent and the exploitation of the indigenous population as farm workers.[77] Different authors would therefore apparently like to see both the hall villa and the non-hall villa as a consequence of the immigration of foreign landowners from the Continent to Britain. In fact it is more likely that winged corridor houses of this type were derived from cottage houses and represent the homes of rich members of the indigenous population. The division of the building into a series of small rooms was a consequence of the growth of a desire for privacy within the Romano-British family and therefore constitutes an indigenous development.

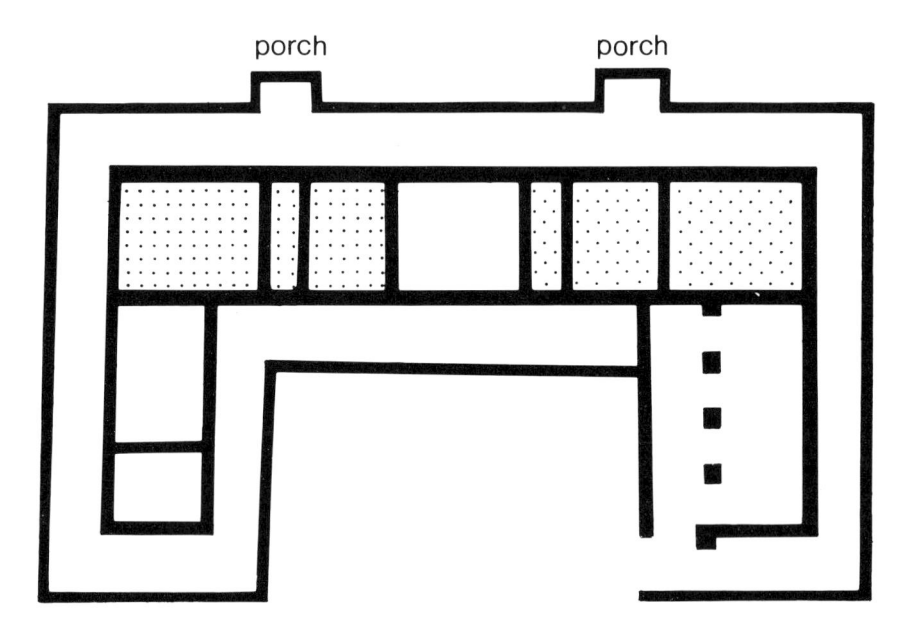

Figure 22 *The unit system applied to a villa at Gadebridge (Herts) showing the rooms occupied by two distinct family groups.*

The possibility that two or more suites of rooms can exist within a single aisled house was discussed above[78] and a similar phenomenon occurs in some winged corridor villa buildings. In some buildings two or more suites of rooms appear to indicate occupation of the building by two or more distinct family groups (*see* Figure 22). These buildings are those which have a symmetry or near-symmetry about a central line. This principle is exemplified at Gadebridge (Herts) where the wings of the villa have almost identical dimensions and where there is a porch at either end of the house. A second possible example of a house of this type occurs at Ditchley (Oxon), and a number of other similar winged corridor buildings are also known.[79] Villas of this type may incorporate two suites of rooms, each for the use of a single family group.[80]

L-SHAPED AND COURTYARD HOUSES (see Figure 23)

Courtyard villas comprise a courtyard which is completely surrounded by buildings forming a connected architectural whole.[81] Villas in which miscellaneous buildings, including a winged corridor house, are grouped around a farmyard – even if these are contained within a continuous enclosing wall[82] – do not represent courtyard villas. On a number of sites L-shaped buildings occur (see Figure 23f, g). Even though these buildings are integrated with other farm buildings into walled farmyards these also are not courtyard houses.

At a number of courtyard villa buildings one or more additional outer courtyards appear to have included agricultural buildings, the residential area being separated from the agricultural area. At Woodchester (Glos) three courtyards existed, although they have not been totally excavated and are not fully understood. The separation of agricultural from residential areas will be discussed in detail below.[83]

The British courtyard house appears to have developed out of indigenous building types, rather than represent a direct copy of a Mediterranean form. It is clear that the majority of courtyard houses in this country developed physically out of earlier cottage or winged corridor buildings.[84] Although courtyard houses are common in the Mediterranean areas of the empire, the courtyard was a garden-court placed within or behind the house and away from the main entrance. In the British courtyard houses the house is entered through the courtyard. This is the case even at the first-century courtyard house at Fishbourne (see Figure 24) which, unlike other British courtyard houses, has obvious continental origins.[85] The British courtyard villa is in effect the reverse of the classical house, with the entrance facing into the yard. The reason for this arrangement lay in the origin of Romano-British courtyard houses. These houses were an indigenous development, even if it occurred under classical influence.

Courtyard houses may have developed in one of two ways. First, winged corridor houses, such as Stroud (Hants), often face onto a farmyard with outbuildings and accommodation for farm hands along the other sides. It is possible that some courtyard houses resulted from the unification of a range of villa buildings and outbuildings into a single architectural unit. An alternative and perhaps more plausible explanation is that individual courtyard houses developed due to the elaboration and extension of the wing rooms of a winged corridor house into the lateral wings of a courtyard house. The villas at Folkestone (Kent) and

52 *Rural Settlement in Roman Britain*

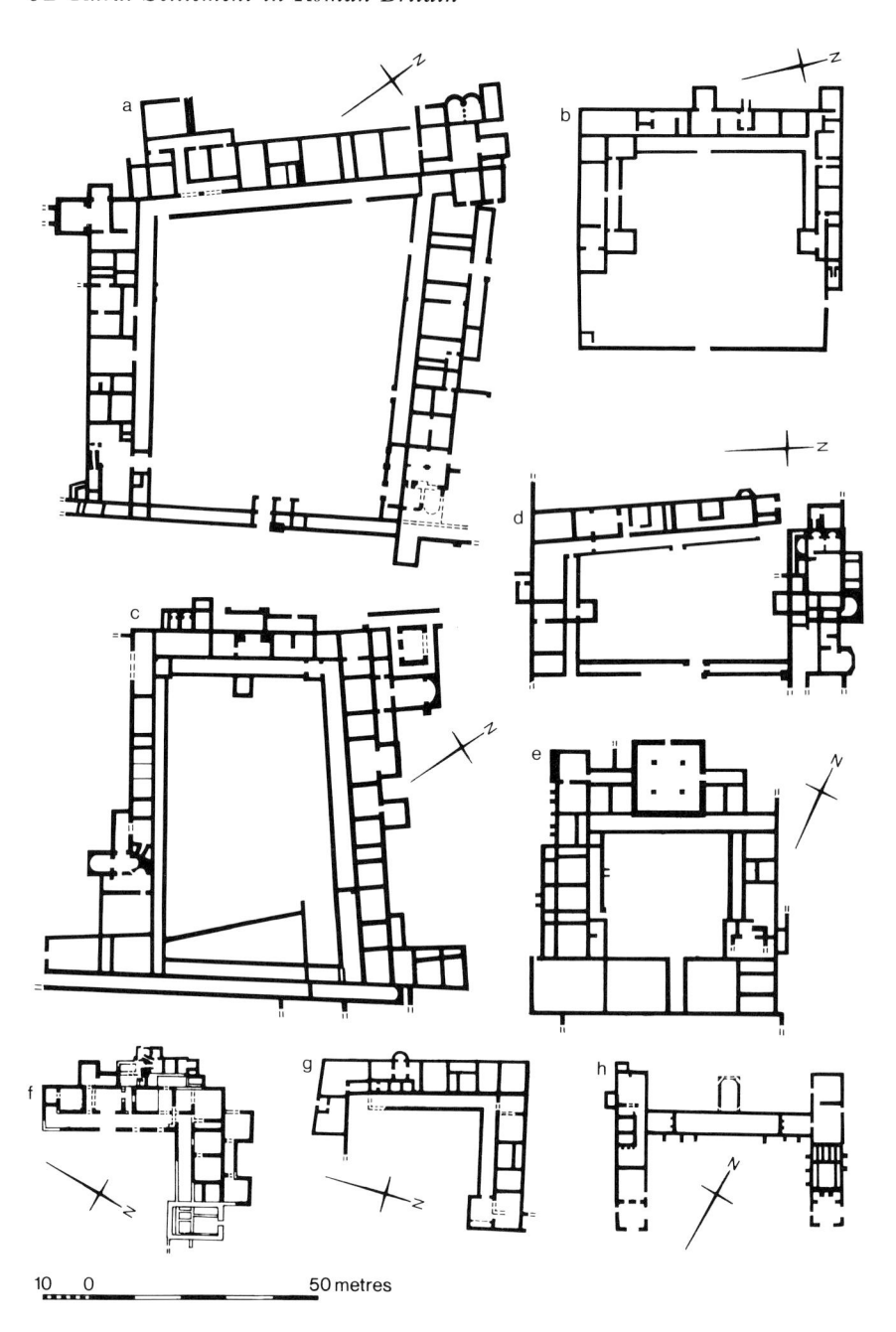

Figure 23 *L-shaped and courtyard houses: a. North Leigh (Oxon); b. Spoonley Wood (Glos); c. Bignor (W Susx); d. Chedworth (Glos); e. Woodchester (Glos); f. Rockbourne (Hants); g. Llantwit Major (S Glam); h. Witcombe (Glos).*

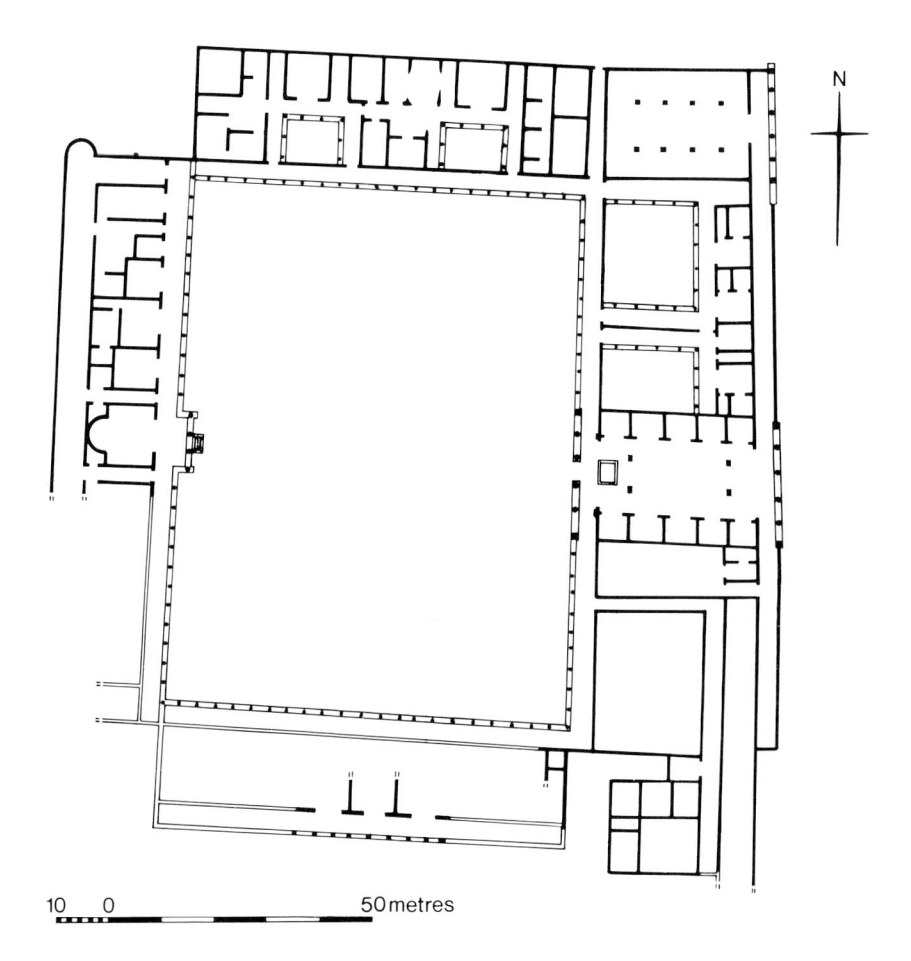

Figure 24 *The Roman palace at Fishbourne (W Susx). (After Cunliffe 1971, figure 42).*

Witcombe (Glos) appear to represent this process in action, as they are half-way between winged corridor and courtyard houses (*see* Figure 23h). The development of courtyard villas from winged corridor villas presumably indicates that many of the owners of the courtyard houses would have been members of an indigenous British élite rather than rich landowners from other provinces who had settled and appropriated large estates in this country.

The 'unit system' model has been mentioned above during the discussion of aisled and winged corridor buildings. This idea is also of relevance to the analysis of courtyard villas. Many, if not all, courtyard villas appear to be made up of two or more houses which were often placed at right-angles to one another. During an early phase in the construction of the villa at Chedworth (Glos) three houses were apparent and were later converted into a single courtyard house.[86] The British courtyard house may represent the home of a number of distinct family units, rather than being the home of one particularly rich family and its servants.

Chapter 4
Compounds – family farms

WHAT IS A COMPOUND?

The 'compound' is a small group of buildings which represented the family farm. Excavation on Romano-British rural sites has often been small-scale and intended to uncover only single house plans and, as a result, the evidence for compounds on Romano-British settlements is not as prolific as that for buildings. These complexes of contemporary and related buildings have been neglected, but nevertheless modern large-scale excavations are beginning to provide some evidence on which discussion can be based.

The significance of the farm and villa compound is that such groups of related buildings represented the dwellings of a single nuclear or extended family. Compounds are known on prehistoric sites in Britain. At the Iron Age lake village of Glastonbury the typical compound had three houses with additional storage structures and working areas, each apparently the home to an extended family of around twenty individuals.[1]

Compounds are also known in the Romano-British countryside. The evidence of Roman sites in southern, northern and western Britain indicates that the individual compound contained a range of buildings including one or two, and on occasion up to five, residential buildings, agricultural and storage buildings and in some cases bath-houses and gatehouses. In many cases compounds were defined by some form of enclosing boundary.

ENCLOSED COMPOUNDS AND OPEN COMPOUNDS

A minority of Romano-British settlements appear to have been open, with no obvious enclosing boundary. Unenclosed non-villa settlements include those at Bradley Hill (Somer), Studland (Dorset), Chysauster (Corn) and the second to third-century settlement at Odell (Beds). Some villa houses also seem to have been unenclosed.[2] In cases where excavated sites appear to have been open this may actually be a result of the limited nature of excavation and the concentration of excavators on stone-walled building. Alternatively, the boundaries could have been hedged and such an arrangement would leave no archaeological trace. It is therefore possible that these sites may also in reality have been enclosed by some form of boundary.

The majority of compounds were defined by some form of enclosing boundary. The origin of the enclosure around the Romano-British farm probably lay in the Iron Age as most farms of that period are known to have been enclosed.[3] Compounds were defined by one of a range of enclosing boundary types. Banks and ditches were the most common type of enclosing boundary on Iron Age settlements in upland and lowland Britain and also occurred around compounds in the Roman province. Stone walls occurred on Iron Age settlements and some compounds in the Roman period of southern and northern Britain were enclosed in this way.

At Woodcuts (Dorset) the farm area was defined by a ditched boundary throughout the period of occupation, although it was recut several times. At Odell (Beds) during the first century BC and first century AD the settlement was defined by a ditched enclosure, but the second and third-century farm appears to have been unenclosed. At Claydon Pike (Glos) two ditched compounds, possibly of differing status, have been identified by excavation.[4] A later settlement on this site was also enclosed. At Catsgore (Somer) six farm compounds have been examined and the boundary ditches of these compounds of the early periods were still in use in the fourth century, although some were replaced with stone walls.

Ditched boundaries defined compounds on many other non-villa settlements in the Roman province. Aerial photographs of Roman settlement sites in the Cambridgeshire and Lincolnshire Fens indicate discrete ditched enclosures which when fieldwalked usually produce a scatter of domestic refuse showing that each is a single farm site.[5] The same appears to be true in many other areas of southern Britain where standing earthworks or aerial photography indicate settlements defined by earthwork enclosures.[6] The typical site usually includes a settlement enclosure which is often associated with trackways and linear boundaries. A distinction clearly occurs in many areas between settlements defined by single enclosures – possibly single farmsteads – and those in which multiple enclosures occur. Some of the settlements with multiple enclosures were made up of a number of farms.[7]

In the north and west of the province enclosures defining non-villa settlements are also very common. In Cornwall, Wales and northern England the small enclosed settlement, often oval or rectangular in form, is the most common settlement type.[8] The enclosures on these sites vary from dry-stone walls to ditches and banks, and the nature of the enclosing earthwork appears often to depend on local geology. Where the local bedrock is close to the surface and ditches are hard to cut a stone enclosing wall was usually constructed. Where the local geology made the digging of a ditch possible and local stone was unavailable a bank-and-ditch was built to enclose the settlement. In northern England stone-built settlement boundaries are common in the uplands, while earth and timber-built enclosures are more common in the major river valleys and lowlands.

Compounds containing villa buildings were also usually defined by a ditch, a wall, or both. Ditchley (Oxon) was enclosed in an early phase by a rectangular ditched enclosure and later a wall was added on the inner lip of the enclosure. Ditched enclosures occur around other villa buildings in the province.[9]

In contrast to the situation at Ditchley a large number of villas had walled enclosures around the farmyard.[10] In some of these cases the buildings of the villa are actually incorporated into the walls. It should be noted that the rectangular walled compound with buildings constructed in the wall is not necessarily a Roman innovation, as some of the stone-walled farm compounds of north-western Wales demonstrate similar characteristics.

Villa settlements sometimes appear to have consisted of multiple settlement enclosures. The clearest examples of sites of this type are the rich and elaborate winged corridor houses and courtyard villas in which a distinction was made between a residential courtyard and an agricultural courtyard.[11]

Compounds at local centres always occurred in multiple groupings and were defined in at least two ways. Ditched enclosures surrounding, or partly surrounding, compounds are common on some sites, while at others compounds appear to have been defined by roads. The definition of building plots by roads is a phenomenon which is also found in the *civitas* capitals of the province.[12]

Compounds marked out by ditched enclosures have recently been located at a number of local centres that have been subject to large-scale excavation.[13] Plots defined wholly or partly by roads are also known at Ashton (Northants), where an area of the town has recently been excavated, and at Scole (Norf). At other sites building plots defined in this way are visible on aerial photographs, or have been located by limited excavation.[14]

It is therefore apparent that compounds can be defined on many settlements and include examples at non-villa settlements, villas and local centres. It would appear, however, that certain settlement compounds are more clearly defined than others. This point can be demonstrated through the discussion of a range of examples. Non-villa settlements in northern England, Wales and Cornwall usually had a substantial banked or walled enclosure and the same is true of villas in central and southern Britain (*see* Figures 26–8, 32–4). Compounds on non-villa settlements in central and southern Britain and at local centres

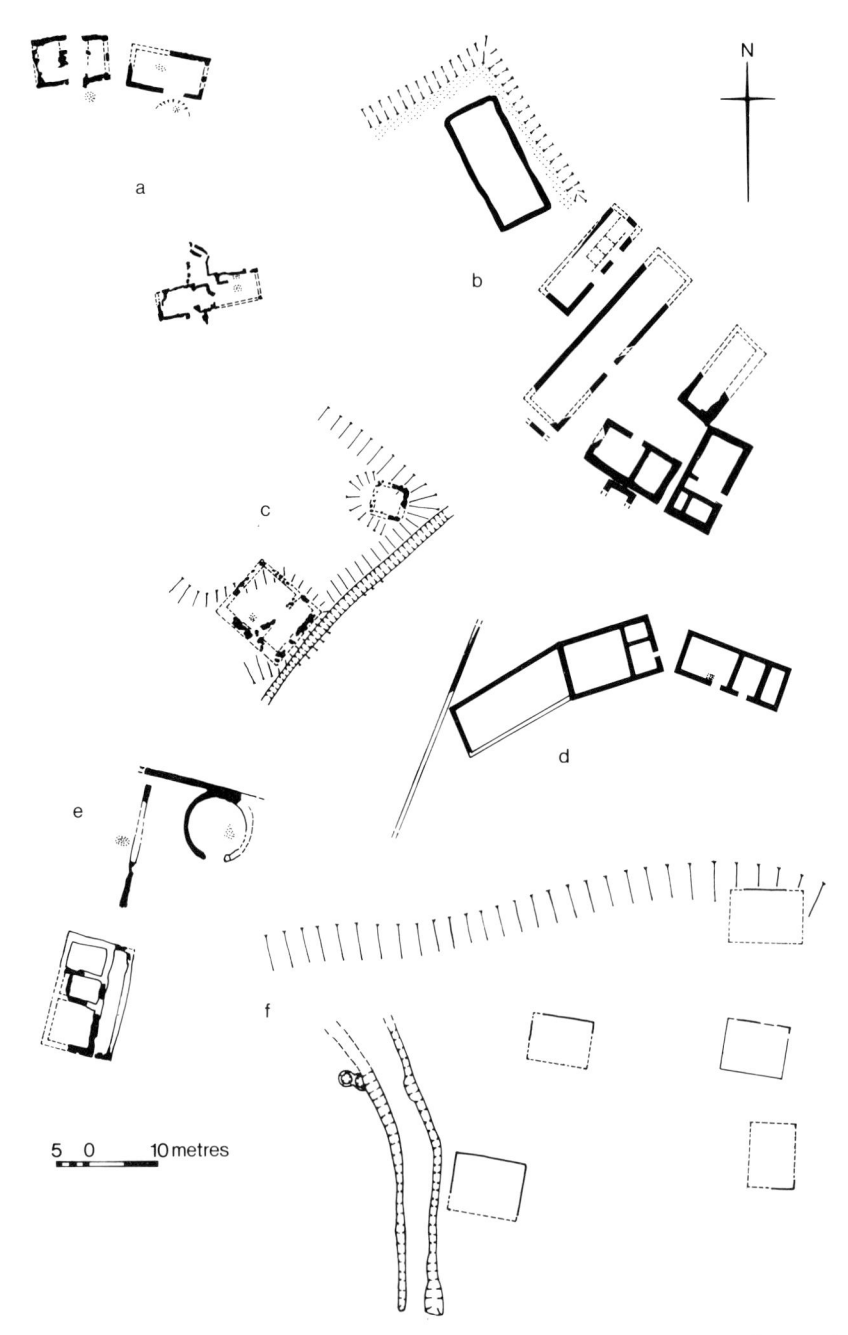

Figure 25 *Compounds on non-villa sites in southern Britain: a. Studland (Dorset); b. Catsgore Complex 1, Period 2 (Somer); c. Overton Down (Wilts); d. Bradley Hill (Somer); e. Clay Lane, Period 3b (Northants); f. Park Brow (W Susx).*

are not usually so clearly defined (*see* Figures 25, 36). The reason for this may lie in the social significance of the enclosure. Recent discussions of the significance of enclosures on Iron Age sites in Britain suggest that a substantial ditched and banked (or walled) enclosure had a symbolic function.[15] It is possible that such an enclosure marked the high status of the Iron Age social group. A broad continuity of social organization between Iron Age and Roman Britain may suggest that this was also the case in the Roman province. A substantial enclosing boundary may therefore provide a way of identifying sites of high status in Roman Britain.

HOUSES, OUTBUILDINGS AND COMPOUNDS

Evidence for the nature and layout of buildings within these compounds will now be considered in greater detail.

Compounds on non-villa and villa settlements

At Catsgore (Somer) the excavator has been able to demonstrate that simple rectangular houses occur in compounds. These compounds consisted of one, or often two, dwelling houses with associated storage houses and workshops. At Catsgore six farm compounds out of an original total of perhaps twelve have been partly or fairly fully excavated. Each compound was clustered within its own ditched or walled enclosure and the boundaries appear to have survived from the foundation of the settlement in the second century AD until its abandonment in the later fourth century. Development can be seen in some of the Catsgore compounds: Complex 1 began in Period 1 (AD 100/120 to 150/180) with only a single round dwelling house, but by Period 2 (late second century to early fourth century) there were two rectangular dwelling houses (*see* Figure 25b). The evidence for Complex 1 could indicate a growth in the size of the family unit represented in the compound from the early to late second century.[16] A number, perhaps the majority, of the other excavated farm compounds at Catsgore contain two dwelling houses in Periods 2 and 3.[17]

A similar farm compound has been excavated at Bradley Hill (Somer), where two dwelling houses and a barn date from the third and fourth centuries (*see* Figure 25d). It is probable that each house contained a single nuclear family[18] and the occurrence of two contemporary houses presumably indicates an extended family. It was noted above that the compound enclosure has not been located on this site, although Leech suggests that it was possibly stone-walled and lay outside the area of the excavation. At Bradley Hill the kin group lived on an isolated hilltop and do not appear to have been grouped together with other families into a larger settlement, as was the case at Catsgore.

At Studland (Dorset) two 'complexes' of buildings were excavated and may form a single farm compound (*see* Figure 25a). It is not clear whether this compound was defined by an enclosure or was open. In the first century AD the settlement consisted of two or three round or oval huts. In the mid-first to second century there would appear to have been two small rectangular dwelling houses on the site. During the third to fourth centuries there were at least three rectangular dwellings, possibly all within the same compound.

Farm compounds exist on other non-villa settlements in southern Britain[19] and in large numbers on excavated and unexcavated sites in northern and western Britain (*see* Figures 26–9). The so-called 'courtyard houses' excavated at Chysauster (Corn), which are not to be confused with courtyard villa houses, provide clear examples. Eight courtyard houses exist as earthworks on the site and six have been excavated. All the houses appear to have a likeness to one another. The main feature is a courtyard area, possibly open to the air. On the side of the courtyard opposing the entrance is a large oval room, and a long narrow room and sometimes other rooms flank the courtyard. The individual courtyard house is clearly a farm compound, as it incorporates a number of distinct buildings of which the large oval room was the living room. One of the Chysauster compounds (Number 3) appears to have been converted into a form which included two living rooms and is thus comparable to the compounds with multiple dwellings at Catsgore, Bradley Hill and Studland (*see* Figure 28d).

Probable farm compounds are also known on many other sites in the north and west.[20] Some of these sites may have had only a single oval or rectangular house (*see* Figures 26c, 27b). Other sites, however, had two or more contemporary dwelling houses.[21] An extreme example is Trethurgy (Corn) which appears to have had as many as five dwelling houses at one stage (*see* Figure 28b). The group resident in the compound at Trethurgy may have consisted of five smaller nuclear families, each resident within an individual roundhouse and forming part of a larger extended family. The size of this extended family unit is uncertain, but could have been similar to the twenty individuals suggested for each compound at the Glastonbury lake village.

In conclusion, it is clear from the evidence discussed above that some farm compounds in Roman Britain contained only a single house[22] and in these cases a nuclear family may be indicated. Throughout Roman Britain non-villa settlements with two or more domestic dwelling houses are common and this indicates the occurrence of extended families on many sites. The way in which extended families developed can also be distinguished. At Catsgore Compound 1 developed from a single house

Compounds – family farms 61

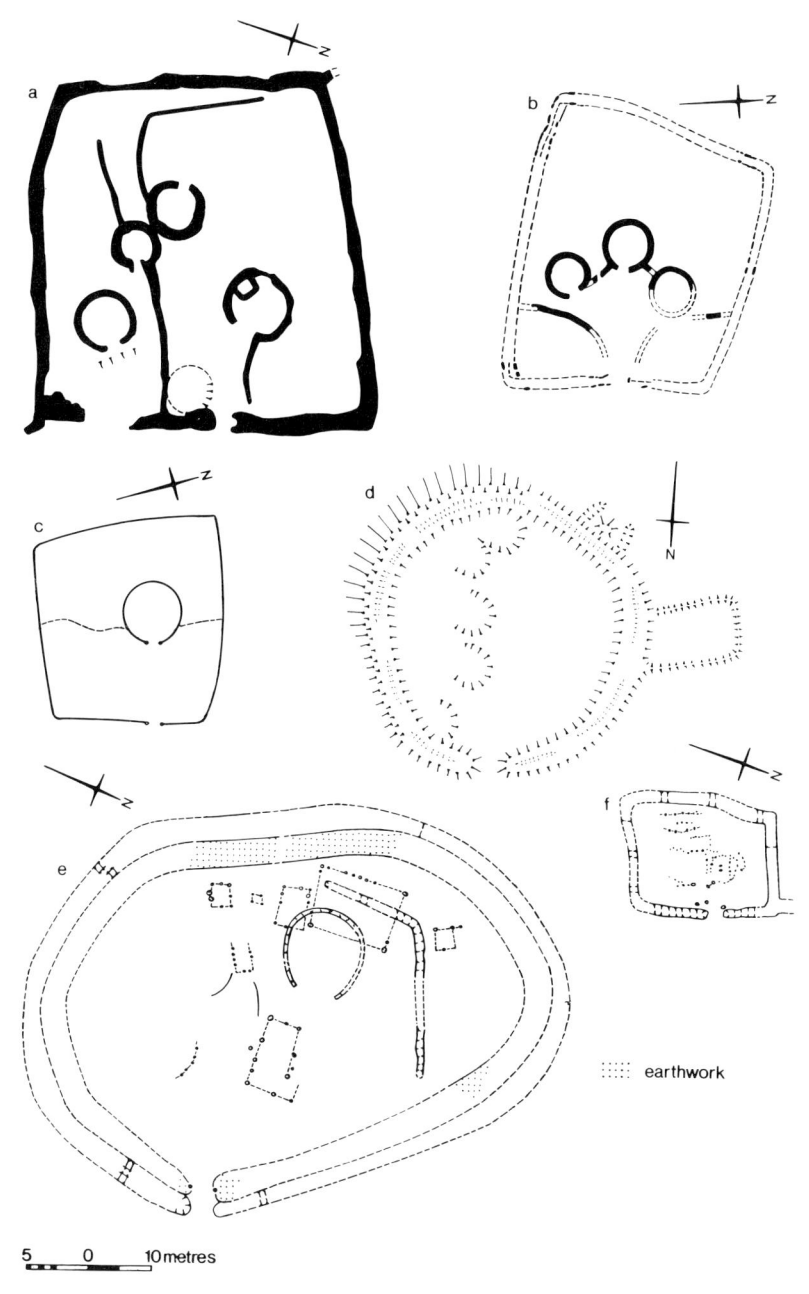

Figure 26 *Compounds on non-villa sites in northern England: a. Middle Gunnar Peak (Northum); b. Tower Knowe (Northum); c. Belling Law, Period 1–2 (Northum); d. Forcegarth Pasture (Durham); e. Penrith (Cumbr); f. Silloth Farm (Cumbr).*

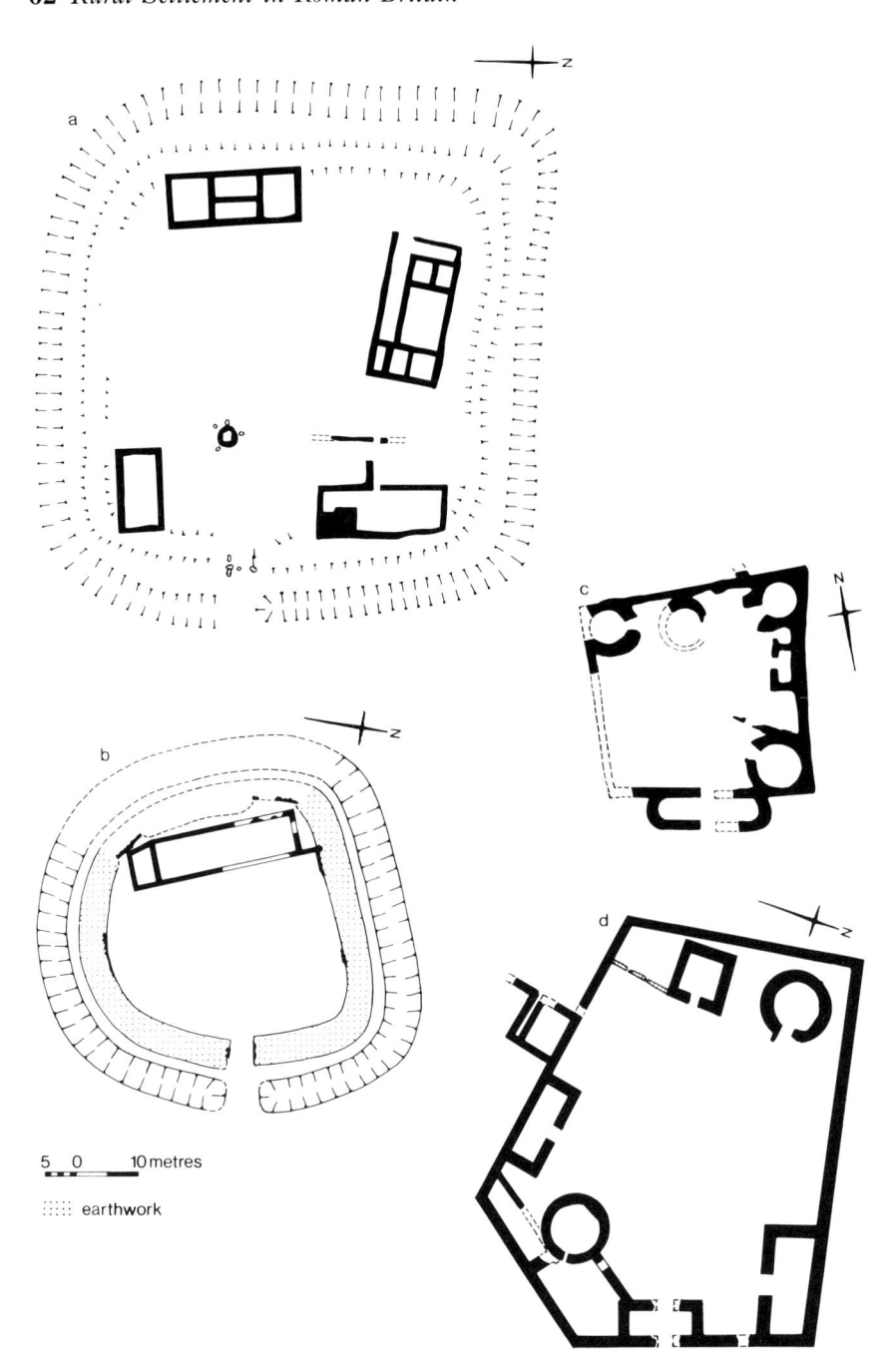

Figure 27 *Compounds on non-villa sites in Wales: a. Whitton, Period X (S Glam); b. Cwmbrwyn (Dyfed); c. Cefn Graeanog (Gwyn); d. Din Lligwy (Gwyn).*

Compounds – family farms 63

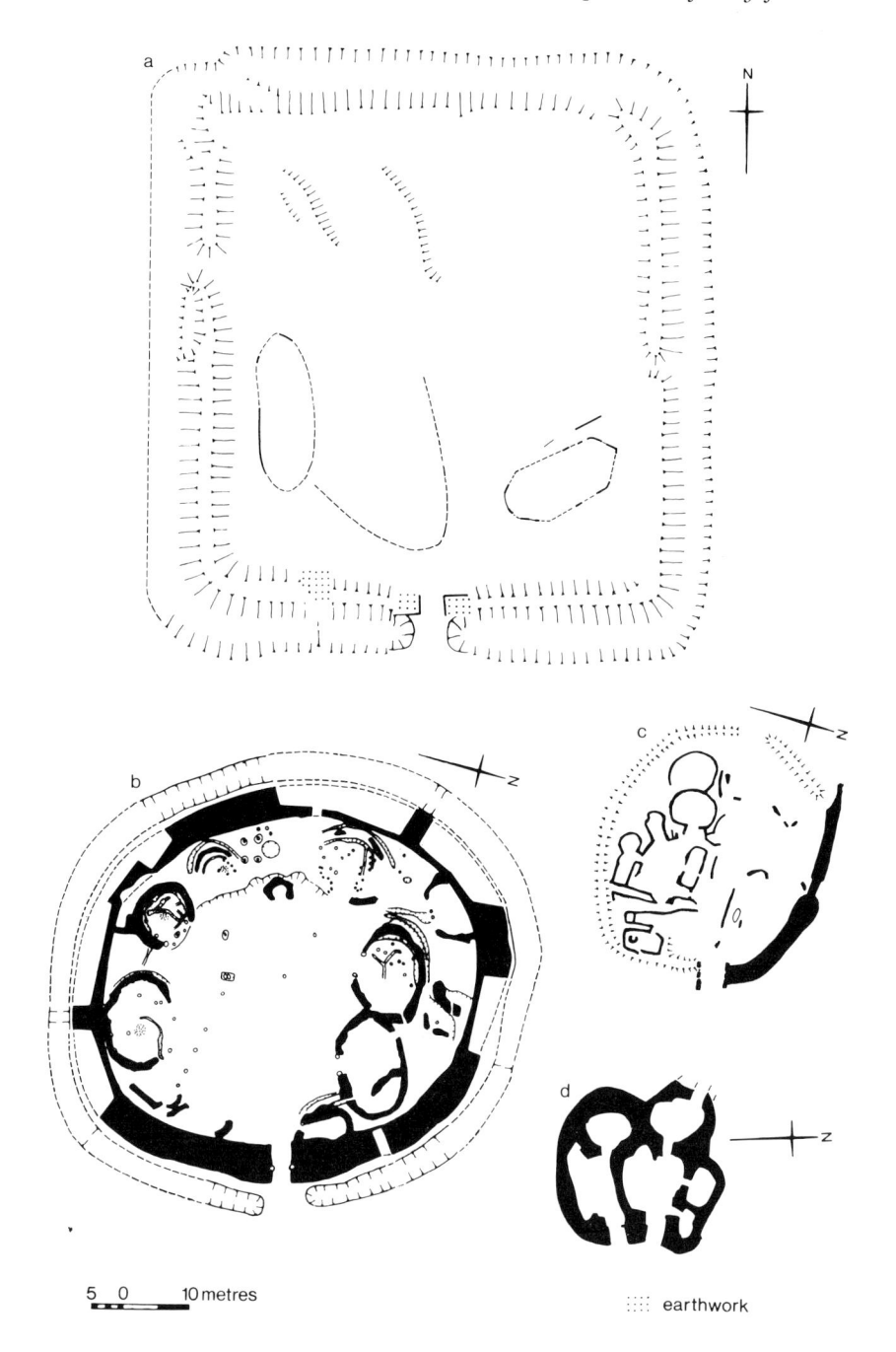

Figure 28 *Compounds on non-villa sites in Cornwall: a. Grambla; b. Trethurgy; c. Goldherring; d. Chysauster House 3.*

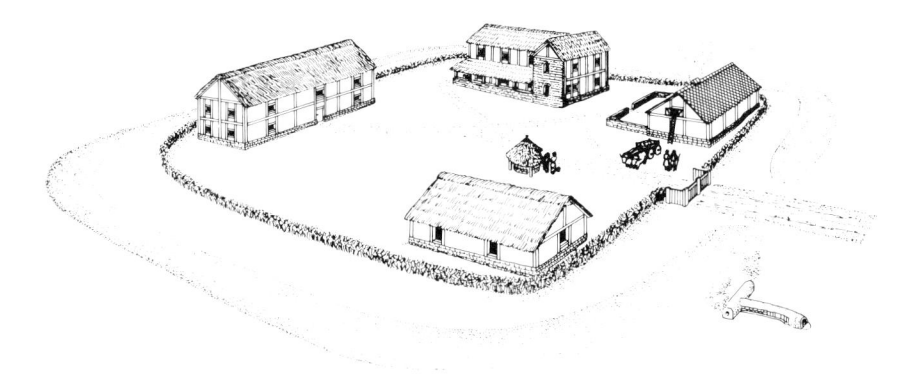

Figure 29 *Reconstruction of a non-villa settlement compound at Whitton (S Glam).*

in Period 1 to two houses in Period 2. This may indicate the creation of an extended family from a nuclear family. At Studland a compound developed from two houses in Period 2 into three houses in Period 3. The maximum number of houses recognized is five and this may represent the maximum size to which the extended family grew in the Romano-British countryside.

Groups of related buildings also exist on sites which have villa buildings and these have been discussed in some detail by other authors.[23] The range of buildings represented are similar to those on non-villa settlements – such as dwelling houses, barns and storage buildings – often with the addition of a bath-house and occasionally also a gatehouse. Several types of villa-farm layout and a range of sites that typify these situations have been defined. Villa buildings and outbuildings occasionally appear to be positioned with no obvious attempt at planning, but in the majority of cases the buildings are set out in a fairly regular manner around a courtyard.[24]

The actual layout of villa compounds will not be discussed in detail; the important point is that these groups of buildings are directly comparable to farm compounds on non-villa settlements. Some villa compounds have only a single internal house (*see* Figures 30–31). It was argued above that a number of the better excavated, or better preserved, farm compounds on non-villa settlements had two or more dwelling houses and exactly the same situation occurs on many villa sites in southern Britain.

The idea that villas often occur in pairs has already been introduced.[25] In some cases a single building can be divided into two equal parts, each of which probably houses a single family and these buildings have been discussed above. In other cases two actual distinct buildings occur within a single compound. On both types of site two or more houses

Figure 30 *Aerial photograph of the villa compound at Islip (Oxon). Copyright Cambridge Committee on Aerial Photography.*

occur, in effect, within the same villa compound (*see* Figures 32–34). Only a few examples of actual pairs of buildings need to be given as the evidence has been discussed in full elsewhere.[26]

At Gayton Thorpe (Norf) two houses situated side by side both had wings (*see* Figure 33e). Although the southern house was considerably smaller than the northern one it appears to be unlikely that it functioned as servants' quarters, being embellished with wing rooms and a mosaic floor.[27] Thus the two halves of the Gayton Thorpe villa building presumably represent a paired household.

The buildings at Marshfield (Glos) fall half-way between, on the one hand, the double villa incorporated within a single building and on the other the two separate villa buildings within a single compound. A corridor house was constructed in Period IIIA (mid-third century to *c.*AD 360–70) and a second corridor house added to one end in Period IIIB (*c.* 360–70 to early fifth century). These two buildings appear to be of equal status and, although attached to each other, faced in opposite directions. Analysis of the buildings may indicate two distinct family groups within each house, suggesting that four distinct families of equal status lived within the two buildings. Although initially of equal status, the evidence appears to indicate that by the late fourth century one of the two family groups became dominant over the other.[28]

At Rockbourne (Hants) the situation is similar to Marshfield as there appear to have been two houses (*see* Figure 33b). The west wing was constructed during the second century and had an associated bath-house.

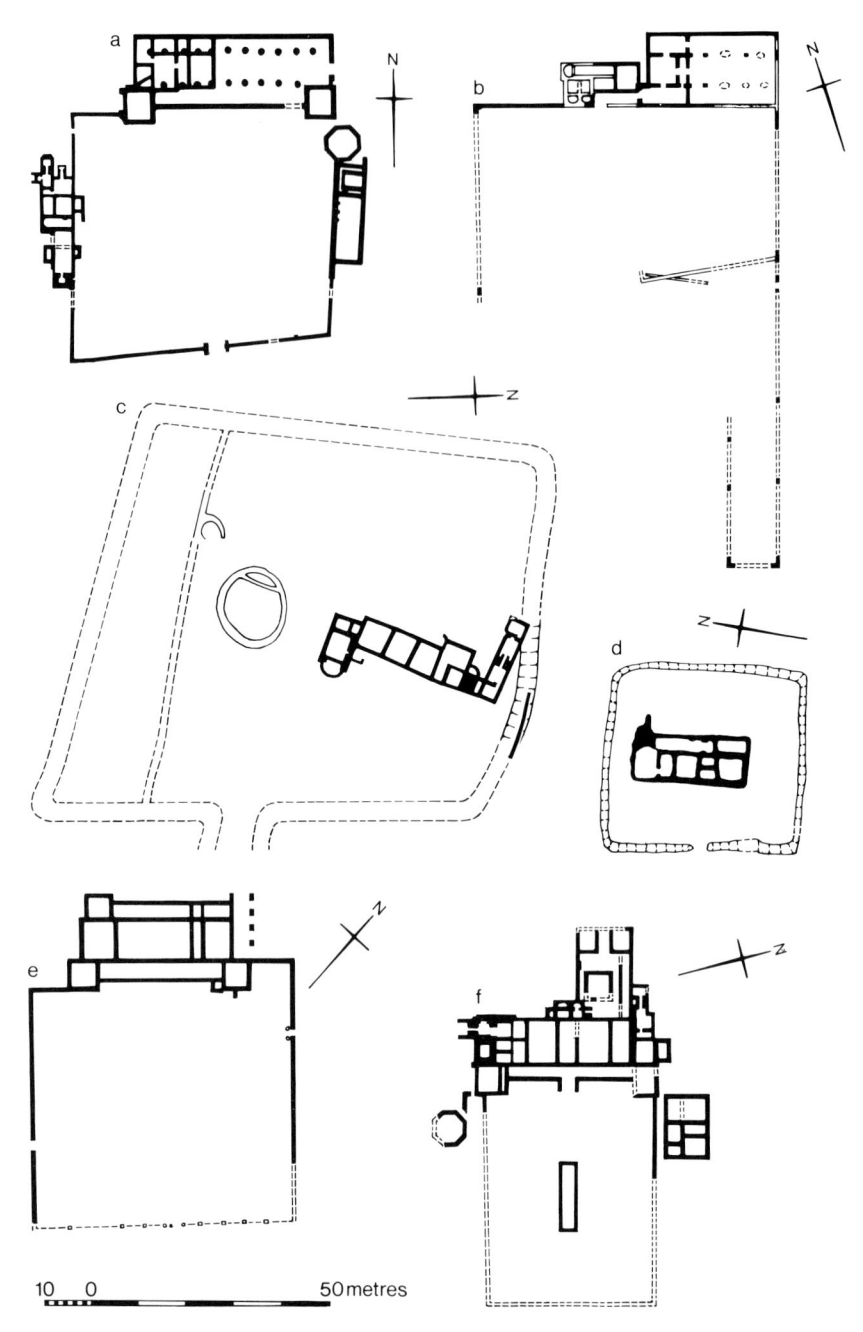

Figure 31 *Villa compounds with a single house: a. Stroud (Hants); b. Combley (I of W); c. Holme House (N Yorks); d. Barton Court (Oxon); e. Frocester Court (Glos); f. Bancroft (Bucks).*

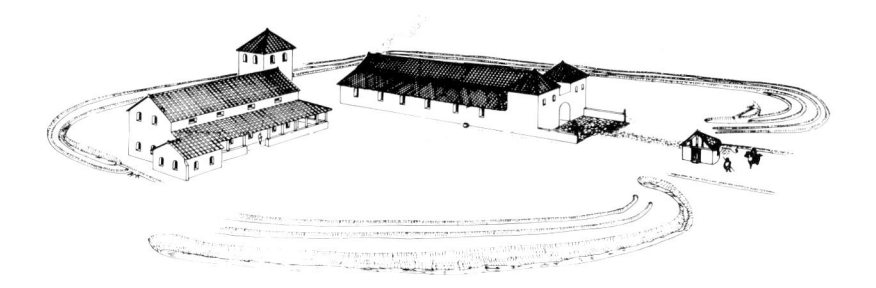

Figure 32 *Reconstruction of a villa compound at Norton Disney (Lincs).*

At the end of the second century or early in the third century a north wing was added with a separate bath-house. These houses were at right-angles to each other with agricultural buildings situated to the south. The Royal Commission has noted the duality of structure of the house and has argued that it relates to the type of social structure expressed in the unit system model.[29] It is possible that on this site the duality originated from the expansion of the family group represented in the western house and its division into two houses. This process is similar to the development of Compound 1 at Catsgore between Periods 1 and 2.[30]

It can be argued that the difference between the L-shaped villa at Rockbourne and the courtyard house at Chedworth, discussed in the previous chapter, is a consequence of the number of households represented in the initial laying-out of the site. At Chedworth there were three houses representing three households and these were joined at right-angles to each other around a courtyard. The two houses at Rockbourne were also laid out at right-angles to one another and formed an L-shaped building with a courtyard in front. A similar development may have occurred on some other villa sites.[31]

On some villa sites, including those reviewed above, two houses of relatively equal status appear to exist. On other sites, however, where two houses occur within the same compound, the evidence may indicate a social distinction between the inhabitants of the two buildings (*see* Figure 34). In this context Richmond's model for the significance of aisled buildings, which was discussed briefly above,[32] requires more detailed consideration. This model specifies that aisled houses were the homes of labourers, tenants and slaves on a villa estate. The alternative model, that aisled houses were the homes of extended kin groupings and that the evidence does not appear to suggest a rigid division between landowner and tenant, has already been considered.[33]

The information for the association of aisled houses with winged corridor and corridor villas on a number of sites will now be discussed. At Norton Disney (Lincs) the aisled house and villa building are joined

68 *Rural Settlement in Roman Britain*

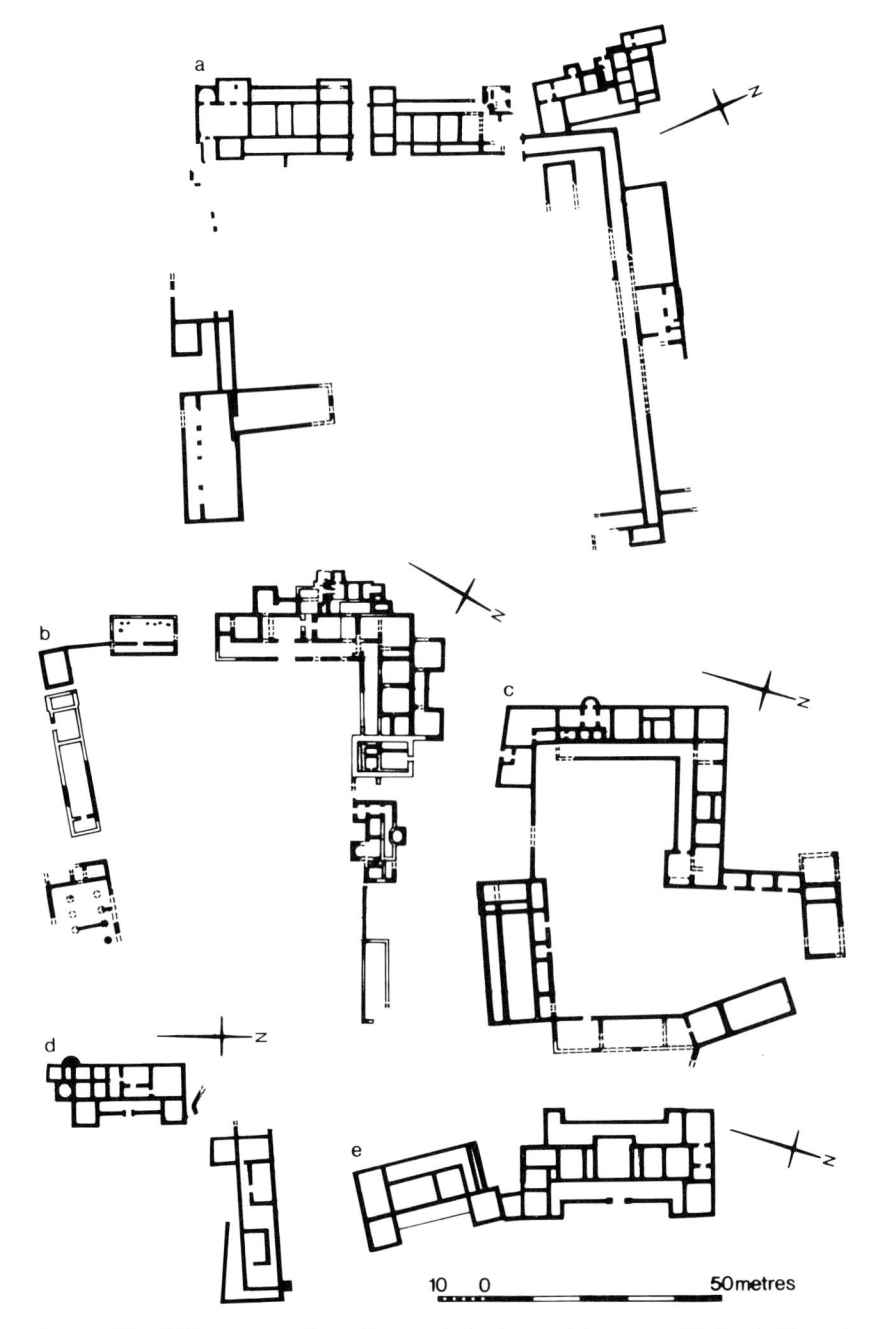

Figure 33 *Villa compounds with two relatively equal houses: a. Halstock (Dorset); b. Rockbourne (Hants); c. Llantwit Major (S Glam); d. Beadlam (N Yorks); e. Gayton Thorpe (Norf).*

by a bath-house (*see* Figure 34c). In the final phase of occupation, around AD 300–360, a luxurious suite of rooms was added to the aisled house and it has been argued that this suggests that there was no clear division between the master in the villa house and slaves or tenants in the aisled house.[34]

At Sparsholt (Hants) a group of houses evolved in a piecemeal fashion (*see* Figure 34b). A second-century house, perhaps an undivided aisled farmhouse, was replaced around AD 200 by an aisled house with living rooms and a bath suite. During the fourth century a winged corridor villa was constructed at right-angles to the aisled house, facing the gateway of a rectangular enclosure which incorporated both buildings. Tessellated pavements were later added to both houses. It is possible to explain the evidence by arguing that the aisled house of the second to third centuries indicates the joint ownership of land by a kin group, and that the construction of the winged corridor house in the fourth century suggests the concentration of wealth and status in the hands of the individual villa owner. The provision of mosaics in the fourth-century aisled house does not, however, support the proposition that the kin group was dispossessed of all rights and status, and it is possible that there was no clear division of wealth between the occupants of the two houses.[35]

At Mansfield Woodhouse (Notts) the reverse of the situation at Sparsholt appears to have occurred (*see* Figure 34d). During the late second century a corridor house was built on the site and in the early fourth century an aisled house was added to the north-east. The aisled house later received mosaics and a hypocaust. It is possible that this indicates a version of the unit system represented on other villa sites and perhaps the creation of a kin group associated with the villa in the fourth century.

Richmond's model of a distinction between masters in winged corridor houses and servants or estate workers in the aisled houses does not appear to be demonstrated clearly on these three sites. It is probable that lowly estate workers would not be provided with hypocausts and mosaic floors. In addition, any of the aisled houses at Norton Disney, Sparsholt or Mansfield Woodhouse would be considered a villa house if it occurred in isolation from a winged corridor building.

On some sites one or more aisled houses without hypocausts and mosaics occur in association with winged corridor buildings (*see* Figure 34a). In these cases the occupants of the aisled houses could have been estate workers, as signs of luxury and status are absent from their dwellings.[36] This evidence requires a fuller discussion than is possible in this book. What does appear to be clear is that when an aisled house occurs alongside a winged corridor house this does not invariably indicate that the status of its occupants was necessarily that of estate

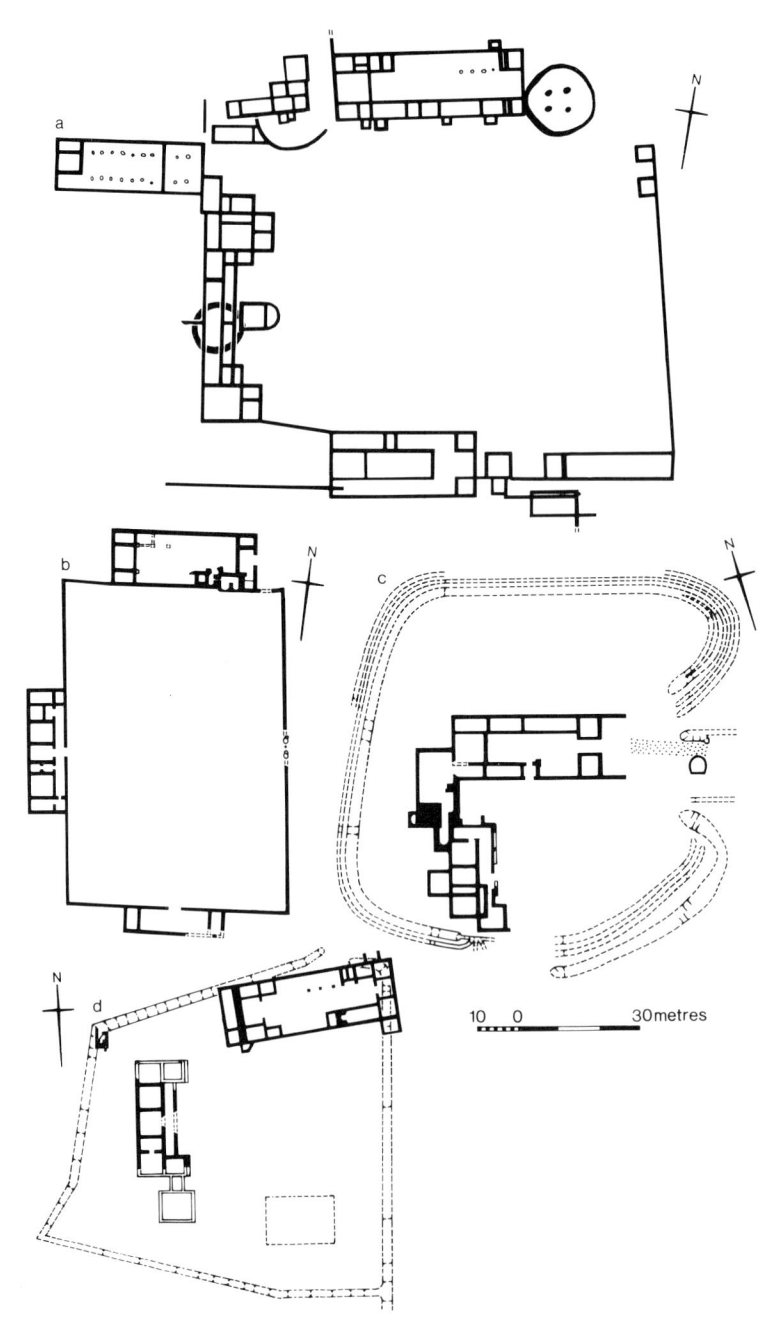

Figure 34 *Villa compounds with winged corridor and aisled houses: a. Winterton (Humbs); b. Sparsholt (Hants); c. Norton Disney (Lincs); d. Mansfield Woodhouse (Notts).*

workers or servants.[37] In fact it is clear that the model for aisled houses as the homes of relatively egalitarian extended families does not preclude the idea that some aisled houses were the homes of estate workers and slaves. In many cases the early aisled buildings were undivided, and the partitioning-off of the upper end and its elaboration with mosaics, hypocausts and painted wall plaster can be observed on some of these sites. This process may indicate the first stage in the degradation of the kin. The addition of a second house of more advanced pattern adjacent to the old aisled house also occurs on some sites, which could indicate a second stage in the process in which the master's lodgings actually became physically isolated from that of his kin, the kin being in effect converted into estate workers. Both stages of the process could indicate the gradual degradation of the kin from an equal status with the head of the household to that of estate workers, or perhaps even servants.[38]

On a number of sites a substantial group of slaves or estate workers associated with a large villa may be indicated. Sites of this type are known in Gaul, Germany and Belgium[39] and there are also examples in Britain.[40] The site at Gatcome (Glos) is a particularly interesting example (*see* Figure 35), although unfortunately the main villa building appears to lie under a railway line and consequently has not been fully excavated. From the available evidence Gatcombe appears to consist of a large villa and a group of subsidiary buildings located within a large walled enclosure. The subsidiary structures probably represent workshops, storage buildings and possibly also dwelling houses for estate workers. A large group of estate workers were in effect resident within the walled compound of the villa.

Compounds at local centres

There is apparently only limited evidence for the nature of farm compounds at local centres (*see* Figure 36). This is a result of the small number of excavations on this type of site, which are usually small-scale in extent. A clearly defined farm compound has been excavated at Braughing (Herts) where, during the first century (*c.* AD 43–61), four buildings were grouped around a small yard and connected by paths (*see* Figure 36e). These buildings were not well preserved and it is uncertain how many of the four were residential and how many related to storage and other activities.

At Ashton (Northants) ten buildings, or parts of buildings, of late second/early third to fourth-century date, have been excavated within the local centre (*see* Figure 36f). The site has only been published in interim form, but it appears possible to identify five compounds on the basis of the distribution of buildings and the roads defining building

72 Rural Settlement in Roman Britain

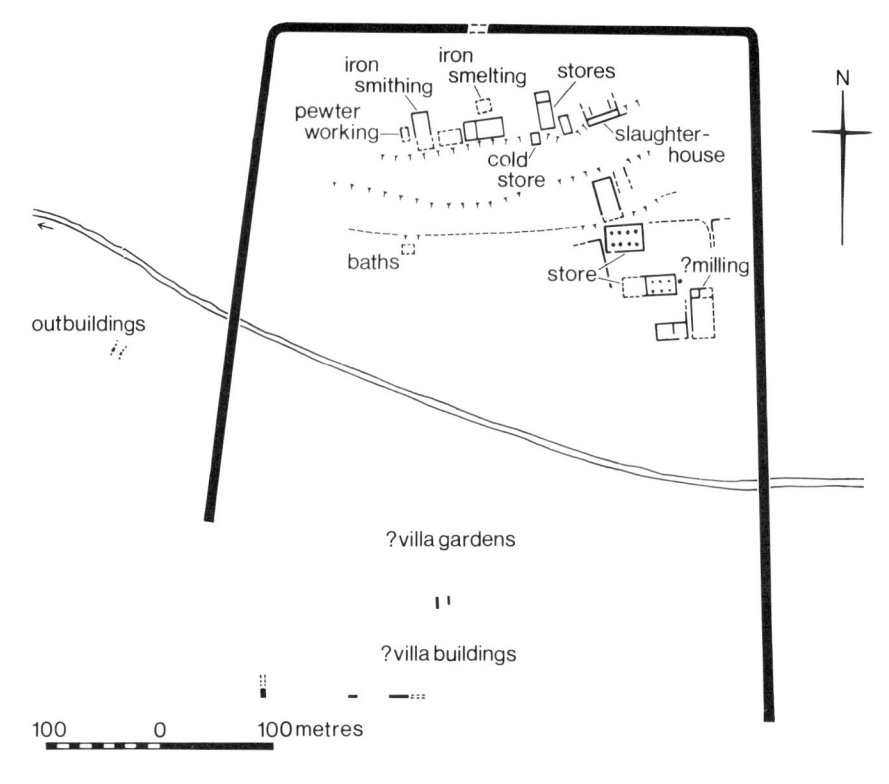

Figure 35 *Villa compound at Gatcombe (Somer). (After Branigan 1977a, figure 33).*

plots, although only two of these compounds have been excavated in anything approaching a complete fashion. One compound seems to have had three buildings incorporating stone walls which define a rectangular courtyard. Three further compounds may have had a pair of buildings. A fifth compound possibly had only a single building, although this is uncertain because the compound was not totally excavated. The results are not fully published and it is uncertain, therefore, whether any of the individual compounds had more than a single dwelling house.

At Dragonby (Lincs) a number of ditched and fenced enclosures have been excavated which are arranged along the frontages of an irregular street network. The enclosure on Site 2 contained only a single building (*see* Figure 36b), although on Site 1 one of the farm compounds appears to have contained at least two buildings (*see* Figure 36a).

Excavations at other local centres have been too small-scale to locate anything larger than the single building.[41] On some sites the buildings were not constructed using techniques that have left clear traces in the archaeological record.[42] As a result it is not clear whether other local centres contained buildings arranged in regular farm compounds,[43]

Compounds – family farms 73

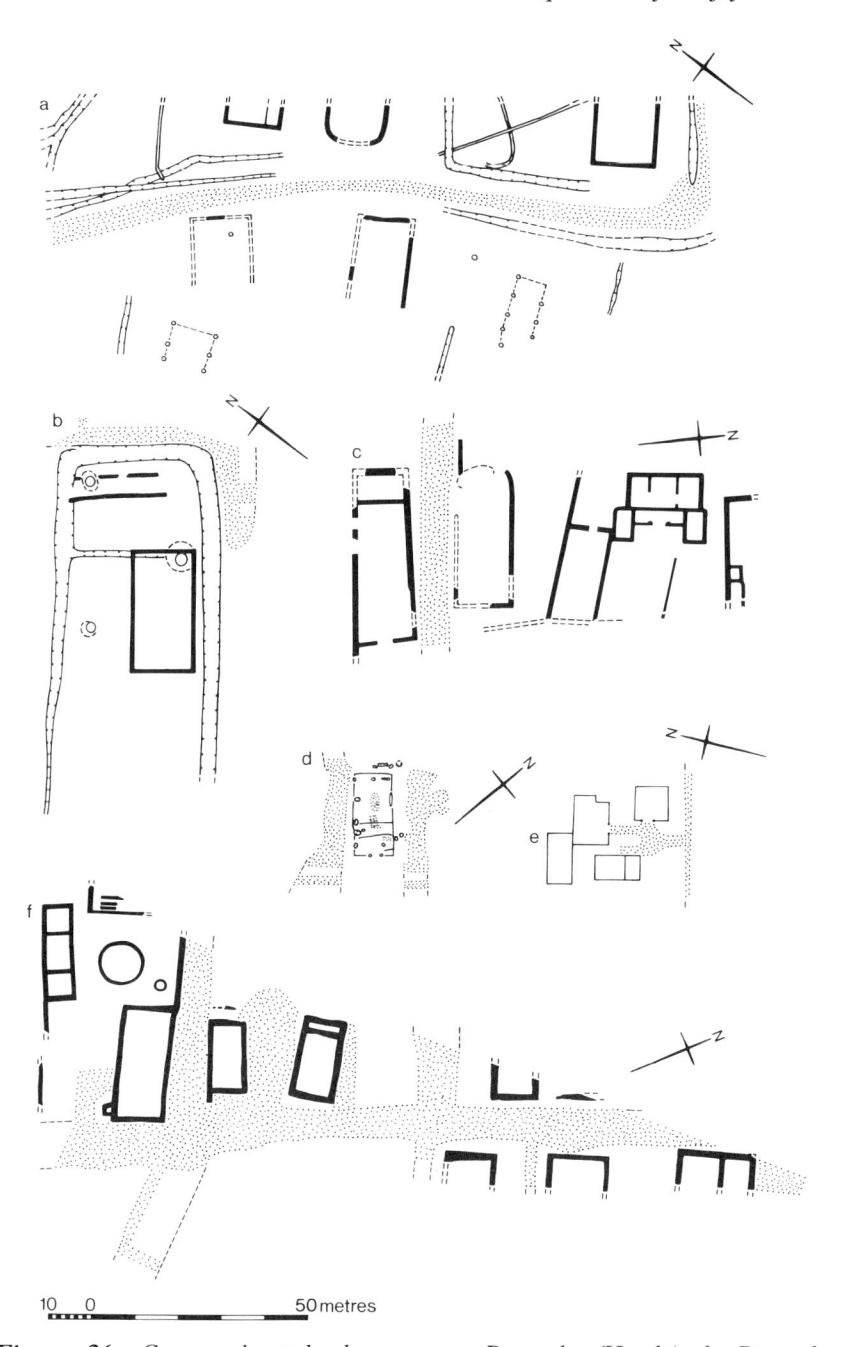

Figure 36 *Compounds at local centres: a. Dragonby (Humbs); b. Dragonby (Humbs); c. Hibaldstow (Humbs); d. Scole (Norf); e. Braughing (Herts); f. Ashton (Northants).*

although some regular properties containing buildings have also been suggested elsewhere.[44] In addition, it is unclear whether more than a single dwelling house occurs within a farm compound at any of these sites. In fact, on the few local centres at which fairly large-scale excavations have been undertaken in recent years, paired dwelling houses are conspicuous by their absence. At Neatham (Hants) a number of distinct ditched properties have been distinguished in the excavated area and most, if not all, of these appear to contain only a single building. The same would seem to be true in both the early (*c.* AD 170–270) and later (*c.*AD 330) phases of the Alchester road suburb at Towcester (Northants). At Hibaldstow (Humbs) ten properties have been defined through excavation and geophysical survey and the majority of these plots appear to contain only a single dwelling, although Plot IX does appear to have included a dwelling house and an ancillary building (*see* Figure 36c). On all these sites individual buildings within small ditched enclosures alongside a Roman road appear to be common.

The evidence of Braughing and Ashton may indicate that farm compounds containing multiple buildings occurred at local centres. At Neatham, Hibaldstow and Towcester, however, farm compounds with paired dwelling houses are notably absent. The evidence for local centres is perhaps too limited to make any definite conclusions about the occurrence or absence and possible significance of farm compounds on these sites and further research will be necessary.

SUMMARY

Compounds can be defined on many of the rural settlements of Roman Britain. The compound represents the family farm and a range of domestic, storage and ancillary buildings occur which vary from site to site. The occurrence of two or more houses within compounds on non-villa and villa sites suggests that large-scale family groups were common in the Romano-British countryside. The evidence for local centres is uncertain as too few of these sites have been excavated on a scale which allows detailed analysis. The evidence available at present may indicate that paired dwellings are not as common at local centres as on non-villa and villa settlements.

Chapter 5
The settlement

WHAT IS A SETTLEMENT?

In many areas of Britain Roman settlements were closely spaced and there are consequent difficulties in defining the boundaries between them. In this chapter a settlement is defined either as a single, isolated compound or as a distinct cluster of a number of compounds. In the latter case the compounds must be clustered together in order that a single settlement may be defined.[1]

The evidence for compounds is more limited than that for building structure, resulting from the comparative ease in excavating a single building rather than a related group of buildings. Some of the rural settlements of Roman Britain appear from the excavated evidence to have consisted of only a single farm compound, while other settlements clearly had two or more compounds and represented 'hamlets' or 'villages'. As a result, many individual settlements cover large areas and few have been excavated on a sufficient scale and in enough detail to provide comprehensive and reliable evidence for the form and chronology of the settlement. The quality of evidence for the organization of Roman rural settlements at the scale discussed in this chapter is even more limited than that for compounds. The purpose of this section, however, is to discuss the limited evidence for a number of themes concerning the organization of the community within the settlement.

THE SIZE OF RURAL SETTLEMENTS

Roman rural settlements vary a great deal in size. The best researched area is the Fenland of Cambridgeshire, Norfolk and Lincolnshire.[2] From the results of aerial photography and an extensive field survey project in the Fenland, Hallam has been able to distinguish 'single farms', 'small hamlets' (two to three farms), 'large hamlets' (four to six farms) and 'small villages' (seven or more farms). The number of farms per settlement by half-century periods has also been calculated and indicates that settlements with single farm compounds fall from almost 70 per cent in the first century to only 35–40 per cent in the late second to early third century.[3] The evidence appears to indicate progressive nucleation of settlement through time until the process was halted by deteriorating drainage conditions in the early third century, after which single farms once more become fairly common.

The limitations of excavation and field survey projects elsewhere in Britain result in comparable evidence for the size of non-villa settlements, villas and local centres being hard to obtain. It is clear, however, that a variety of settlements of the sizes discussed by Hallam do occur in the province. The evidence from earthwork survey in north-western Wales and Dartmoor show a similar variation in settlement size to the Fenland data.[4] Evidence for variation in settlement size also occurs on settlements over the rest of Britain.

Single farms

Settlements which consisted of a single compound are common in the north and west of the province and include enclosed sites in Northumbria, Cumbria, north and central Wales and Cornwall (see Figures 26–8). In some areas these compounds were not totally isolated as a number of compounds occur close to one another. Farms of more than a single conjoined compound appear, however, not to be very common.

In southern Britain farms with a single compound do not seem to have been quite so common. Bradley Hill (Somer) has already been mentioned as an isolated farm[5] and other possible examples are known.[6] Even in cases such as Bradley Hill, however, excavation has often not been extensive enough to prove that additional compounds did not once exist within 150 metres of the excavated buildings. Other non-villa settlements in southern Britain consisted of two or more compounds.

In many cases villa compounds also appear to occur in physical isolation from other settlements, as for instance at Barton Court (Oxon).[7] Where only a single villa compound is present the site is of comparable size to a non-villa farmstead.

Hamlets and small villages

On sites with villa buildings multiple compounds are not uncommon. Some of the larger winged corridor and courtyard villas appear to have two compounds – the villa compound itself and a second compound which housed estate workers attached to the villa. At some sites two or more distinct areas of settlement of varying status, a villa and a non-villa compound, occur close together. These sites are comparable in size to the small non-villa hamlet as they consist of two or three compounds.

Non-villa settlements that can be designated as small hamlets were quite common in the province. Large hamlets also occur (see Figure 37)

The settlement 77

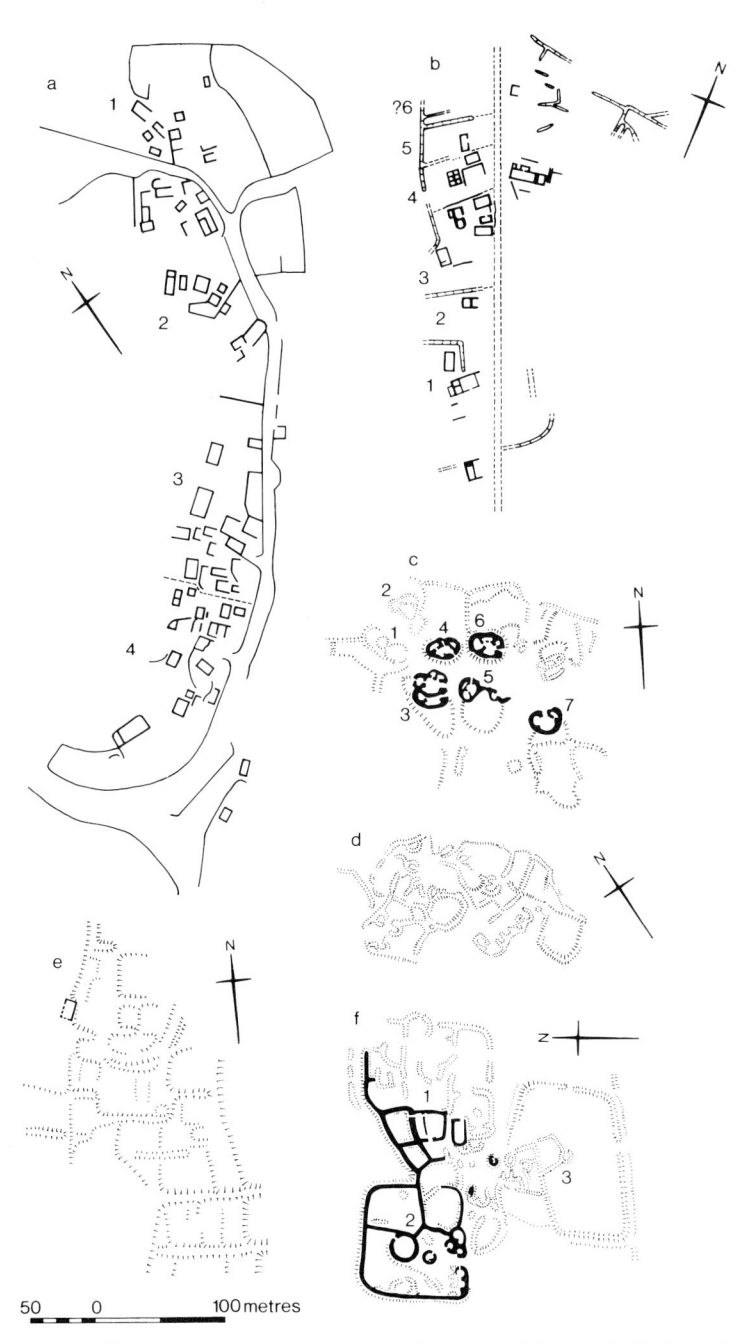

Figure 37 *Hamlets and small villages: a. Chisenbury Warren (Wilts); b. Catsgore (Somer); c. Chysauster (Corn); d. Crosby Ravensworth (Cumbr); e. Chalton (Hants); f. Crosby Ravensworth (Cumbr).*

78 *Rural Settlement in Roman Britain*

Figure 38 *Aerial photograph of the non-villa settlement at Chysauster (Corn). Copyright Royal Commission on Historical Monuments (England).*

and a number of sites of this type are known.[8] If they are contemporary, the eight courtyard houses at Chysauster formed a small village (*see* Figure 38). The most extensively excavated non-villa settlement at Catsgore (Somer), which is estimated to have had twelve farm compounds, is one of the larger small villages.

Large villages and towns

It is clear that local centres are at least comparable to small villages in size, and some evidently had considerably larger populations than the largest non-villa settlements (*see* Figures 39–41).

It has been argued that the recently excavated local centre at Neatham (Hants) had a population as high as 2,270–3,972 people during the third and fourth centuries.[9] This figure was determined by multiplying the number of buildings on the excavated part of the site, which formed about 2.6 per cent of the total area of the settlement, to give an estimate of the total number of buildings on the whole of the site. It was then assumed that each building would have housed five people. It can be calculated that a figure of 3,000 people indicates between 150 and 600 farm compounds, depending on the size of the family within the individual compound.[10]

The settlement 79

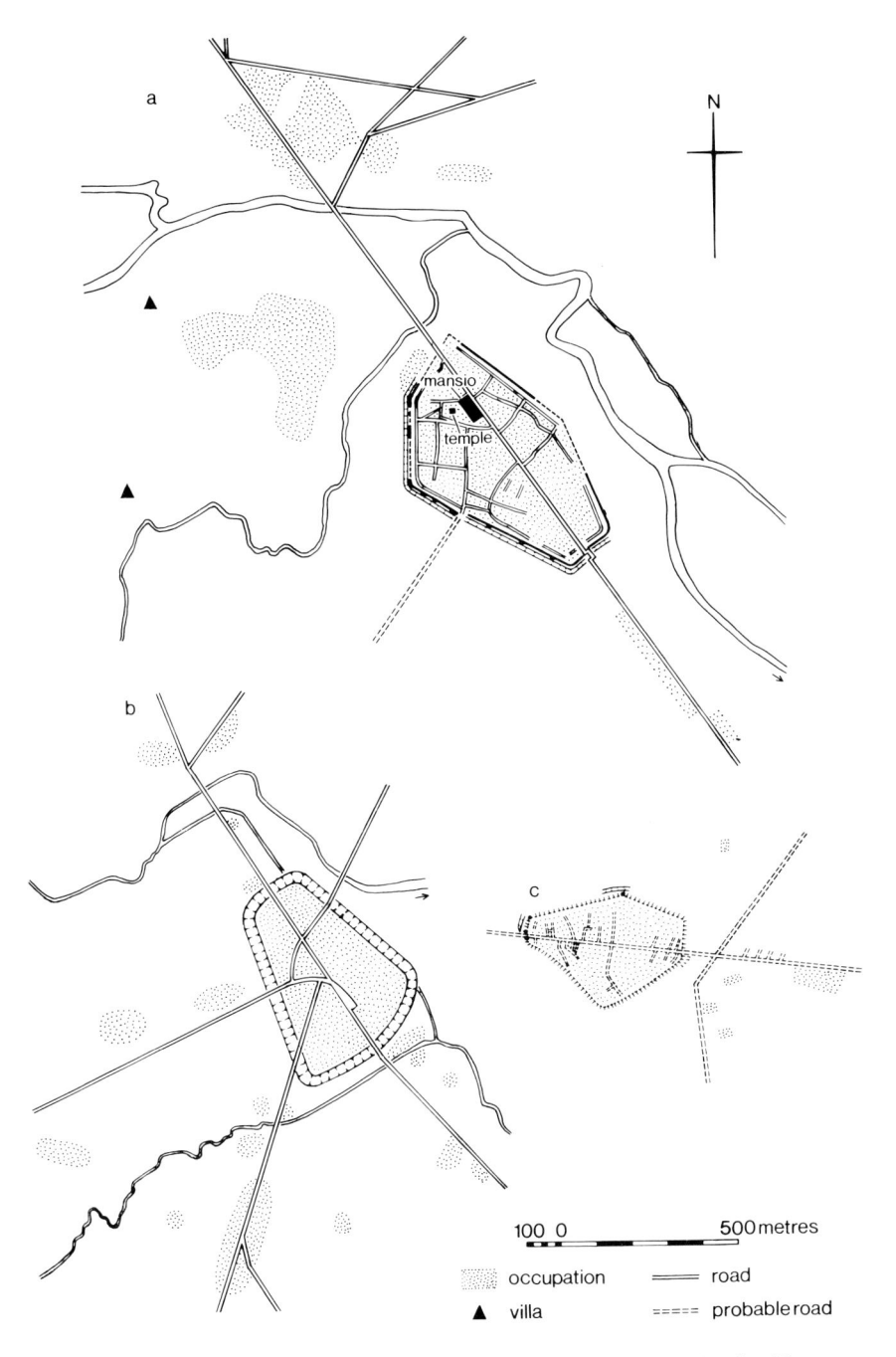

Figure 39 *Local centres: a. Water Newton/Castor (Cambs); b. Towcester (Northants); c. Kenchester (Here & Worc).*

If this figure is even approximately correct it suggests that the population of some local centres could have been considerable. Neatham is a comparatively minor local centre of between eight and fourteen hectares (*see* Figure 40b) and other sites cover considerably larger areas, some as much as forty hectares.[11] Sites of this size could on this basis have had populations of at least 10,000 inhabitants and this would indicate 500–2,000 farm compounds.[12]

In reality the figure for Neatham is based on inadequate data and the population of the settlement could actually have been considerably lower. A population estimate as low as 200 individuals has been made for the local centre at Godmanchester (Cambs) in the second century. Nevertheless it would appear that many of the larger local centres will have had considerable populations indicating large numbers of compounds.[13]

THE LAYOUT OF VILLA AND NON-VILLA SETTLEMENTS

The evidence for the layout of compounds within sites that consist of more than a single compound will now be discussed. A simple model will be explored for non-villa and villa settlements; this is the evidence for the division of some sites into two or more distinct compounds that differ in wealth.

The majority of non-villa settlements are fairly simple in form. As has been argued above some sites, particularly in the north and west, consisted of only a single farm compound, although many sites in southern Britain appear to have had two or more compounds. On some southern British hamlet and village sites the groups of compounds appear to have been spaced out to either side of one or more tracks.[14]

In some of these settlements a division into areas of differing wealth occurred. The recently excavated non-villa settlement at Claydon Pike (Glos) demonstrates this principle (*see* Figure 42). A Late Iron Age settlement existed on the site which was reorganized during the late first or early second century AD, possibly with occupants of differing status to each side of a trackway. In the higher status compound an aisled house and aisled barn have been excavated and the finds from these are fairly rich. The excavator has suggested a military presence, although the evidence does not appear to be fully conclusive.[15] In contrast, the second compound had smaller and less elaborate buildings, perhaps the dwellings of farm workers or slaves, and rich artefactual material is less common in this area.[16]

A possible difference in status between compounds also exists at Catsgore, where one of the six farm compounds that has been excavated appears to have been rather different from the others and has been called a 'villa'.[17] In this supposedly richer farm compound three

The settlement 81

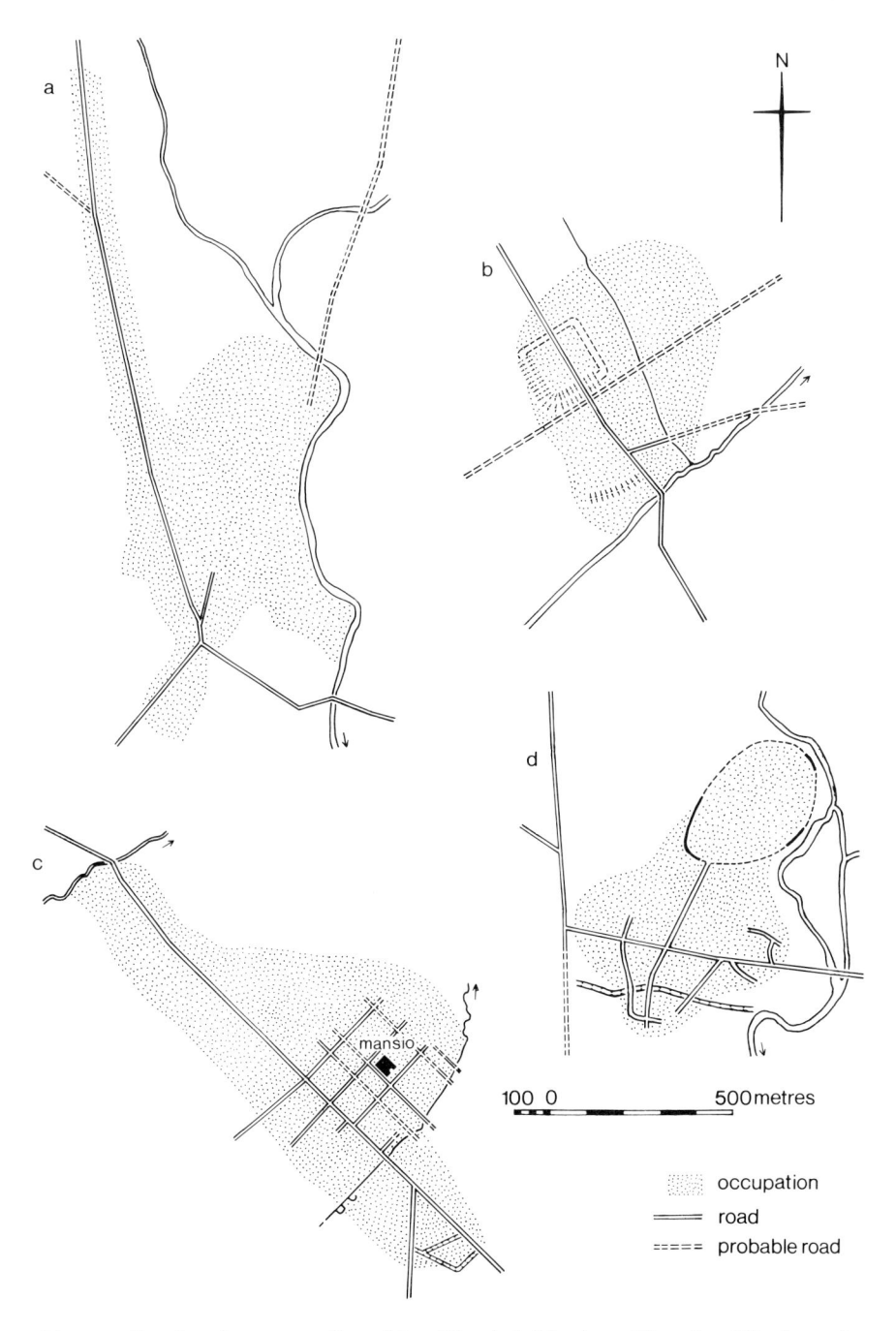

Figure 40 *Local centres: a. Braughing (Herts); b. Neatham (Hants); c. Wanborough (Wilts); d. Alcester (Warw).*

82 *Rural Settlement in Roman Britain*

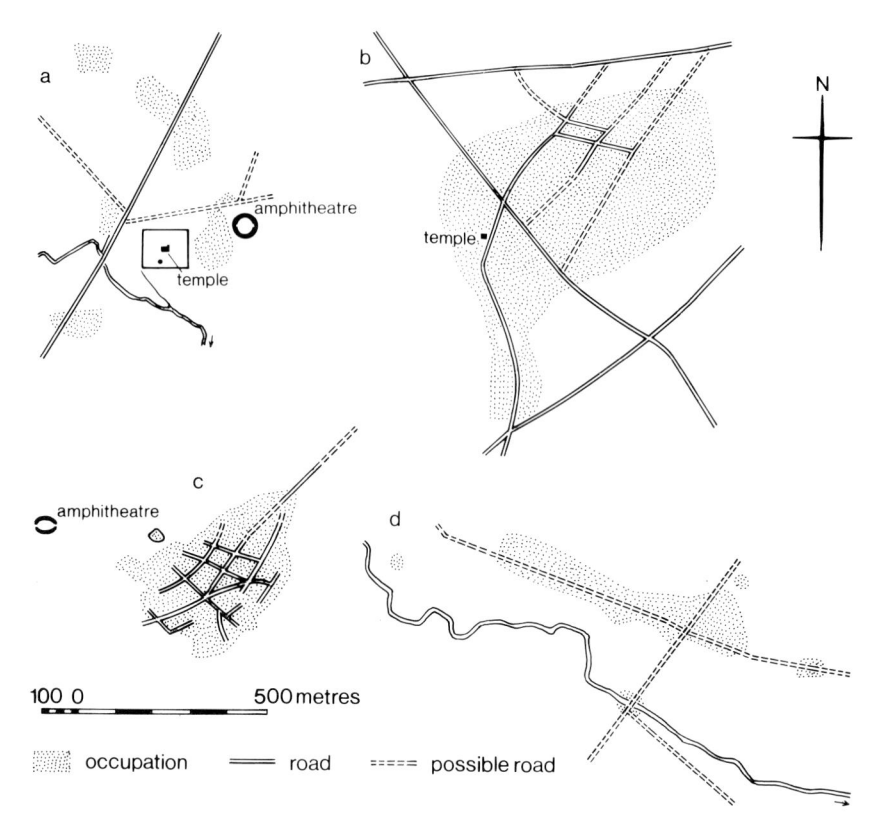

Figure 41 *Local centres: a. Frilford (Oxon); b. Baldock (Herts); c. Charterhouse-on-Mendip (Avon); d. Scole (Norf).*

buildings were situated around a courtyard. One building has been excavated and was of greater size and elaboration than the simple two to three-roomed dwellings of the other five farm compounds. It has been suggested that the owner of this compound owned the whole settlement at Catsgore and that the occupants of the other compounds were his tenants.[18] This compound does not, however, appear to be very much richer in material terms than the other farms and does not have any of the additional symbols of wealth that distinguish the archaeological definition of a villa.[19] It is possible that the occupant of this farm was only marginally richer than the occupants of the other compounds. In this case the difference in settlement form has no certain tenurial significance.

The evidence from Dinorben (Clwyd) indicates that a similar distinction of status between farm compounds may have occurred in Roman Wales (*see* Figure 43). It has been suggested that a large round

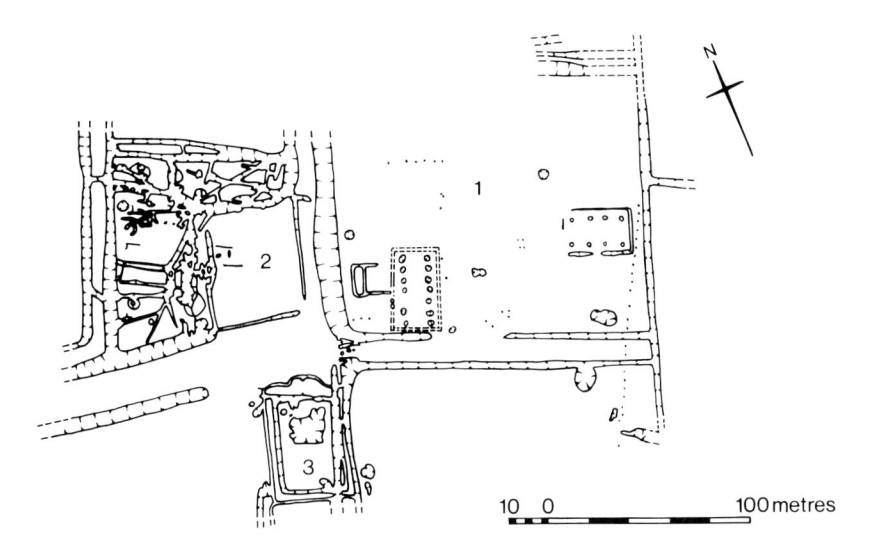

Figure 42 *Non-villa settlement at Claydon Pike (Glos): 1. higher status compound; 2. lower status compound; 3. shrine. (After Miles 1984a, figure 4).*

hut with rich finds represents the home of the landowner or landowning family and an occupation area, possibly the site of the houses of tenants, has been located to the south of the hill fort.[20] This evidence is incomplete, for it is unclear whether the rich family and its tenants lived in a single farm compound with the poorer kin or tenants – as in the southern British cases reviewed above – or whether there were two distinct compounds with different levels of wealth, as at Claydon Pike.

At least two types of situation can be defined for villa settlements. Some villas had only a single compound and these have been discussed in the previous chapter. On a number of other sites the villa compound had a second compound attached to it (*see* Figure 44).

Villas that are divided into a residential and an agricultural compound appear to have been more common in Gaul than in Britain.[21] Indeed in Britain only a few villas, including some of the larger and more elaborate examples, have this division. A number of corridor and winged corridor houses had secondary agricultural courtyards,[22] and the double compound also occurs in association with a number of courtyard houses in Britain.[23] This second compound contained poorer houses which probably represented the dwellings of farm workers and also the agricultural buildings of the settlement and it is usually called 'the agricultural courtyard'. The two compounds on these settlements varied in status. One of the compounds contained elaborate villa buildings which were probably the home of the individual or family who owned the estate, while the second contained agricultural buildings and also the

84 *Rural Settlement in Roman Britain*

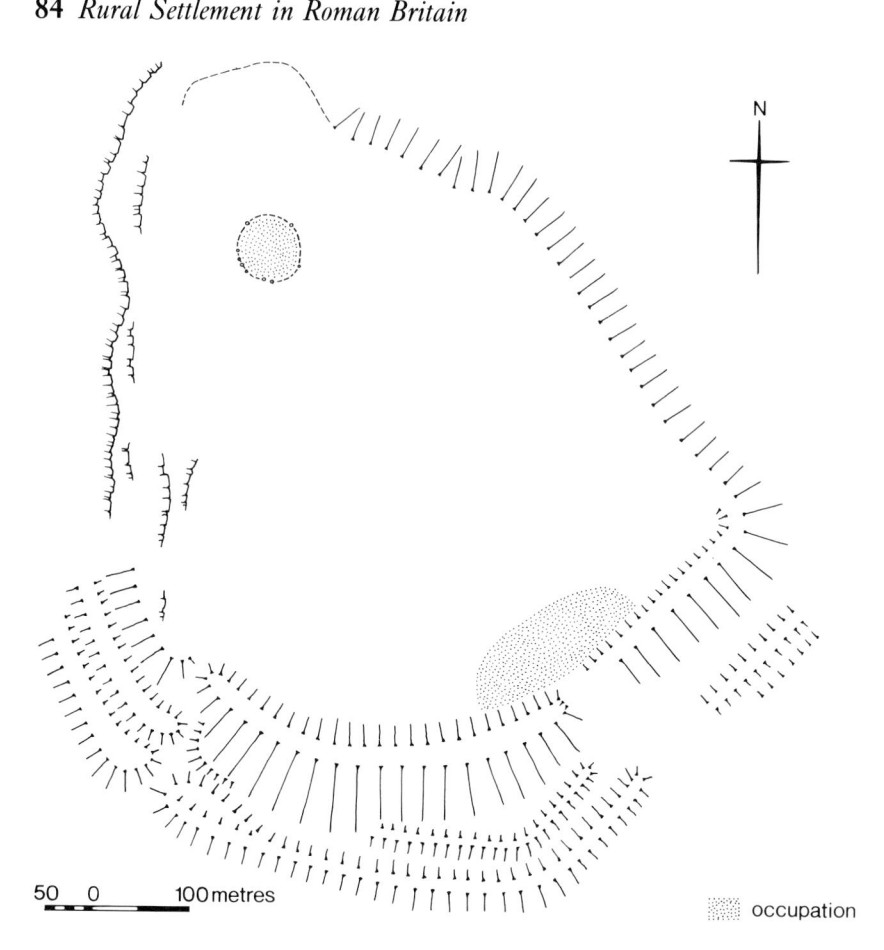

Figure 43 *Third to fourth-century settlement at Dinorben (Clwyd). (After Gardner and Savory 1964, figure 3).*

homes of the farm workers. The situation on these sites is directly comparable to that observed at the non-villa settlement at Claydon Pike (Glos).

An Iron Age origin for the two-compound division appears to have been demonstrated at Gorhambury (Herts). At this site in the Late Iron Age there were two ditched compounds (*see* Figure 45). One contained a building which was later overlain by the villa, the other an Iron Age aisled house underlying a later Roman aisled house. There was possibly a distinction on this site during the Iron Age between the compound of the owner and that of the estate workers, a division which survived into the Roman period. It is probably socially significant, however, that the workers' compound was supplied with a fairly elaborate bath-house.[24]

The settlement 85

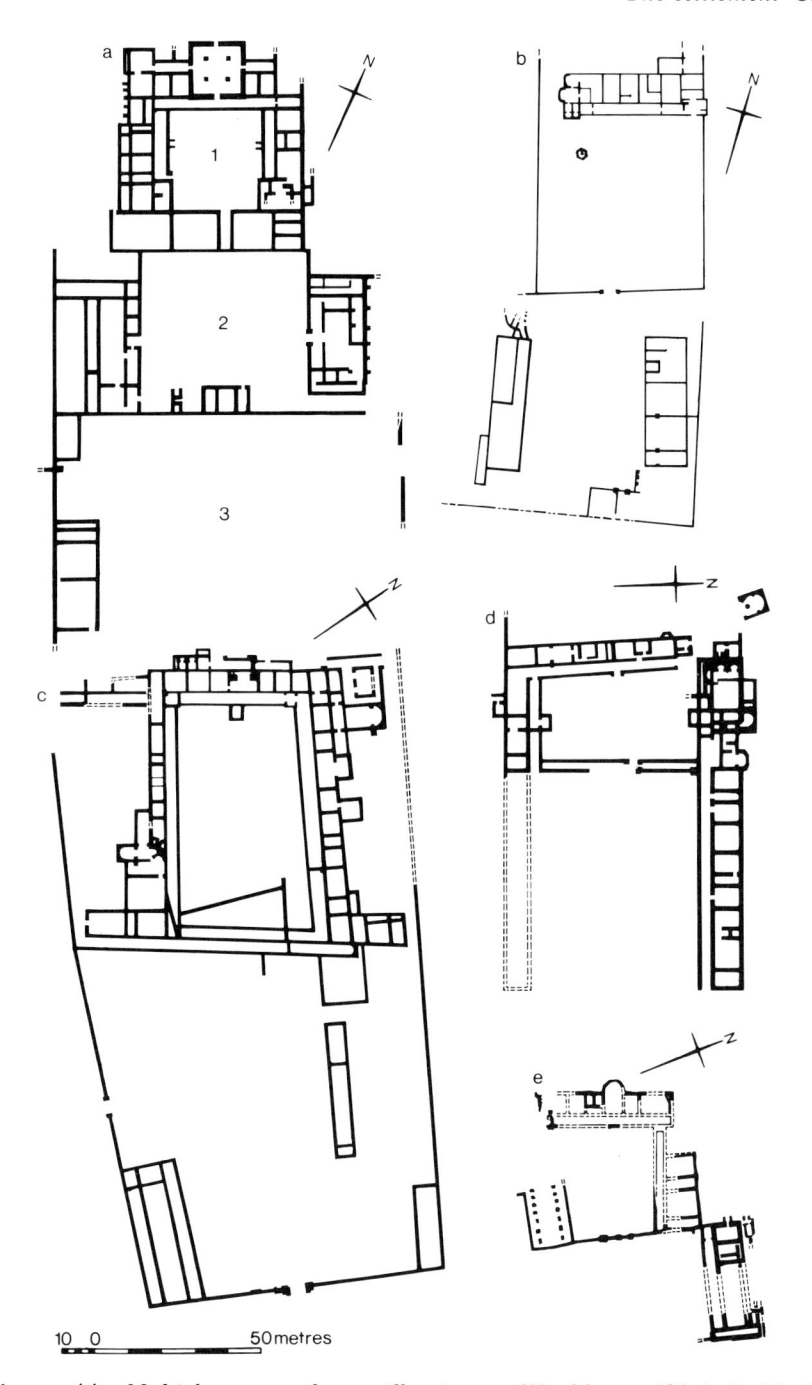

Figure 44 *Multiple compounds on villa sites: a. Woodchester (Glos); b. North Wraxhall (Wilts); c. Bignor (W Susx); d. Chedworth (Glos); e. Norfolk Street (Leic).*

86 *Rural Settlement in Roman Britain*

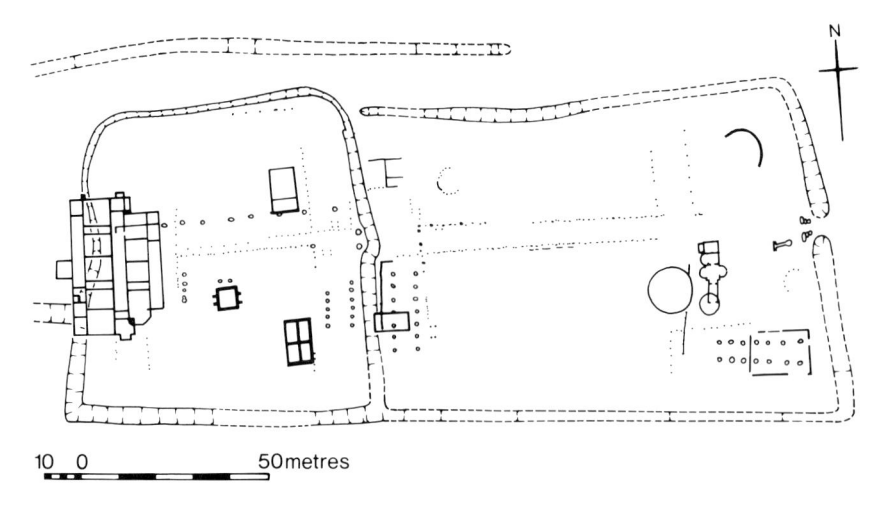

Figure 45 *Villa at Gorhambury (Herts). (After Selkirk 1983, figure on p 116).*

Woodchester (Glos) is the most interesting courtyard villa as it has three compounds, of which only two are known in any detail (*see* Figure 44a). In the third century the villa appears to have had only two courtyards (marked 2 and 3 on Figure 44a), a situation probably directly comparable to Brading (I of W) and Norfolk Street (Leic), with the main accommodation at the head of an inner courtyard flanked by two aisled buildings, and with an outer agricultural courtyard. At a later stage an inner courtyard was added to the main dwelling (marked as 1) and this in effect formed one residential and two agricultural courtyards.

THE LAYOUT OF LOCAL CENTRES

Local centres were extensive settlements and few excavations have been sufficiently large to produce evidence of the organization of the whole settlement.[25] In fact, from the excavated and published examples of local centres it is impossible to reconstruct more than ten properties in detail.[26] Consequently, the quantity of evidence available for reconstructing the pattern of settlement at local centres is very limited.

Variations in wealth

The evidence for villa and non-villa settlements has been explored by studying the layout of these sites in terms of distinct compounds with differing levels of wealth. Separate compounds with varying levels of wealth also exist at local centres. Evidence for the variation in wealth at local centres is provided by villa-type buildings on a number of these sites.

The typical buildings at the majority of local centres appear to be simple rectangular buildings of no more than a few rooms.[27] Stone-winged corridor buildings are, however, known on local centres.[28] At Hibaldstow (Humbs) the winged corridor building occurred within one of the compounds discussed above, while the buildings in the other farm compounds were simpler rectangular structures (*see* Figure 36c).

The significance of a villa building occurring within a local centre may be considered in two ways. First, it is possible that the nucleated settlement may have been the home of farm workers on an estate that was the property of the villa owner.[29] This explanation seems fairly probable on nucleated settlements where the winged corridor building is large and exhibits a high level of wealth, while the other buildings appear fairly poor; this is probably the case at Gatcombe (Glos).

At sites such as Tiddington (Warw), Hibaldstow (Humbs), Camerton (Avon) and Ilchester (Somer), however, the 'villas' are only marginally larger and more ornate than the standard dwellings on the sites. At Hibaldstow it is evident that the building developed from an earlier, simpler house and within a pre-existing compound. A possible second explanation of these sites may be that the villa owner was merely a villager who had managed to accumulate slightly more surplus than his neighbours. The owner of the villa-type building may originally have had a similar level of wealth to his neighbours, but have subsequently been able to acquire enough surplus to construct a more elaborate dwelling. This type of explanation also appears likely for the wealthy buildings at Water Newton (Cambs) and Kenchester (Here & Worc), which appear to have in-filled sparsely settled areas of the town enclosures at some date, presumably during the second to fourth centuries. These buildings do appear to indicate an unequal distribution of wealth within local centres, but the differences were probably not very great and did not necessarily have tenurial connotations.

Zoning of activities

It appears that distinctions in wealth occur between compounds at local centres. The evidence indicates that other forms of zoning also occur on these sites, and these will be discussed briefly.

Unlike the tribal capitals of Roman Britain, town planning in the local centres was rudimentary.[30] The limited evidence indicates that the compounds in which the buildings were located were often fairly irregular and were usually located along both sides of a road or street.

Properties, represented by ditched compounds, have been discussed above.[31] On recently excavated sites the excavators have claimed evidence for recurring regular dimensions in the laying out of compounds. At the Alchester road suburb of Towcester (Northants) some evidence exists to indicate that properties had a road frontage of about nineteen metres after a major reorganization of the area around AD 170. At Neatham (Hants) a regular roadside width of twenty five metres has been claimed for the Silchester-Chichester road on the basis of the spacing of pits and wells, and regular spacing has also been claimed for the Winchester-London road. Frere has suggested that although the settlement at Neatham appears at first glance to be haphazard, the evidence for the regularity of the spacing of properties may represent a type of formal organization,[32] which may also apply to the Towcester suburb.

Frere asks questions about these plots, which at present are impossible to answer. Were plots marked out and then let or sold to incomers? Did each acquire as much as they could afford? Was the land appropriated at one time or successively, perhaps by an estate owner? Or were there officials of the *vicus* with planning powers?[33] At Hibaldstow the sizes of the ten properties do not appear to be so standardized and the excavator has suggested that the dimensions of the compound may have been related to the price that the occupier could afford when he bought the plot.[34] Frere has stated that it will be impossible to gain a full understanding of these matters until a number of additional large-scale excavations have been undertaken.[35]

The excavated areas at Hibaldstow, Neatham and Towcester in effect constitute the largest areas for which there is a fairly detailed understanding of local centres. When an attempt is made to study whole sites, rather than parts of sites, the evidence is less reliable, as it is based largely on aerial photography. Some evidence occurs for the division of the area of the local centre into zones with distinct functions, although this zoning appears often to have been fairly rudimentary.[36]

There is evidence for the street systems of local centres (*see* Figures 39–41). Aerial photography and excavation on a number of sites have shown irregular networks of paved and metalled roads defining irregular plots within which buildings were located.[37] In general these street systems are very different from the regular *insulae* of the *civitas* capitals of the province and may indicate that many local centres developed organically, without the officially imposed street system typical of the major towns. Formal control of ownership and planning might well have created property boundaries and street systems with a more regular layout, possibly indicating that the planning of local centres was not as formal as Frere has suggested.

Sites with regular street systems, such as Wanborough (Wilts, *see* Figure 40c) are far less common than those with irregular street systems,[38] and it seems possible that they were controlled by some tribal or sub-tribal administrative body.[39]

The impression is that some local centres consisted of little more than

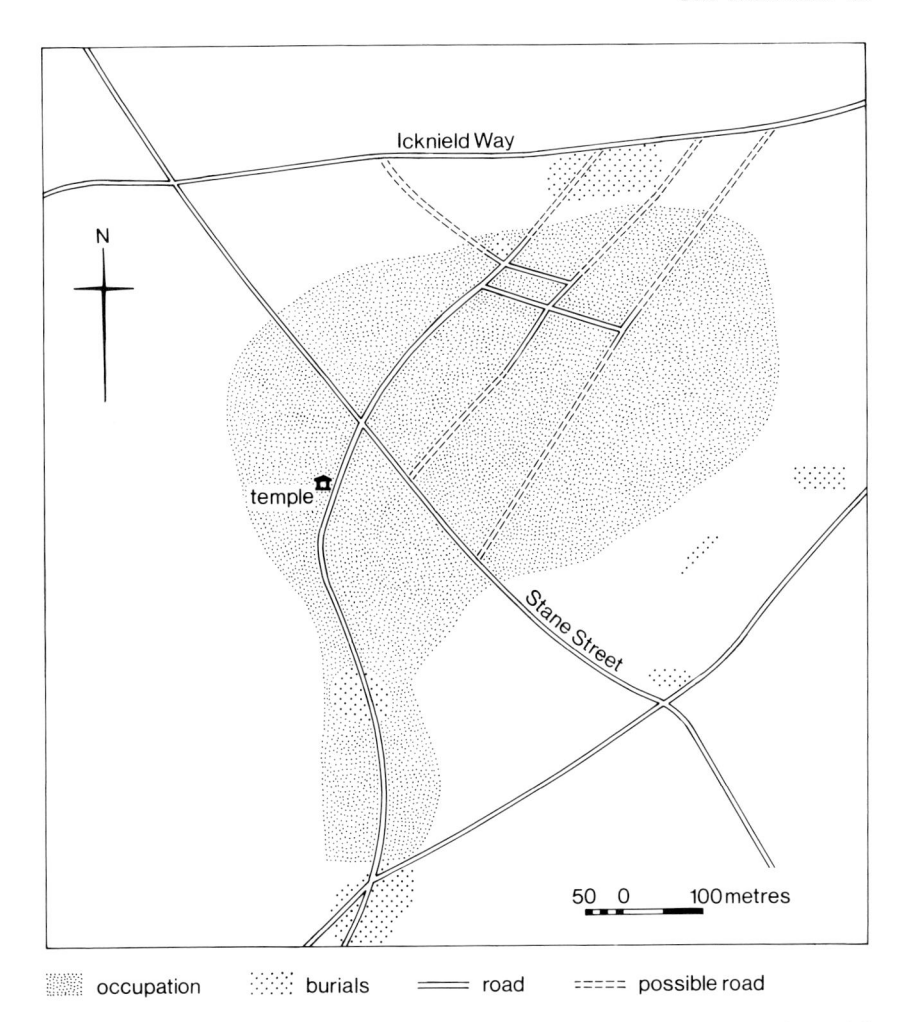

Figure 46 *Local centre at Baldock (Herts). (After Rom. Brit. in 1985, figure 21).*

farm compounds spaced out irregularly along the streets, with the occasional side street dividing up blocks of properties. This pattern is similar to that at the larger non-villa settlements such as Chisenbury Warren and Catsgore. Baldock (Herts) is an example of a local centre of this type that has been excavated on a fairly large scale and for which the approximate layout and extent are known (*see* Figure 46). Many other local centres were probably broadly comparable to Baldock, although few of these are known in any detail.[40] Sites of this type are remarkably ordinary and have few special features to attract the excavator.[41] As a consequence of their apparent poverty these sites have received relatively little attention. In contrast to this the local centres with special

90 Rural Settlement in Roman Britain

features, such as public buildings, administrative buildings and town walls, have been studied in greater detail, although the evidence will only be discussed briefly here.

In the *civitas* capitals and *coloniae* of Britain, forum-basilica complexes were constructed at the centre of the settlement forming a separate zone.[42] Evidence for the development of a differentiated central zone at local centres is very limited, although some local centres do appear to have distinctive buildings in a central location. These buildings usually included one or more large and important buildings, or some form of temple or temple-complex.[43] Water Newton (Cambs) has two large courtyard buildings of uncertain function at its centre (marked 1 and 2 on Figure 47). Likely explanations for the function of these buildings are a *mansio*, a market-hall, or perhaps even a forum-complex. Corbridge (Northum) also appears to have a planned central core with one or more large rectangular buildings. Bath (Avon), with its major temple complex and bathing establishment, is another example as is Stonea (Cambs) which has a monumental tower of uncertain significance at its centre. *Mansiones* also occur at some local centres.[44] At these sites the centre of the town appears to have had some form of official significance and it is possible to draw a contrast with other sites which have an 'economic' focus.[45]

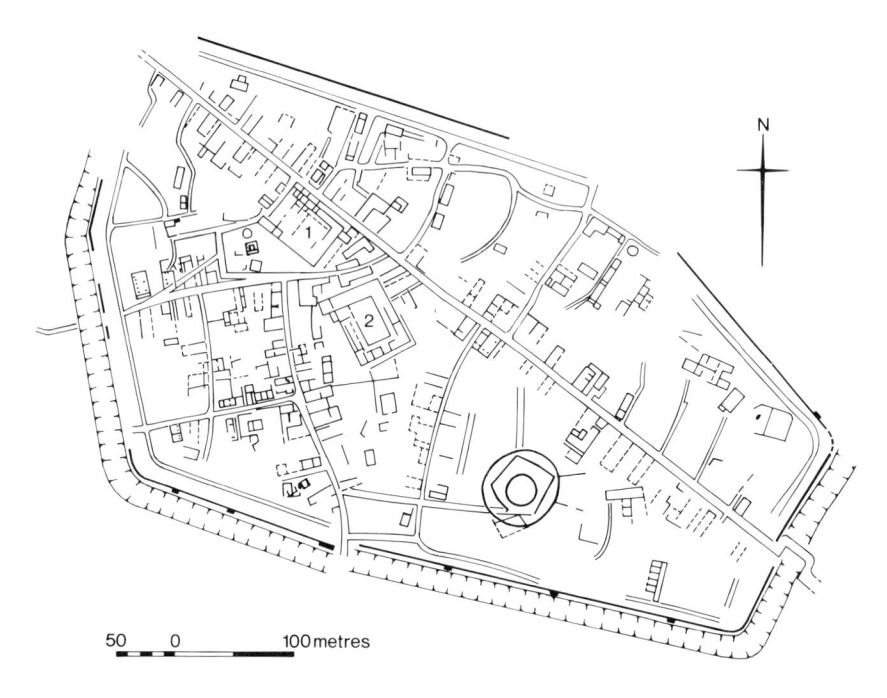

Figure 47 *Local centre at Water Newton (Cambs). (After Mackreth 1979, figure 11).*

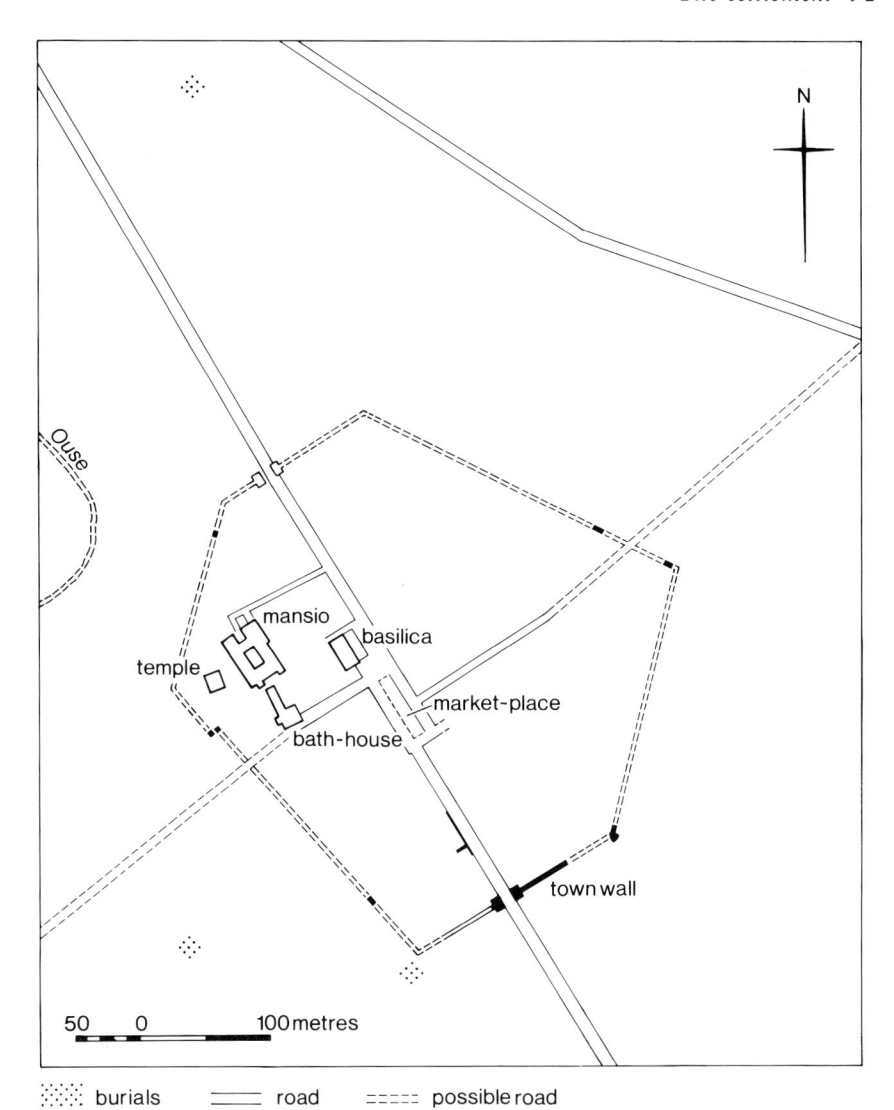

Figure 48 *Local centre at Godmanchester (Cambs). (After Green 1975, figure 10).*

At Godmanchester (Cambs), for example, the economic focus appears to consist of an open market with a 'basilica', or market-hall, of second to fourth-century date (*see* Figure 48). Possible open market areas have also been suggested at Stonea (Cambs) and Dorchester-on-Thames (Oxon), while a market building has been claimed at Towcester (Northants).[46] It is likely that an economic focus will have been a common factor at the local centres of the province, although a formal market-place may only have existed at the most successful centres.[47]

92 Rural Settlement in Roman Britain

A temple occurs at the centre of many sites,[48] and indeed on some the religious focus may have had a major part in the development of the centre. At Frilford (Oxon) it is probable that the religious complex formed a primary attraction for traders and that the local centre grew up as a consequence (*see* Figure 49). It is of importance that in all cases of temples and temple complexes within local centres the temples would have provided social and economic attractions in addition to religious functions.[49]

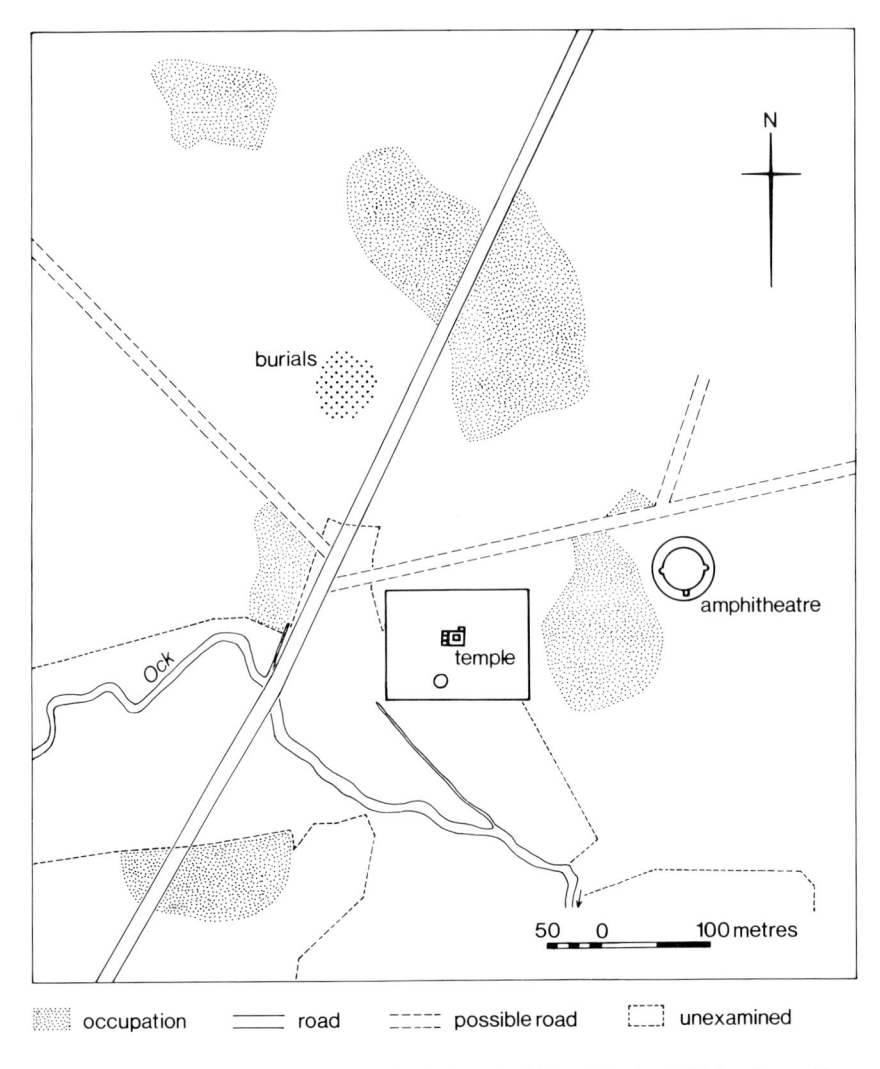

Figure 49 *Local centre at Frilford (Oxon). (After Hingley 1985a, figure 3).*

The settlement 93

Industry was important on many small towns and in some cases appears to occur intermingled with domestic dwellings.[50] On some sites, however, there is evidence that industrial production was confined to a particular area of the settlement, usually the outskirts (*see* Figure 50). This can be clearly seen in the pottery industries at Water Newton/ Castor (Cambs), Brampton (Norfolk) and Mancetter/Hartshill (Warw). At each site the pottery kilns are situated on the edge of the local centre. At Water Newton/Castor other industrial activities, such as iron working, were also conducted in the suburbs, while at Alcester (Warw) buildings of an industrial nature with evidence for tanning and metalworking occur in the south of the town.

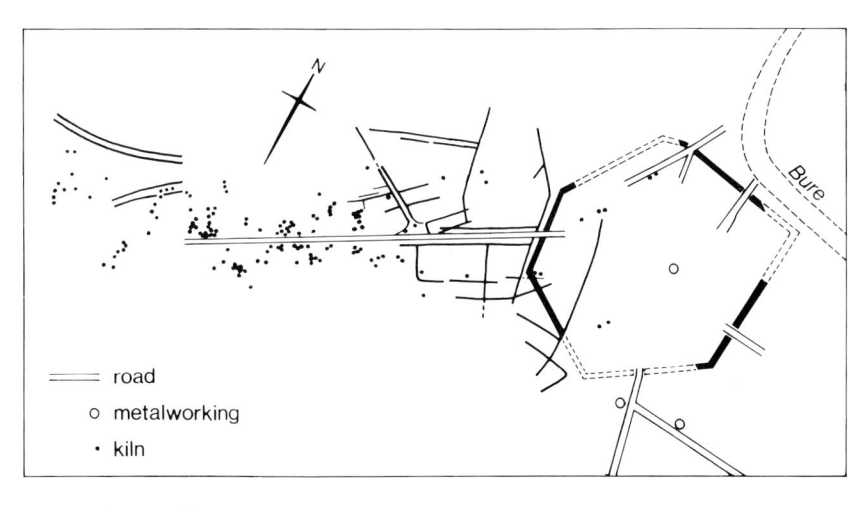

Figure 50 *Local centre at Brampton (Norf) showing pottery kilns. (After Knowles 1977, figure 1).*

Presumably the isolation of industrial activities to the periphery of the settlement was a consequence of the amount of smoke produced during the firing of a kiln and possibly also the risk of fire. It should be noted, however, that evidence for the zoning of industrial and residential areas does not necessarily indicate deliberate town planning.

SUMMARY

Some settlements consisted of only a single farm or villa compound, while others had multiple compounds. On some sites the settlement was divided into distinct areas of differing wealth. Local centres are often more complex in form and provide evidence for the division of the settlement into areas with distinct functions, such as domestic, industrial, administrative and trading. On these sites, however, the planning is fairly haphazard and rudimentary.

Chapter 6
Local groupings of settlement

The discussion in this chapter will be restricted to local groupings of settlements. Two particular models will be considered in relation to the settlement evidence. The initial discussion is concerned with non-villa settlements which, it will be argued, occur in groups, of which a proportion represented communities holding land or other important resources in common. Second, the evidence for estates consisting of villas with associated non-villa settlements will be discussed.

GROUPS OF NON-VILLA SETTLEMENTS

Information for the population of Britain was considered above and this indicates a very densely settled landscape.[1] In some areas sites are so close together that some direct association between them is indicated (*see* Figure 51); indeed, it appears to be a characteristic of non-villa settlements that they often cluster together in groups. The region where this has been demonstrated most clearly is the Norfolk, Cambridgeshire and Lincolnshire Fenland. From the first century AD onwards individual settlements appear to agglomerate and there is a tendency for loose complexes to form with members not more than about 500 metres apart.

Outside the area of the Fenland the evidence for the grouping of non-villa settlements has received little attention. In a number of areas of southern Britain, however, settlements appear to have occurred in groups comparable to those in the Fens.[2] Groups of sites also clearly occur in many areas in the north and west of Britain.[3] With rare exceptions, however, excavators have studied sites that occur within groupings of this type as if they were isolated from other contemporary settlements and did not form part of a broader settlement landscape.[4]

As there is an absence of classical literary evidence for the communities based in non-villa settlements, these sites are usually forced into either the villa estate or the imperial estate model.[5] It is necessary to consider whether these estate models are valid in each particular case. Second, even if the estate model is valid this does not mean that the social and economic organization of those who lived on these sites is of no interest. In this section a model that describes and explains so-called 'girdle patterns' of settlement will be applied to some

96 *Rural Settlement in Roman Britain*

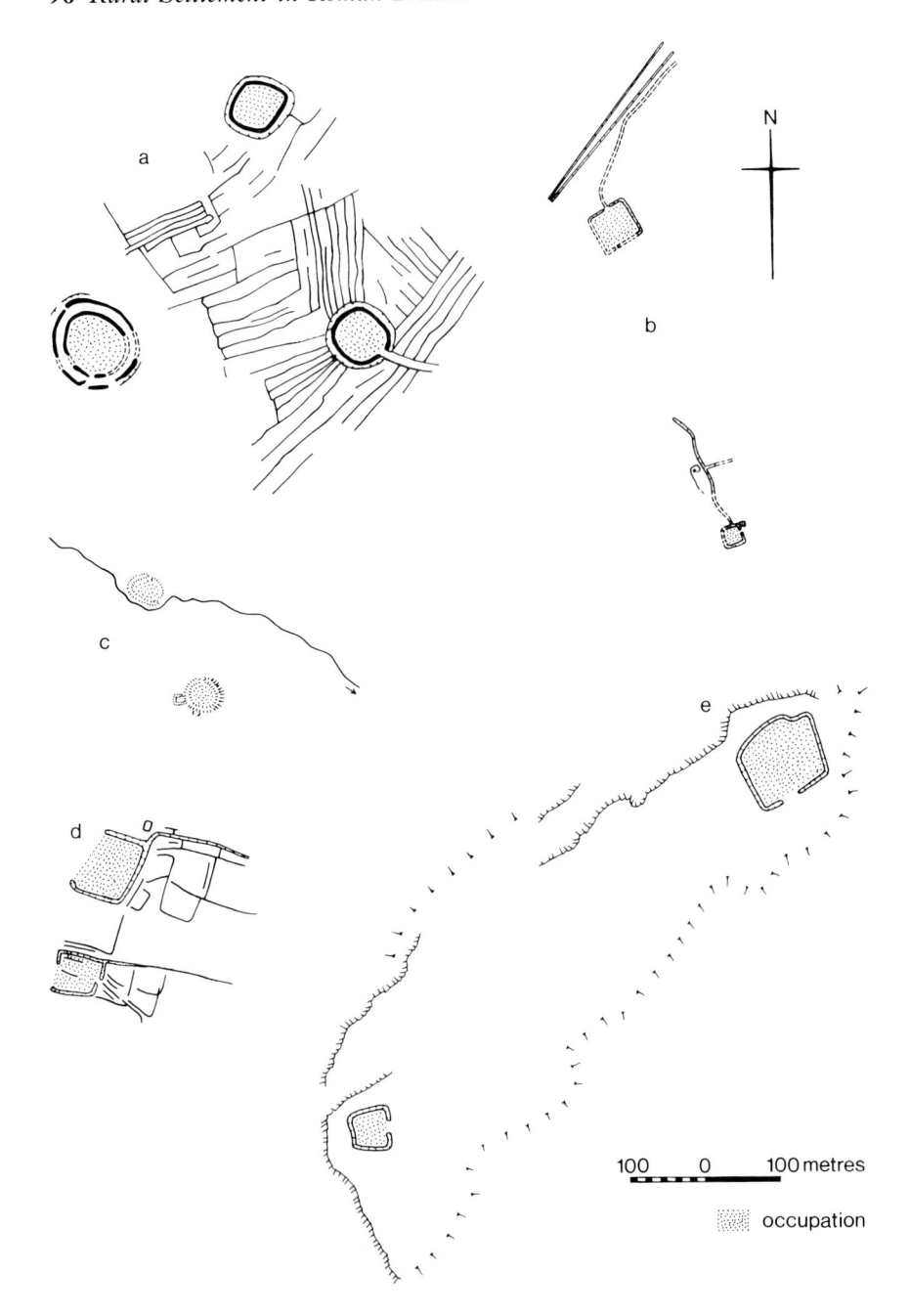

Figure 51 *Groups of non-villa settlements: a. Tregonning (Corn); b. Silloth (Cumb); c. Forcegarth Pasture (Durham); d. Dunston's Clump (Notts); e. Middle Gunnar Peak (Northum).*

of the evidence for southern Britain. The model does not specify the tenurial organization of the community. The girdle pattern model could relate either to communities who owned rights to land outright or to tenants with long-term leases from the Emperor or some other landowner.

It has been shown above that on some Romano-British settlements individual farm compounds were combined into nucleated settlements consisting of a number of compounds. It is possible that this occurred through family ties, perhaps descent from a common ancestor. At Catsgore (Somer) a number of separate family groups remained together on a single site and the nucleated nature of the single settlement may have been a result of divided inheritance of land, or of rights to land.[6]

Some nucleated settlements occur in the Fenland. Hallam has suggested that the Roman inhabitants of this area may have considered the local groupings of settlements to be a more relevant social and economic unit than the individual settlement.[7] It is possible that in some areas dispersed but closely associated groups of settlements had a similar significance to that of the nucleated settlement. Some groups of settlements may have constituted the homes of large-scale kinship groupings based on the divided inheritance of an area of land.

The idea that multiple groupings of settlements in the Romano-British countryside comprised communities derived from common descent will be discussed in this section, along with the evidence for the significance of groupings of settlements as productive units. This model fits particularly well at Wetwang Slack (Humbs), where three farms in close proximity have been excavated (*see* Figure 52, Sites a, c and d). Two of these (c and d) and an additional farm known through field survey and aerial photography (Site b) appear to have been occupied from the first to fourth centuries AD. These three settlements developed on the ditched periphery of a pre-existing area of land. In the centre of this area was an Iron Age and Roman period farm (Site a) which was abandoned in the first century AD, at about the time when the other settlements came into existence. On this site three settlements developed from a single settlement on the periphery of the lands of the original one, possibly suggesting that the inhabitants of the three separate settlements maintained fairly close ties with one another.

What were these ties? There are no clearly defined sub-divisions of the enclosed area between the settlements at Wetwang Slack. That the settlements developed on the periphery of the pre-existing land unit and the lack of clear evidence for subdivision of this land could indicate that this area was held in joint ownership. The three settlements may have shared and had equal rights to the area of arable and/or pasture within the ditched enclosure around which they developed. Shared ownership,

98 Rural Settlement in Roman Britain

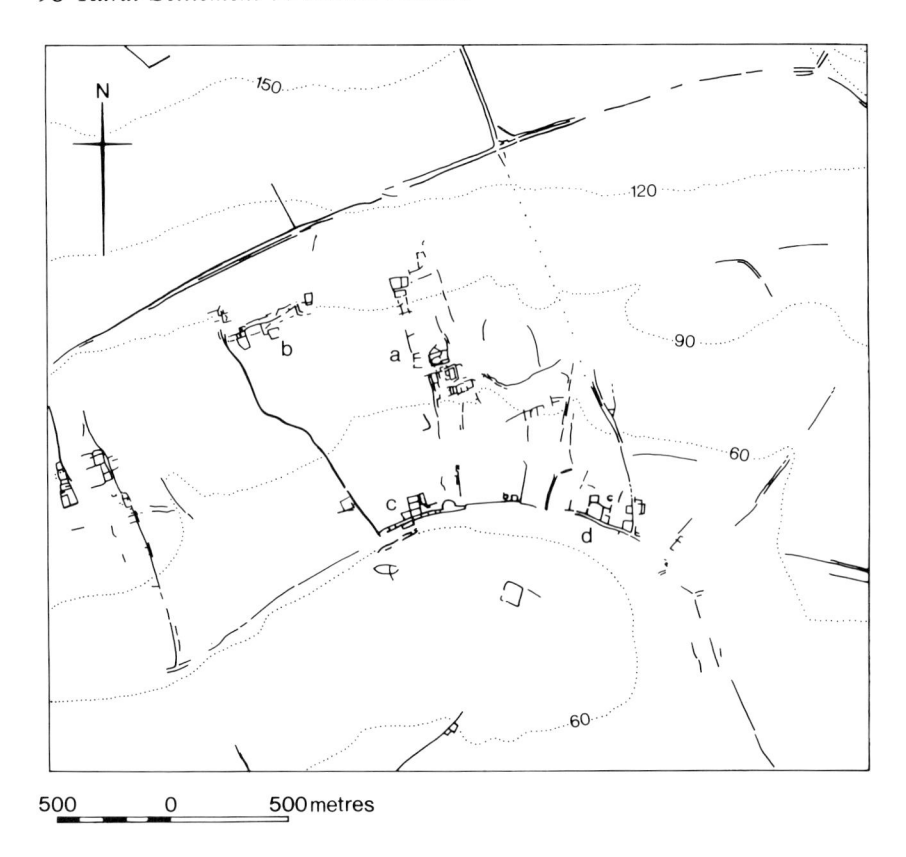

Figure 52 Roman settlement patterns at Wetwang Slack (Humbs). (After Dent 1983a, figure 3).

or control, of a single area of land may have been the basis of kinship at Wetwang Slack.

The situation at Wetwang Slack during the first to fourth centuries appears to fit a model which has been derived from medieval Welsh settlement evidence. According to GR Jones a type of settlement grouping which he calls 'girdle pattern' was once very common, but has rarely survived in the modern Welsh landscape. The girdle pattern can be typified by the group of medieval/post-medieval settlements at Bryngwyn Caerwys in north-east Wales (*see* Figure 53). Originally this group of settlements consisted of one large arable field, which was almost encompassed by a roadway providing access to a group of farmsteads. The budding-off of settlements, once the area of common land became too small to feed an expanding population, presumably caused the development of additional secondary girdle pattern settle-

Local groupings of settlement 99

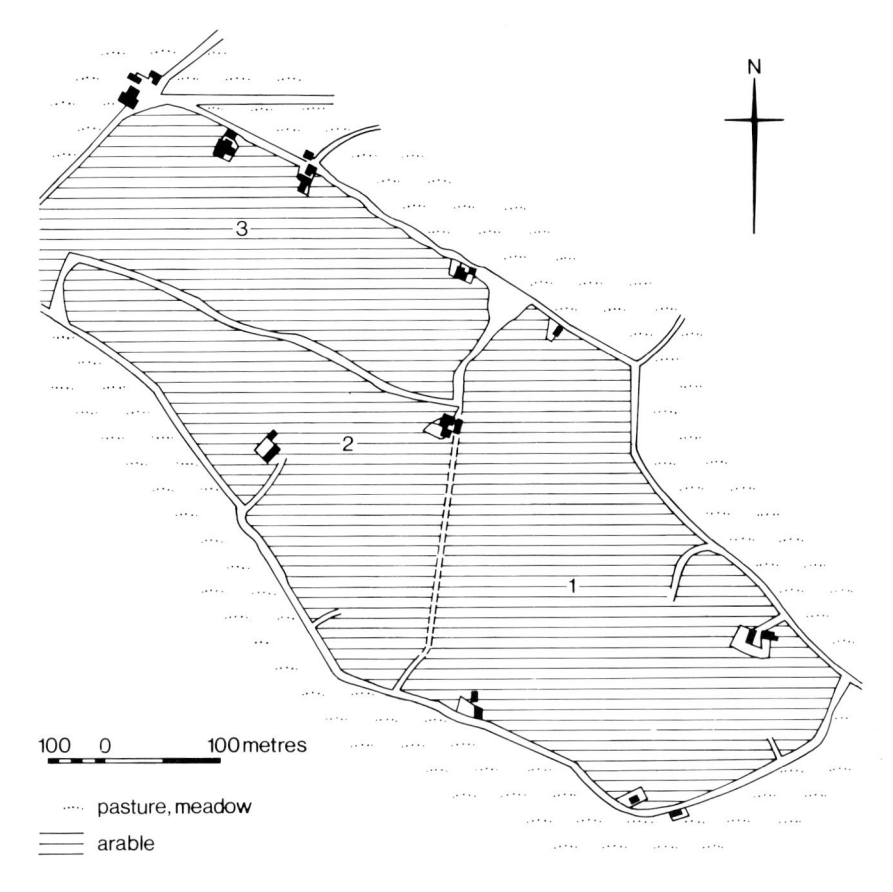

Figure 53 *Girdle pattern model. The numbers represent the sequence in which the three patterns developed. (Based on Hingley 1988 and GR Jones 1985, figure 11.2).*

ments peripheral to the original group. In this way a network of girdle patterns developed.[8]

The pattern is similar to that at Wetwang Slack. The area of common land defined by the settlements and roadway at Bryngwyn Caerwys, usually lies on well-drained fertile soils suitable for crop production. The girdle pattern of settlement and access roads form a division between the arable land and the pasture. The pasture lay outside the ring of settlement, often on less well-drained or less fertile soil.

The Fenland of Norfolk and Cambridgeshire and Lincolnshire was typified by non-villa settlements during the Roman period. Patterns of settlement are fairly complete, although they are only known from aerial photography and field survey. Settlement patterns appear to be fairly simple, being uncomplicated by earlier and subsequent occupation.

Probable girdle patterns of settlement can be recognised on the low-lying soils of the Fenland and indeed the maps provided in Hallam's survey indicate that the majority of the Roman Fenland settlements can be fitted into these settlement groupings (*see* Figure 54). As in the case of the medieval Welsh examples, these comprise areas of settlement with trackways forming a boundary with the arable land of the community, and usually occur in multiple groups as if created by expansion from a single original core settlement grouping.

The author has suggested that the girdle pattern of settlement characterizes the Iron Age settlement record on the gravels of the Upper Thames Valley. This area is typified by non-villa settlements in the Roman period and there are some indications that they fit the girdle pattern model, although the evidence is not as clear as that for the Fenland. Further research will be necessary if these patterns are to be analyzed more fully.[9]

It is probable that the girdle pattern settlements of Wales are related to common descent and to control and ownership of some areas of land by the community resident within a group of settlements. The same pattern in the Roman province may have a similar explanation.[10] This would indicate that many or most of the Roman settlements in the Fenland were bound into broader communities based on common descent and possibly on common ownership of land.

It was mentioned above that archaeologists usually study individual settlements as if they occurred in isolated locations and had little contact with other settlements.[11] At present the suggested occurrence of girdle pattern settlements in Roman Britain is dependent on aerial photographic evidence and limited fieldwork, and none of these potential groupings have been investigated in detail. If the suggestions made in this section are to be assessed more fully, it will be necessary to examine a group of these settlements through large-scale excavation and intensive survey.

VILLAS, NON-VILLA SETTLEMENTS AND ESTATES

It has been shown in previous chapters that a division occurs on many sites between a compound which contains a villa building and a second non-villa compound. It has been suggested that this division could be between the land-owning dominant family and their subservient kin or servants. The evidence indicates that these relations also existed between groups of settlements.

It is probable that land was the basis of the wealth of many élites of the Roman Empire. For many, economic wealth was accumulated through the ownership of an area of agricultural land. It is likely that this land was often cultivated for the wealthy individual or family by tenants or slaves. It has been argued that the landed estate with associated farm

Local groupings of settlement 101

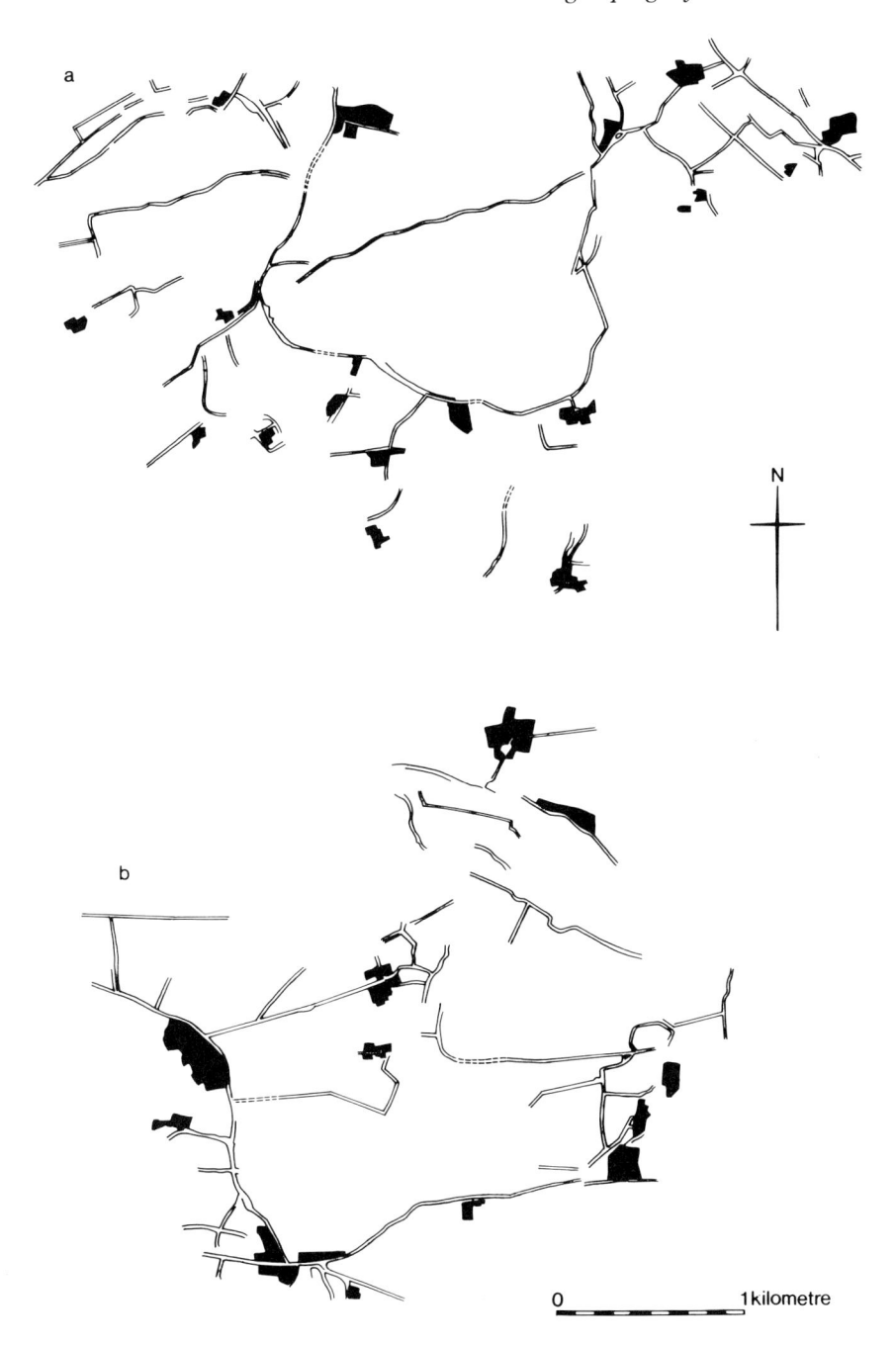

Figure 54 *Girdle pattern settlement in the Fenland. (After C Phillips ed., 1970, fold-out maps 2 and 10).*

workers was probably the economic basis for the largest villas in Britain.[12]

Applebaum has suggested that it may be possible to identify a tenurial connection between villa and non-villa settlements in at least two types of situation. First, on some sites a villa and non-villa settlement are located in close proximity to each other, and it is probable that the latter was the home of estate workers on land owned by the owner or owners of the villa. Second, Applebaum has developed a model called 'peripheral holdings' in order to examine the extent and structure of the estate.[13] In this section the evidence for both types of pattern will be considered. The final discussion is of the evidence for estates associated with large and wealthy villas.

Close associations between villas and non-villa settlements

A tenurial relationship may be indicated when a villa occurs in close association with a non-villa settlement, although the extent and boundaries of the associated estate are not known (*see* Figure 55). In this situation it is possible that the inhabitants of the non-villa settlement were tenants or slaves and worked on the lands of a villa-owning individual or family.[14] Several examples of close associations between villas and non-villa settlements are known in Britain.[15] It is possible that in some instances the two settlements could have been successive, and that the villa replaced an earlier non-villa settlement on a neighbouring site, as was possibly the case at Lockington (Leic).

Specific areas also exist in which villa and non-villa settlements occur alongside one another. This appears to be the case in the valley of the River Dene around Kineton in Warwickshire, the area around Fotheringhay in the Lower Nene valley of Cambridgeshire, and the Corallian Ridge around Frilford in Oxfordshire (*see* Figure 56). The quality of the evidence available for analysis is low, as in none of these examples have associated groups of villa and non-villa settlements been excavated on a large scale.

Evidence for localized estates

Direct evidence for the extent of the land units which were associated with settlements is absent in Britain. In a number of cases, however, it has been argued that Roman land units survived in the medieval landscape of southern Britain and it may be possible to identify the extent of Romano-British estates. The thesis comprises the local estate units surviving the end of Roman Britain to become the basic units in the Anglo-Saxon estate system. Roman estates can therefore be reconstructed from the local estates recorded in Anglo-Saxon and

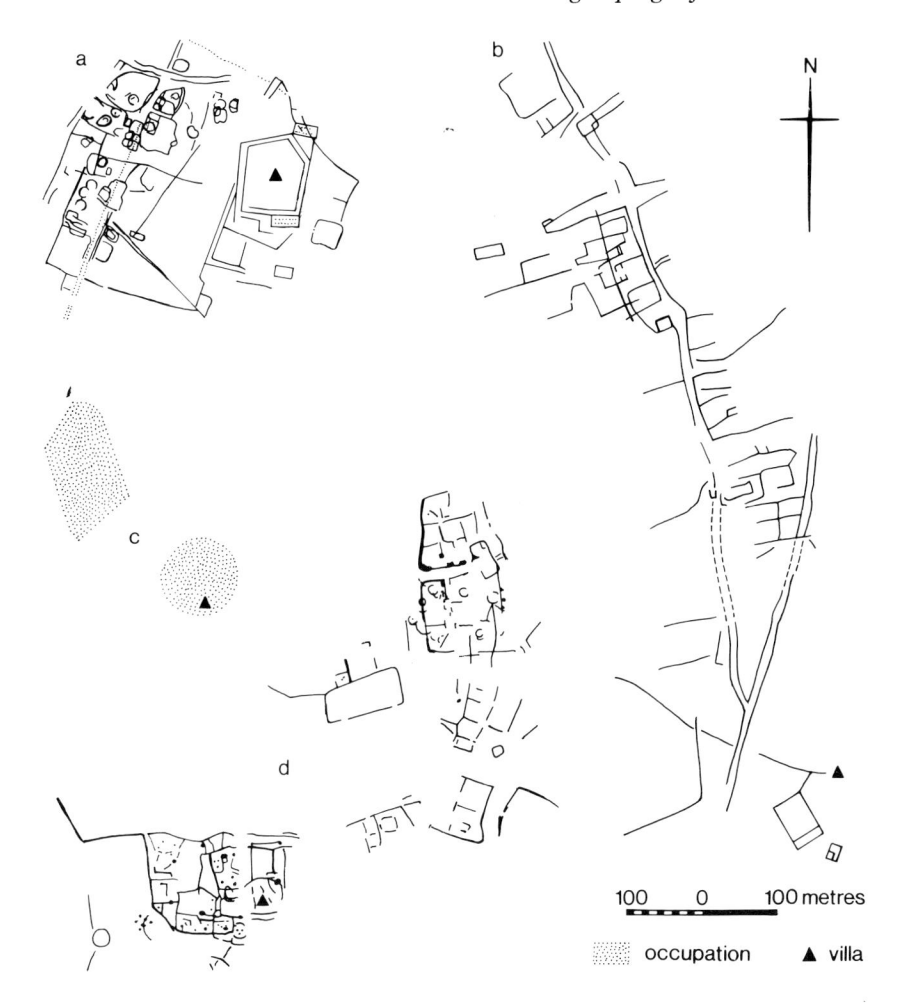

Figure 55 *Association of non-villa settlements with villa settlements: a. Lockington (Leic); b. Fotheringhay (Northants); c. Whitminster (Glos); d. Frilford villa (Oxon).*

medieval estate boundary documents. This idea was first suggested for Withington (Glos) and has more recently been argued for a number of other areas such as northern Somerset, Northamptonshire and Oxfordshire.[16]

In a number of these areas it may be possible to establish the extent of the lands associated with Roman period settlements, and something of the tenurial relations between villas and non-villa sites. It is possible that medieval parish/township boundaries around Frilford (Oxon) and in the Vale of Wrington (Somer) represent the approximate extent of Roman

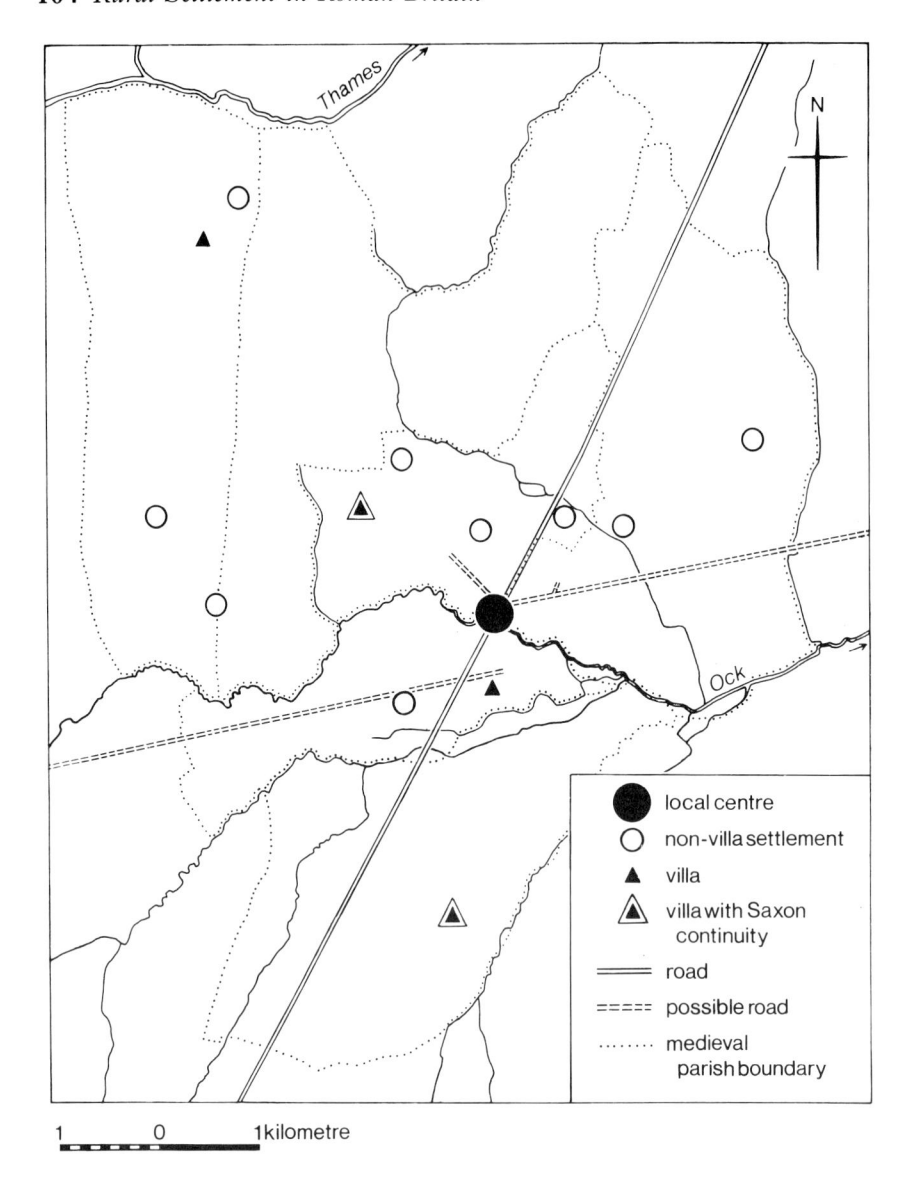

Figure 56 *Possible villa estates around Frilford (Oxon). (Hingley, work in progress).*

villa lands. In both of these areas non-villa settlements are known to have existed within the land unit.

In the Vale of Wrington the villas occur on the valley floor and non-villa settlements on the northern slopes. It has been suggested that the Lye Hole villa had a link with the non-villa settlement of Scars Farm, and a number of the other possible Roman villa estates appear to include non-villa settlements.[17] In this case it may be possible to recognize the extent of a villa estate and to identify a further settlement which was tenurially dependent on the villa. The same pattern appears in the most fully investigated parishes around Frilford in Oxfordshire (*see* Figure 56). In these parishes one villa is known per parish, but non-villa settlements also occur in close association and it seems likely that they were the homes of tenants or slaves of the villa owners.

These possible Romano-British land units are at a local scale and may represent either the lands of fairly small-scale landowners, or the lowest level of an estate system with individual villas tenurially dependent on landowners based in larger villas. Fieldwork in the areas that have produced possible evidence for continuity of land units has not been extensive enough to have distinguished settlement patterns at a scale above that of the individual local estate.

The estates of large landowners

In France evidence exists for estate patterns at a rather larger scale than the individual land unit indicated by parish/township-sized areas. Percival has reviewed the evidence for possible estates around the villas of Chiragan and Montmaurin (Hte-Garonne) and on a number of other sites in France and Belgium. At Chiragan the supposed estate is defined largely by the natural topography of streams and hills, within which are four smaller villas, at least three 'villages' and numerous other possible settlement sites. At Montmaurin the villa estate can be defined not only from archaeological and topographical considerations but also from documentary evidence. The group of parishes in which the villa and associated settlements are situated is known from medieval times by a name derived from that of the Roman estate. It seems probable that the group of medieval parishes preserves the boundaries of the estate of the Montmaurin villa.[18] Many other Romano-Gallic estate names survive in the countryside of France, Belgium and to a lesser degree Germany, often appearing to indicate the location of Roman villa estates.[19]

The density of Roman settlement in lowland Roman Britain suggests that it would be incorrect to attempt to define the extent of Roman villa estates by topographical features. The whole landscape of southern Britain was intensively settled and exploited and in many areas there were probably no unoccupied areas between estates. Evidence for the survival of place-names derived from Roman estates is absent in Britain. While in Gaul the Roman estates often appear to have continued and to have formed tenurial units in Carolingian times,[20] in Britain it is generally considered that the villa system of hierarchically organized estates collapsed in the fifth century.[21] The possible evidence for the

106 *Rural Settlement in Roman Britain*

▲ large villa
▲ small villa
○ non-villa settlement

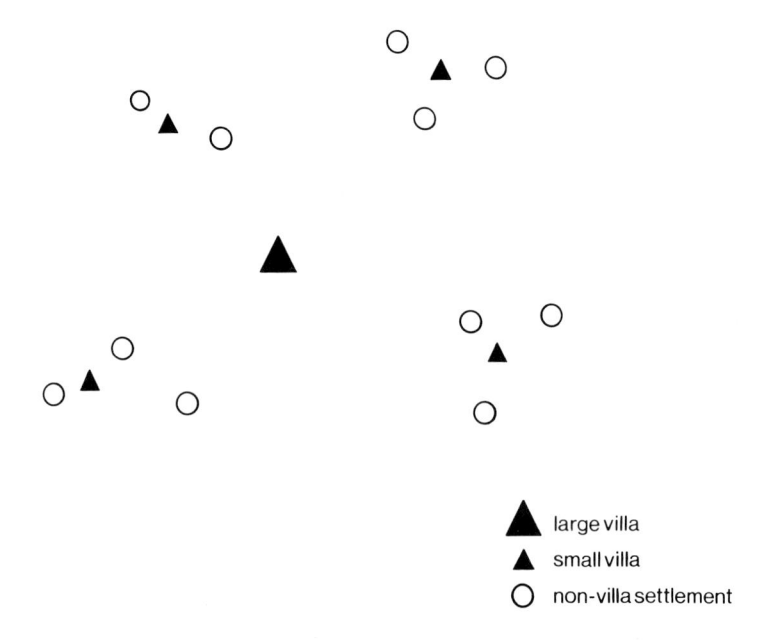

Figure 57 *Peripheral holdings model. (After Applebaum 1963).*

survival of parish/township-sized estates which was discussed above may indicate the level beyond which the fragmentation of estates during the fifth century did not occur.

Applebaum has suggested that estate patterns may be characterized in the archaeological evidence by peripheral distributions of tenurially dependent settlements around an estate centre, usually a large villa. These peripheral holdings can be recognized in the Carolingian cartularies of Gaul, and Applebaum has argued that these Carolingian estate patterns were derived from late Roman estates.[22] This is the type of model that has been used to analyze the Romano-Gallic estates centred on large villas in Gaul and Belgium. Under this approach the parish/township-sized land units discussed above would be integrated into larger estates, centred on a large villa (*see* Figure 57). The Gallic evidence appears to indicate that villas could in some cases represent the homes of tenants of the landowner or land-owning family, so that the tenurially dependent settlements may have included non-villa settlements and examples of the more modest villas. In other words, large-scale land owners existed holding large estates made up of multiple parish-sized units. This might suggest a three-tier hierarchy comprising landowners in rich extensive villas, tenants in smaller villas and agricultural servants and slaves in non-villa settlements, although a two-tier hierarchy is also possible.

Can patterns of the peripheral holdings type be recognized in Britain? The evidence is totally inadequate, as few projects covering large areas of the landscape have been conducted. Applebaum, however, has discussed a range of sites at which peripheral holdings may occur.[23] He has estimated the area of land belonging to the courtyard villa at Bignor (W Susx) on the basis of granary capacity, ox-stalls and possible natural boundaries. This estate probably covered about 800 hectares and included some areas suitable for arable and others for pasture. Within the supposed boundaries of this estate five or six additional Roman sites have been found, and Applebaum has argued that it seems likely that they constituted the homes of sub-tenants of the villa owner.[24] He has also discussed the villa at Wiggonholt (W Susx), where there were four minor sites nearby, each commanding a distinct area of fertile arable soil.[25] The case studies of Bignor and Wiggonholt do not actually appear to involve areas much larger than the individual medieval parish.

Branigan, however, has attempted to reconstruct the estate of the villa at Gatcombe (Glos) on the basis of local topography and limits implied by neighbouring villa lands (*see* Figure 58). This hypothetical estate covers 6,000 hectares and includes possible areas of arable, pasture, sheep pasture and woodland. In addition the estate includes the sites of at least eight 'native' or non-villa settlements. In this hypothetical model of the Gatcombe estate these non-villa settlements are seen as the homes of dependent labourers or slaves rather than tenants, as the full potential of the estate could not be realized unless it was organized as a single economic entity.[26]

Other courtyard and large winged corridor villas probably have comparable densities of settlements in the immediate vicinities. At Woodchester (Glos) a high density of settlement includes winged corridor villas and non-villa settlements,[27] but for the majority of courtyard and large winged corridor villas these patterns have not been studied in detail.

The pattern of estates may not always have been as simple as the peripheral holdings model suggests. There are indications in the classical literary sources that estates often did not form coherent, concentrated land units.[28] Individuals often appear to have owned numerous distinct areas of land isolated from one another and located throughout the province.[29] Estates of this fragmented type will be impossible to reconstruct from archaeological evidence alone.

More complex forms of territorial organization than the simple peripheral holdings model may, however, be indicated by the archaeological evidence. One example is suggested by the pattern of large villas, winged corridor villas and non-villa farms in the area of the North Oxfordshire Grim's Ditch (Oxon). In this area (*see* Figure 59) three rich villas occur at the core of a territory, while more modest villas and

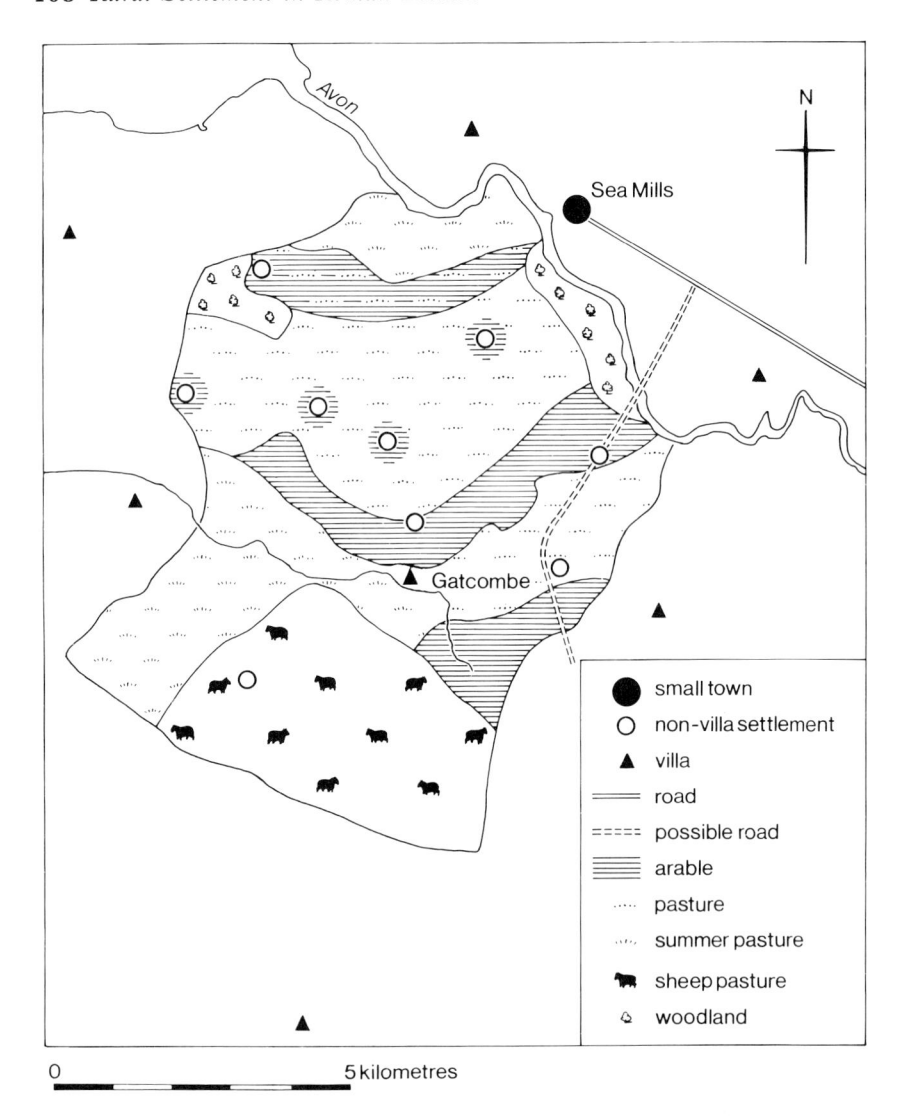

Figure 58 *A possible 'villa estate' at Gatcombe (Somer). (After Branigan 1977a, figure 34).*

non-villa settlements occur in a peripheral distribution around these sites. It seems possible that this provides evidence for the division of a large estate between three large land-owning families living in the rich villas, with tenants and slaves in the smaller villas and farms.[30] If this interpretation is correct the North Oxfordshire Grim's Ditch area indicates a type of multiple peripheral holdings model, as a single original estate has become divided between a number of distinct owners.

Figure 59 *Settlement patterns in the area of the North Oxfordshire Grim's Ditch: a. North Leigh; b. Stonesfield; c. Ditchley; d. Shakenoak; e. Callow Hill; f. Oaklands Farm. (After Hingley 1988, figure 7:12).*

SUMMARY

Some evidence for local patterns of settlement exist, and it is possible to attempt to interpret this patterning by considering how agricultural production was organized at a local scale. In this chapter two particular approaches have been considered. First, it has been argued that some relatively egalitarian communities based on nucleated settlements or groups of settlements could have held important resources in common. Second, the limited evidence for the organization of rural estates controlled by villa-owners has been discussed.

Chapter 7
The network of local markets

The term 'local centre' is reserved for sites in the 'civilian' zone of Britain. The *vicus* centres of northern Britain are of limited relevance to the discussion in this chapter, as they appear to have existed mainly as markets for the military rather than the civilian population. These sites will be discussed further below.[1] Two alternative models, a restricted and a broader model, have been discussed for the distribution and significance of local centres in southern and eastern Britain. The significance of local centre distribution will now be considered. The economic relationship between villas and local centres must be studied, as the local market may often have provided the source of the surplus with which villas were built.

MARKET NETWORKS

The two models for Romano-British local centres which were introduced in Chapter 2 differ fundamentally. The restricted model is the more traditional of the two and stresses the scarcity and isolation of the Romano-British local centre. It was remarked above, however, that those who adopt this approach do not define the category of sites that are being considered in a consistent and coherent way, but merely discuss the most obvious or best preserved sites.[2]

If a more objective definition of the concept is attempted it becomes difficult to exclude a far wider range of settlements from the category. If the extent of the settlement and a position on a known Roman road are taken to indicate a local centre, then a wide range of sites on which little detailed archaeological work has been conducted should be defined in this way.

The difficulty with studying sites as defined by the broader classification is that too little work has been carried out on the majority to positively identify a market function and that they were anything more than non-villa settlements. Only large-scale excavation can prove this point.[3] A great deal of detailed fieldwork and excavation will be necessary if a full understanding of the distribution, significance and status of local centres as a whole is to be obtained.

The broader definition of local centres has, however, been implemented in two areas of southern Britain. These two areas are the territory of the

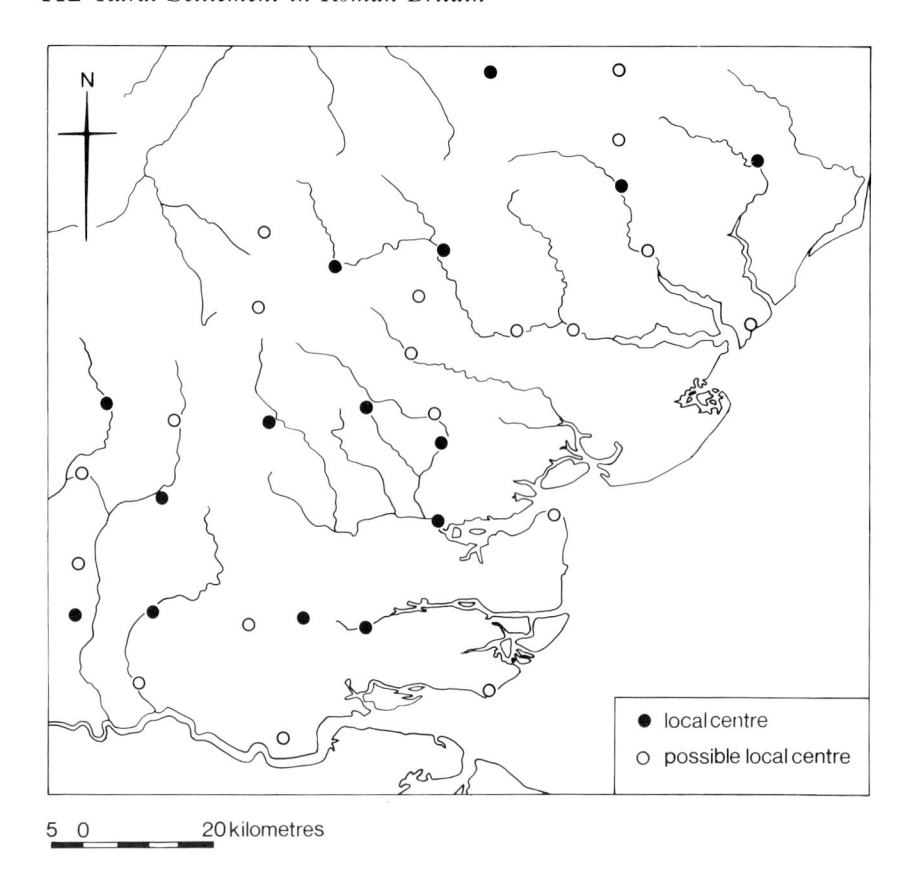

Figure 60 *The distribution of local centres among the Trinovantes. (After W Rodwell 1975, figure 1).*

Trinovantes – present-day Essex, southern and eastern Sussex and the fringe areas of Herefordshire and Cambridgeshire (*see* Figure 60) – and the area of the Upper Thames Valley and southern Cotswolds which constituted the territory of the south-eastern Dobunni (*see* Figure 61).

The Trinovantian local centres include some well-known and some very poorly known sites.[4] The extent, location, structure and chronology of these local centres have been discussed in some detail elsewhere.[5] In the Upper Thames Valley/south Warwickshire an equally dense distribution of local centres has been located, although again the amount of information varies from site to site.[6]

The distribution of local centres in the area of the Trinovantes and the south-eastern Dobunni appears to fit a model for the distribution of 'lowest order market centres' or local market centres. The model is derived from the study of medieval local markets in southern Britain and

The network of local markets 113

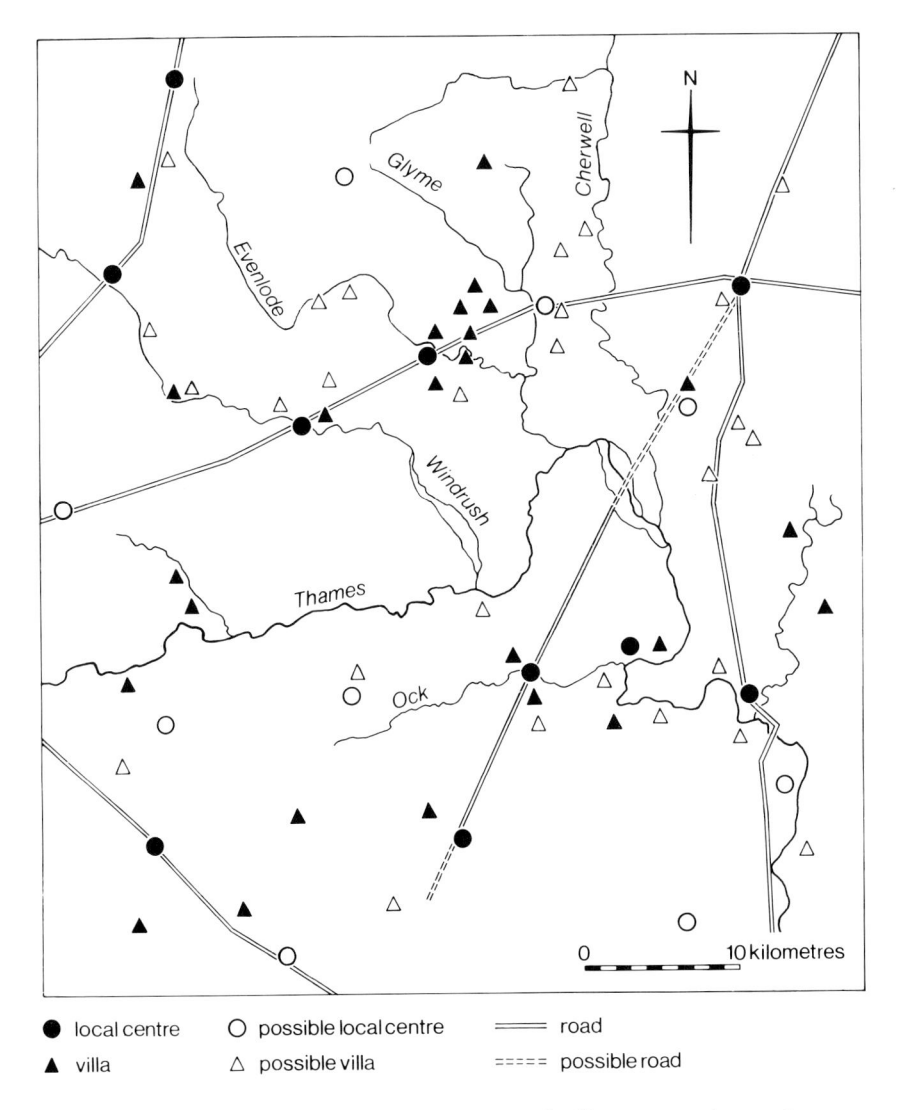

Figure 61 *The distribution of local centres and villas among the south-eastern Dobunni. (After Hingley 1988, figure 7:15).*

other areas of the world.[7] This model appears to be relevant for societies which have a high population density, an absence of self-sufficiency amongst individual communities and pre-industrial methods of transport. All of these factors are relevant in the southern area of Roman Britain. It has been suggested above that the population of Roman Britain was approximately as dense as that of medieval England at a period shortly before the Black Death in the mid-fourteenth century. The importance of exchange within rural communities and absence of self-sufficiency is indicated by the fact that even the poorest Romano-British settlements in southern Britain had access to industrially produced pottery and metalwork. In societies of this type it is often found that rural peasants will not travel more than about seven to ten kilometres to obtain and exchange basic agricultural and manufactured goods. At this distance the peasant can reach the market and return home within one day. As a consequence, where there is enough demand rural marketing centres develop at fairly regular intervals of ten to fourteen kilometres.

The information for the distribution of extensive settlements among the Trinovantes and south-eastern Dobunni indicates the validity of the local market centre model for these areas. It is suggested below that the model will also be found of use in other areas in the south of the province, although it still remains for the evidence to be researched and published.[8]

It is probable that this local distribution of market centres did not exist in all areas of the province. The model is not applicable to the military regions of northern England and Wales and Cornwall,[9] due to the lack of economic growth in these areas. There may also be areas of southern Britain, such as the Fenland, in which local centres are rare or completely absent.[10]

It has been suggested that the administrative and military structure imposed on the Roman province and the functions of local centres that derived from it should lead the Roman archaeologist to be sceptical of analogies taken from societies not subject to these types of formal external control.[11] This would suggest that the basis of the argument for local centres as local markets is incorrect. Local centres actually appear to be far more common than has been previously considered, which weakens the correlation between military establishments and local centres.[12] The majority of local centres were unwalled, and imposed administrative factors may have been of limited significance in relation to economic factors. The distribution of unwalled local centres in Roman Britain may thus have been conditioned largely by economic rather than administrative considerations. Formal control of Romano-British rural settlement need not have been great once the Roman army had moved northwards in the first century.

A second point of importance concerns the source of the model for lowest-order market centres. The model has been developed in the context of the medieval landscape of Britain, at a time when free market forces were certainly not dominant.[13] In the medieval period, as in Roman Britain, market forces were constrained by military and administrative factors. Many medieval markets developed outside castles and monasteries, a situation directly comparable to the Roman province in which many of the local centres grew up in association with forts and religious centres. The grant of a royal charter to a local lord was a prerequisite for the establishment of a market in the medieval period.[14] The existence of a local medieval market will therefore have been at the will of the local landlord, rather than according to purely economic principles. The landlord will presumably have been interested in making a profit through the market and will have located it at some distance from other markets, or at least have tried to make his local market competitive. Any Roman landlord who set up a market will presumably also have been guided by similar principles of common sense. Indeed the situation in medieval southern Britain may not have been very different from that in the Roman Empire, where local markets were presumably under the control of local landlords.

Archaeology can provide no details of the size or timing of the markets and fairs held in the local centres of Roman Britain. Large markets would, however, presumably have drawn traders and customers from a larger area than minor markets. It seems probable that the markets of some local centres were larger and of greater significance than the markets of others. The size and wealth of the local centre may indicate something of the importance of its market. Extensive, wealthy small towns such as Water Newton (Cambs), Alchester (Oxon) and Kenchester (Here & Worc) may have had more important markets than smaller or poorer local centres such as Chesterton-on-Fosse (Warw), Churchover (Warw), Abingdon (Oxon) or Baldock (Herts). A positive correlation may be expected between the size and wealth of a settlement and the scale and success of a market.

The range of goods sold at the more important markets would probably have been wider, with exotic goods brought from a distance as well as local goods. Archaeological excavations provide information on the range of goods available at the settlements, but whether work can provide information on detailed matters such as the frequency and timing of markets and the organization of market networks is yet to be seen.

If the medieval parallel is extended further it would suggest that markets within Romano-British local centres would have been held on particular days, perhaps on a weekly cycle. If this was so then networks of markets may be expected, with neighbouring markets held on different days and market circuits developing. These circuits developed for the convenience of the trader, who could travel between markets on a weekly cycle. It is known that markets of this sort existed in Roman Africa,[15] and the archaeological evidence for the number of local centres in Roman Britain probably suggests that a similar situation existed in the province.

The fair was a market that was held on a regular day, or days, in a year. In some areas of the north and west of the province there is a possibility that a barter economy survived the Roman occupation and that periodic markets existed that were not associated with extensive settlements. Davies has discussed the situation in Wales, where she has suggested that major fairs occurred at the great tribal and religious assemblies which met regularly to celebrate festivals.[16] Festivals constituted a traditional Celtic practice, and it is assumed that such events were also held in south-western, northern and southern England. Trading at festivals of this type may explain how some of the artefacts that occur on rural sites in the north and west found their way to sites.

It is likely that a number of local centres in southern Britain had periodic fairs in addition to their regular markets. Frilford (Oxon) is one of the best known of these, where an extensive temple complex occurred in the middle of the local centre (*see* Figure 49). The complex includes an amphitheatre, which has not been fully excavated, but has been estimated to have had a potential seating capacity of around 4,000.[17] It is to be assumed, therefore, that sizeable gatherings of hundreds, or thousands, of visitors are indicated for this site.[18] The temple-complex at Frilford was probably used for major and perhaps tribal religious festivals, and presumably a major fair would also have been held on such occasions. Other local centres also included large-scale temple complexes,[19] where it is likely that tribal or sub-tribal festivals were held. These festivals would also have encouraged the establishment of fairs.[20]

THE VILLA AND THE MARKET

The surplus agricultural goods produced on a villa estate were converted into surplus wealth through trade at the local or regional market.[21] It is possible, therefore, that the proximity of a settlement to a local market could have been important in the economic growth of that settlement. A model can be proposed in which two settlements of equal status existed, one close to a town and one distant from the town. The inhabitants of the former might find greater encouragement to create an agricultural surplus and thus have been able to construct villa buildings, while the inhabitants of the latter might have had greater difficulty in marketing any surplus. It is clear that the nature of the communications network will also have been important – proximity to a well maintained road or track will have facilitated access to the market.

The significance of the proximity of villas to towns has been discussed by a number of authors. Two types of studies can be considered. First, in many cases the landscape of an individual local centre has been studied and the association of a villa or villas to the local centre discussed.[22] Second, the general pattern of villas and their association with towns over a single tribe or the whole of the civilian province have been analyzed.[23] It is clear that groups of villas occur close to many local centres (*see* Figure 62) and it is possible that in many cases the villas were in origin non-villa settlements which had profited from their proximity to a market.[24]

Some local centres may have been the homes of *coloni*, or slaves, associated with a villa estate.[25] This model has already been discussed for the association of non-villa settlements with villas.[26] The villa was not necessarily always economically dependent on the local centre, as in some cases the local centre may actually have been tenurially dependent on the villa.

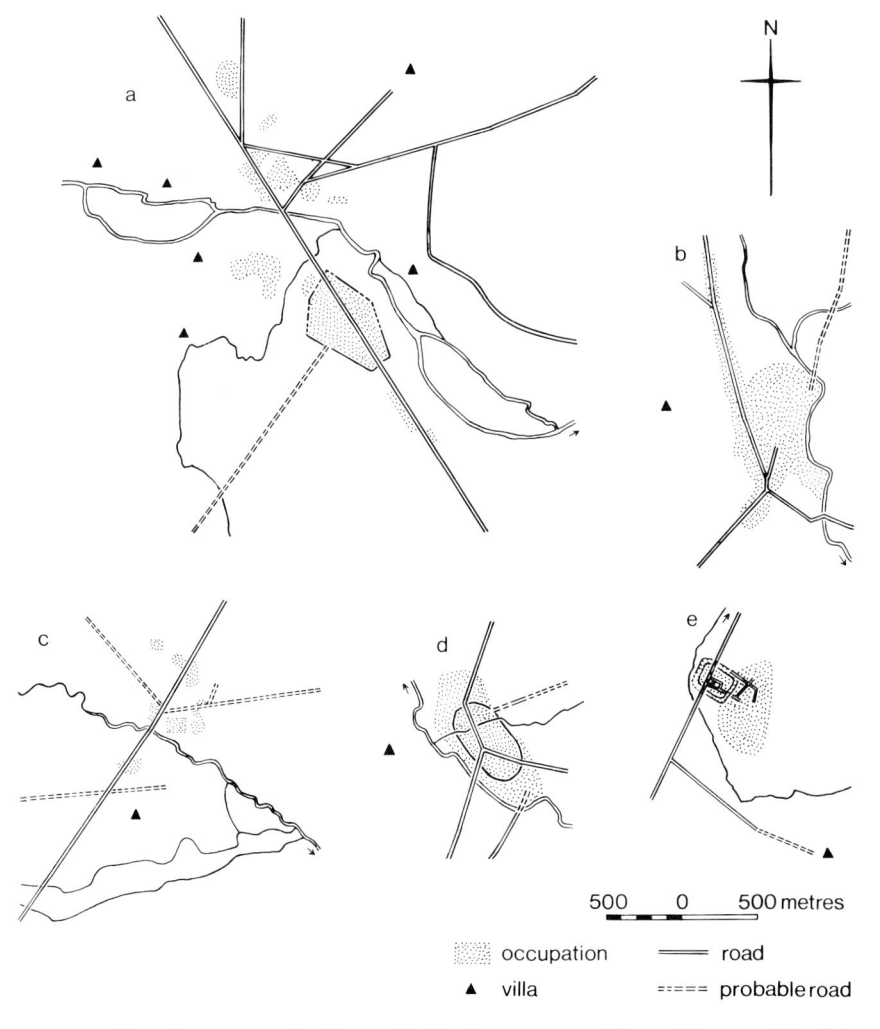

Figure 62 *Association of villas with local centres: a. Water Newton (Cambs); b. Braughing (Herts); c. Frilford (Oxon); d. Great Chesterford (Essex); e. Chesterton-on-Fosse (Warw).*

More information is needed on the surroundings of local centres in Britain. A full understanding of local centres will only follow from a detailed study of the association of villas and non-villa settlements in the area surrounding the local centre. The size and importance of the villa may be of significance. It therefore seems improbable that a small corridor/winged corridor villa, such as those at Godmanchester (Cambs) or Frilford (Oxon), would have had tenurial control over the neighbouring local centre. Large and wealthy villas such as those close to Water Newton (Cambs) are more likely to have been the centres of estates, perhaps with estate workers living in the local centre. The understanding of this type of patterning requires further and more detailed study. The problem was discussed in detail by Todd in 1970, but subsequent surveys of local centres in Britain have done very little to improve understanding of the relationship of villas to local centres.[27]

An alternative approach to the study of villas and local centres has been utilized by a number of authors.[28] This approach attempts to explore the general patterning of villas in relation to local centres over a single tribal territory or the whole of the civilian province. Rivet's comments were derived from visual inspection of information from the 1956 edition of the *Ordnance Survey Map of Roman Britain*, while other studies draw on a much larger body of information for local centres and villas. Recently a 'systematic analysis' has been conducted by Hodder and Millett, based once again on the limited body of information shown on the Ordnance Survey map, but attempting a numerical analysis of the fall-off in the density of villas by considering their distance from Roman towns.

A number of observations were derived from this detailed analysis. It is suggested that the larger towns, for example the *coloniae*, *municipia* and *civitas* capitals, appear to have attracted villas to a wider surrounding area than did the local centres. This may be a consequence of the provision by the more important towns of a wider range of functions and their larger, more important markets. The problem with this analysis is again the inadequate nature of the available data. It is not certain, for example, quite how large a proportion of all the Roman villas that once existed have been located. The information on which the analysis was based is an unknown sample of the original information for villa distribution. The fifty eight towns considered in this study form a restricted sample of the original total of local centres in the province.[29] This analysis provides a number of proposals that require assessment through further data collection.

In the territory of the Trinovantes the broader definition of local centres has been adopted, and it is possible to study the distribution of villas in relation to these centres (*see* Figure 63). Although villas and local centres appear to occur within the same general area there are no

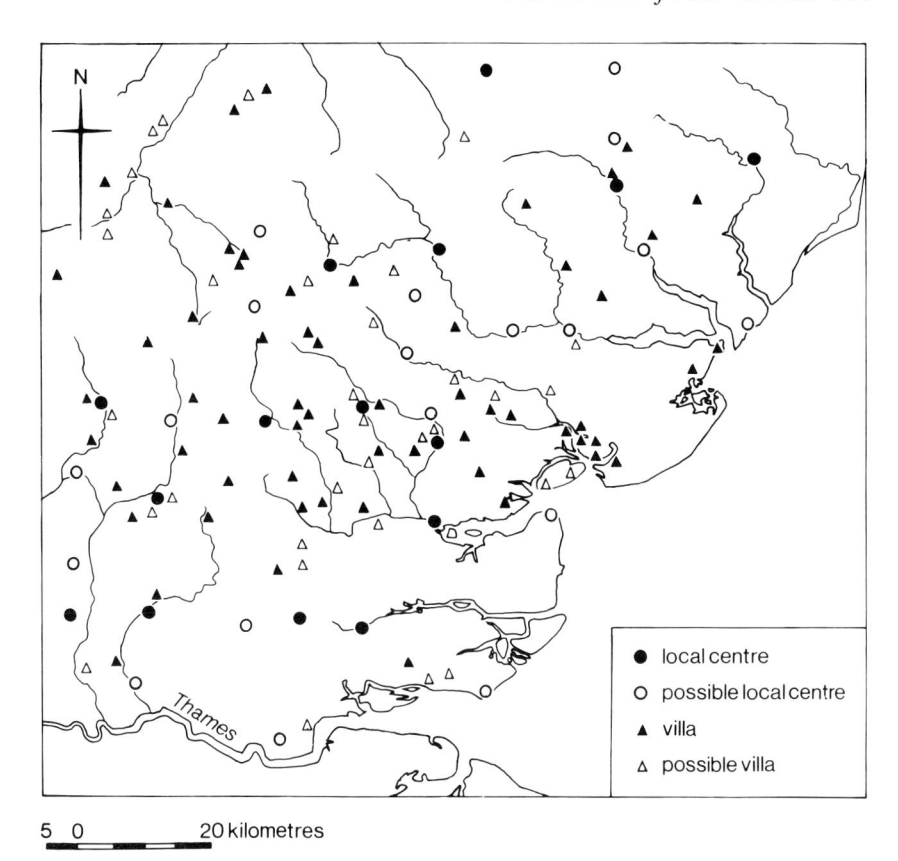

Figure 63 *The distribution of local centres and villas among the Trinovantes. (After W Rodwell 1975, figure 6).*

obvious signs of satellite formations of villas around local centres.[30] Villas and local centres are distributed fairly regularly with little indication that proximity to a local market was a vital factor for villa development. This is presumably because the market landscape over much of the area was fully developed and all villas and non-villa settlements had easy access to their local market. The pattern of villas in relation to local centres appears very similar in the area of the south-eastern Dobunni, with villas and local centres occurring in similar areas, but with no obvious clustering of villas in the immediate vicinity of the local centre (*see* Figure 61).

As non-villa settlements also occur around local centres in both of these areas, proximity to a local centre may not have been the only reason behind ability to accumulate the wealth necessary to build a villa; many family groups who lived close to the market did not acquire the wealth to do so. The area around the Frilford temple site and local centre indicates this clearly (*see* Figure 56), and it has already been mentioned that the simplest explanation for the villas and non-villa settlements in this area is that the latter fell into the estates of the former.[31]

SUMMARY

The presence and location of the local market were doubtlessly important factors behind the distribution, wealth and form of rural settlement in Britain. The evidence may indicate economic growth in southern Britain. In some areas a very dense and even distribution of local market centres and villas developed, and a similar pattern may be expected in other areas when sufficiently detailed fieldwork has been undertaken. It will be argued below, however, that in northern Britain and Wales markets were dependent on the army and that local communities were less dependent on trade.

Chapter 8
Regions of the south and east

It is likely that each local region of Britain was characterized by its own unique type of settlement pattern which differed from that of other regions.[1] It would require a fairly complete pattern of settlement and a detailed local analysis of each distinct region to interpret these types of settlement pattern in full. In the absence of more complete information, the evidence will be considered for regions which are characterized by the occurrence of either villa or non-villa settlements.

The development of villa settlements is a trend that Rivet has described as 'normal'.[2] This suggests that the majority of settlements in southern Britain became villas. In fact, villa buildings were not constructed on the majority of settlements throughout Britain and material culture remained fairly poor.[3] It is simplistic to describe the development of the villa as 'normal'.

Two common types of situation can be defined for non-villa settlements. The non-villa settlement could occur in a landscape which included villa settlements. This type of pattern has already been discussed in connection with the proposition that in many cases the non-villa settlement was the home of tenants or slaves on an estate owned by villa-dwellers.[4] Much of the south and east of the province had this type of settlement patterning. The development of regions in which villas occur alongside non-villa settlements is the trend that should be defined as 'normal' rather than the conversion of the non-villa settlement into a villa.

The second situation is that in which there is a distinct region defined by non-villa settlements and the absolute or relative absence of villas. Some areas of the south of the province fall into this category and are discussed in this chapter. In addition most of the upland areas of northern and western Britain are regions of this type and this is discussed in the next chapter.

VILLA REGIONS

The presence of villas and local centres indicates economic growth within that region. This growth is probably based on more intensive agricultural production, surplus creation, the development of exchange and consumption.

Some of the villas of Roman Britain will have been the homes of families who exploited the new conditions created by the Roman conquest. A model was proposed by R Collingwood in 1937 when he argued that the isolated family groups on the periphery of Cranborne Chase (Dorset and Wilts) could have exploited new conditions by expanding the scale of their agricultural activities, thus creating an agricultural surplus for exchange. These groups were able to accumulate the surplus wealth with which to construct villas. Collingwood contrasted this to the densely occupied 'village' settlements of the Chase, where agricultural expansion and surplus creation were impossible and villas are consequently absent.[5] It is possible, therefore, that in areas of the province physically isolated families were able to expand the scale of their agricultural activities and were thus able to build villas.

At a local level this model has been used to explain patterns of settlement in the area around Ewell (Surrey). In this area two contrasting agricultural zones are formed by the chalk, which appears to have been heavily settled by the second century BC, and heavy clay soils to either side which seem to have been unoccupied during the Iron Age (*see* Figure 64). Two of the three Roman villas in the region occur in areas which were marginal to the Iron Age settlement distribution, while many of the known Iron Age sites continue to be occupied but are non-villa settlements. It has been suggested that the chalk remained occupied by relatively small-scale farms which did not have the productive capacity to rise to villa status, while the villas came into existence through the initiative of individuals who exploited marginal land.[6]

Settlement patterns of the Sussex coastal plain and in the Upper Thames Valley in the Roman period may have a similar explanation. The Sussex Plain appears to have been relatively unsettled in the Iron Age and was colonized during the later first millennium BC and the first and second centuries AD. This newly-colonized area provided the type of environment in which agricultural expansion and the development of villas were possible.[7] In the Upper Thames Valley it appears that in the Oxford Uplands, for instance in the North Oxfordshire Grim's Ditch area, individual family groups controlled the immediate area of land around their isolated settlements during the Iron Age and Roman period. Once incorporated into the Roman Empire these family groups were able to adopt an expanded economic strategy. This is presumably characterized by the expansion of the area under cultivation and by its more intensive use. The resulting agricultural surplus was then marketed and the generated wealth could be invested in a villa building.[8]

Over much of southern Britain the most fertile areas were already intensively settled by the Roman conquest and in these Iron Age heartlands of settlement the expansion of the agricultural economy was hindered by the density of population. It seems possible, therefore, that

Regions of the south and east **123**

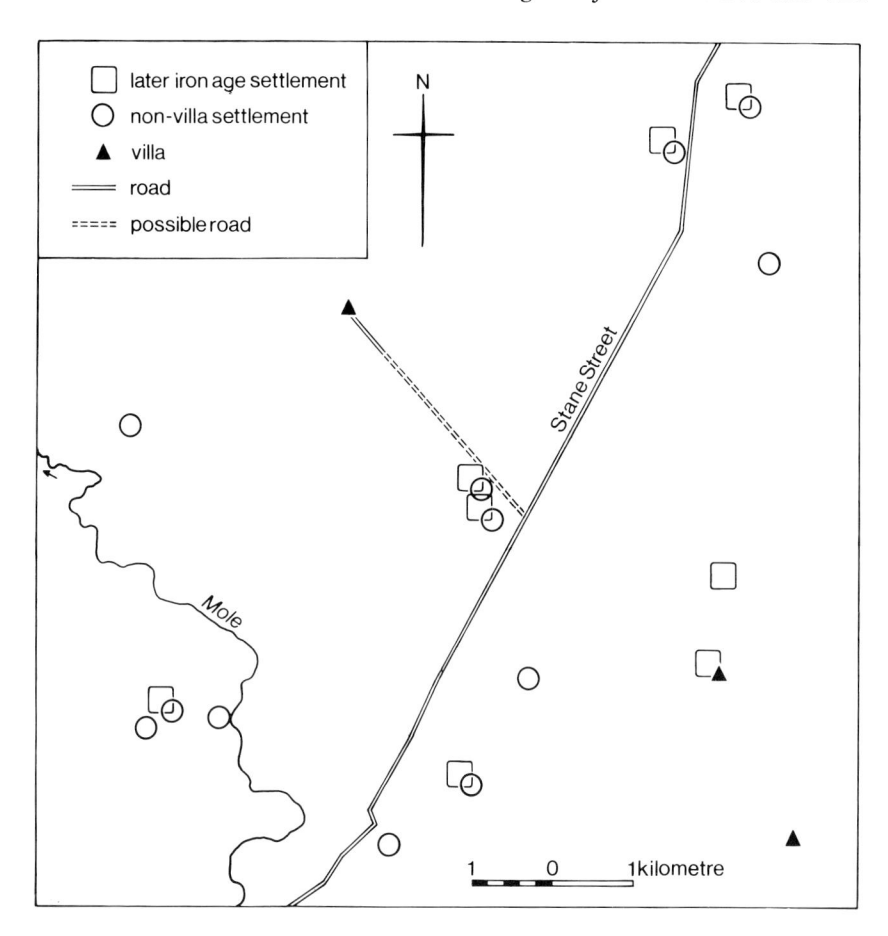

Figure 64 *The Ewell area (Surrey) in the Late Iron Age and Roman period. (After Black 1987, figure 26).*

in some areas of Roman Britain greater potential for agricultural expansion existed in marginal regions, areas that were relatively sparsely occupied. Some marginal areas contrast with the densely settled areas in that a new Romano-British élite developed by colonizing unused, or underused, areas of land and by expanding agricultural production.[9] This may be the basis of the economy in many areas of the province for, as already discussed, in the south and east of Britain landscapes with villas are typical rather than rare (*see* Figures 61, 63).

REGIONS OF NON-VILLA SETTLEMENTS

In some areas villas and local centres do not occur. The economy in these areas was stagnant, any expansion of agricultural production limited and there was little creation of new wealth. There are perhaps three possible explanations for this stagnation in the economy. Either physical factors limited the wealth of these areas; or any wealth which was created belonged to people other than those who created it; or these societies were organized in a different way from those in the villa regions, and wealth creation and display was not encouraged.

Physical factors, such as poor climate and soil conditions in the upland areas and over-dense settlement in southern Britain, may have constrained economic expansion and development. It has been argued above that the physical distance from a market and difficulties of communication may have prevented agricultural expansion, therefore constraining surplus creation and the construction of villas.[10] Another possibility is that types of land tenure may have been significant. In some areas excess agricultural production may have belonged to an estate owner or owners who controlled production and surplus over the whole region. In particular it has been suggested that a number of areas of southern Britain were the property of the Emperor. Third and finally, in some cases social factors may have been of relevance, preventing initial surplus production or constraining the investment of any surplus in material symbols of the wealth of one family.

A number of areas of southern Britain appear to be characterized by non-villa settlements. In these areas villas and local centres are either totally absent or very scarce. The best known non-villa region is the Fenland of Cambridgeshire, Lincolnshire and Norfolk. Detailed aerial photographic coverage and field survey projects provide useful information on the distribution and chronology of the non-villa sites.[11] The dense non-villa settlements of the Fenland form a regional pattern which is distinct from the villa areas on its eastern margins (*see* Figure 65). The details of the organization of settlement in the Fens are limited, however, as a consequence of the lack of excavation.[12]

Other non-villa regions in Britain are even less well-known than the Fenland. Aerial photographic and field survey evidence is more limited and all of these areas are typified by a lack of excavation. Cranborne Chase and Salisbury Plain in Dorset and Wiltshire constitute a region identified by Collingwood as characterized by non-villa settlements to the virtual exclusion of villas and small towns.[13] The evidence on the most recent edition of the *Ordnance Survey Map of Roman Britain* indicates that this is still the case. Information on non-villa settlements in this region is very limited.[14] As in the Fenland, the absence of villas on Salisbury Plain/Cranborne Chase contrasts with the occurrence of villas in the surrounding area.

Other areas appear to lack villas. The gravel soil of the Upper Thames Valley in Oxfordshire forms a non-villa zone.[15] Sites in this area are known from aerial photography and limited field survey, and recently

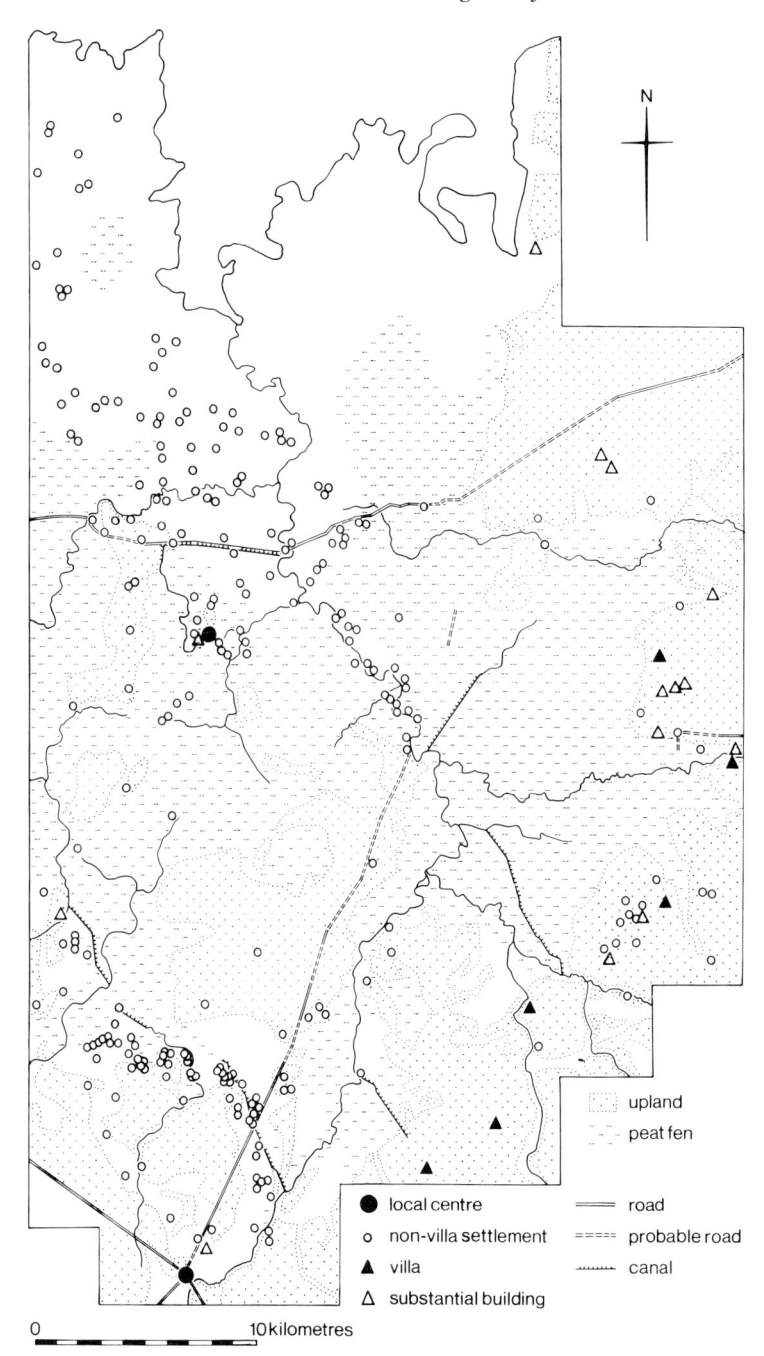

Figure 65 *Settlement patterns in the Fenland and its eastern margins. (After C Phillips ed. 1970, fold-out map K).*

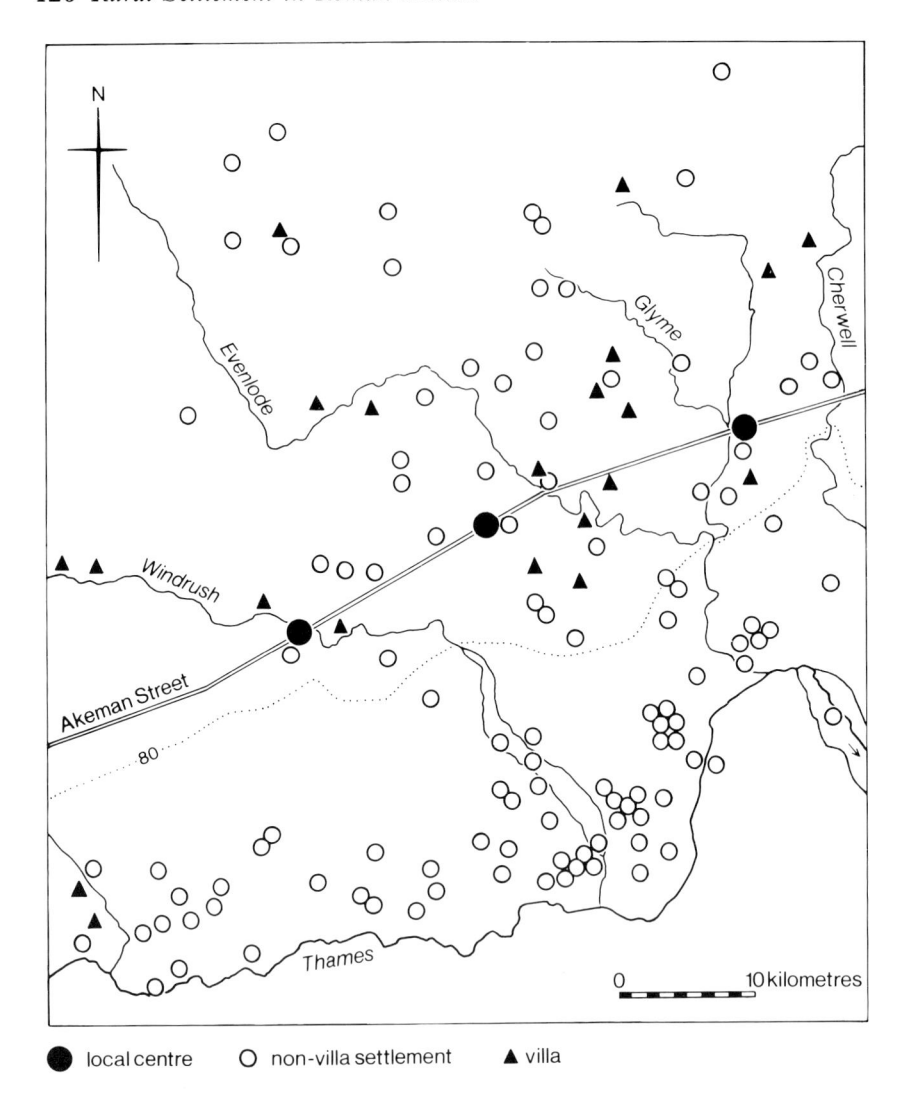

Figure 66 *Settlement patterns in the Upper Thames Valley. (After Hingley 1988, figure 7:10).*

excavations have been undertaken on a number of non-villa settlements in the west of the region.[16] There is a clear contrast between this and the villa zone of north Oxfordshire which was discussed above (*see* Figure 66).

Another area where non-villa settlements appear to predominate are the downlands of Sussex, although initial work on these sites during the 1930s and 40s has not been followed up in more recent years.[17] The Sussex Downlands contrast with the Sussex Coastal Plain between Bognor and Worthing, where non-villa settlements occur but where villas are also common. Other areas of southern Britain where non-villa settlements predominate can be distinguished on the Ordnance Survey map.[18]

Regions characterized by non-villa settlements appear from present evidence to be fairly common in southern Britain. It is also apparent that these areas are often close to other regions that supported vigorous villa economies. What is the explanation for regions of non-villa settlements?

Imperial estates

The most common explanation given for these areas is that they formed imperial estates, the property of the Emperor. Imperial estates included areas of farming land and areas with resources such as forests and minerals. The original nucleus of the imperial estate was usually the property of previous rulers, which was taken over by the Emperor after conquest by the Roman army. These lands were apt to be enlarged by later inheritance, confiscation and gift, and diminished by various forms of alienation from the Emperor.[19] Imperial estates frequently also included the lands of individuals and communities who had actively resisted annexation.[20] Imperial lands comprised a wide variety of forms ranging from very large estates to single farms.[21] It is probable that large areas of Roman Britain were imperial property, as it has been estimated that 15 per cent of the land area of the empire constituted imperial property by AD 300.[22]

The method of farming the imperial estate appears from literary sources to have varied between estates. Some imperial lands will have been cultivated by slaves under the control of an imperial official, while others were leased or even sold to private individuals.[23] It is also likely that the conditions of any leases held by the tenants would have varied between estates[24]. Indeed, peasant holdings on some imperial estates may have varied very little in material terms from the estates of lesser landlords, as the distinction was a legal rather than material one.[25]

Imperial estates can only be identified with certainty where inscriptions have been found referring to the estate or to the officials connected with it.[26] It has been argued that inscriptions from Chew Stoke (Avon) and Combe Down (Avon) indicate the location of imperial property, although the exact location and nature of the proposed estate is uncertain.[27] Suggestions have also been made, on the basis of archaeological evidence alone, that other areas of southern Britain formed imperial estates. It has been suggested that Salisbury Plain was an imperial estate due to the concentration of villages and the absence of villas in the area.[28] A similar suggestion has been made for the area of gravels in the Upper Thames Valley of Oxfordshire, where villas are apparently absent.[29]

The area for which this argument has been proposed most forcefully and by the largest number of modern authors is, however, the Fenland.[30] The main reasons for the suggestion that the Fenland formed an imperial estate are the dense concentration of poor peasant settlements in the area and a total absence of villas and local centres. An associated point which may have some significance is the apparent evidence for the involvement of the administration in draining the Fens during the early second century AD. The Fens were unsettled and poorly drained in the period prior to the late first century AD and appear to have been settled during the late first/early second century. The waterways which were constructed in the Fens presumably represent a rather greater investment and co-ordination of labour than would have been possible by individual farmers, or even large-scale private landowners.[31] This extensive investment of labour may support the idea that this land was the property of the Emperor.

A number of points can be made from this brief review of imperial estates and the attempts of previous authors to identify imperial estates in Roman Britain. First, they should not be seen as a fixed and invariable institution. Large regions characterized by peasant settlement are not the only form of imperial property that would be expected in the province. The Emperor would also have possessed numerous smaller estates, some no larger than the individual farmstead. Second, conditions would have varied between estates; while some were probably run with slave labour, others would have been let out to tenants on long-term leases, and some would have been sold to new independent owners.

The existence of an imperial estate should not be accepted uncritically from archaeological evidence alone. Settlement patterns within imperial estates need not have differed greatly from those on privately owned lands, and the evidence should be reviewed critically and other possible explanations considered for such areas of peasant settlement.

Physical constraints and social organization

Four areas of non-villa settlement will be considered in more detail and a possible alternative model developed in some detail. The areas to be considered are Cranborne Chase, the Fenland, the Sussex Downlands and the Upper Thames Valley. The discussion will be based on a model which was proposed by R Collingwood in 1937 to explain the distribution of settlement on Cranborne Chase.[32] This model has been introduced above[33] and provides an alternative, or perhaps a complementary explanation for regions of non-villa settlements to the idea of the imperial estate.

The model specifies that nucleated village-type communities occurred on Cranborne Chase with isolated villa settlements on the periphery. The village economy was rigid and unprogressive, because the minute subdivision of land and the smallness of 'capital' (surplus wealth) commanded by any individual made reform of the economic system all but impossible. In other words the inhabitants of Cranborne Chase in their nucleated settlements did not have sufficient land to increase production and, by marketing the surplus, to accumulate sufficient wealth to build a villa. As has been shown, the more substantial and independent farmers lived in isolated farms and after the conquest gradually acquired Roman ways of living by expanding production, increasing the area under cultivation, thus accumulating the necessary surplus to build villas.[34]

This model has subsequently been dismissed by other writers. It has in fact been demonstrated that many of Collingwood's 'villages' were small isolated farms.[35] The abandonment of Collingwood's model has resulted in the use of another of his suggestions to explain the absence of villas in the area, that Cranborne Chase was an imperial estate.[36]

Despite this criticism, Collingwood's Cranborne Chase model appears to have some value in the analysis of regions of non-villa settlement. The contrast between the non-villa zone on the Sussex Downlands and the villa zone of the Sussex Coastal Plain has already been described.[37] On the Downs, continuity of settlement and agricultural organization appears to occur from the Bronze Age into the Roman period. This continuity is demonstrated graphically at Park Brow, where a group of settlements appear to represent the movement of a single settlement over a period of more than 1,000 years (*see* Figure 67). Cunliffe has argued that most of the productive land of the region was densely occupied by long-established farming communities by the early Roman period. In contrast to this, as has already been described, the coastal plain between Worthing and Bognor was relatively unsettled and supported villa as well as non-villa settlements during the Roman period.

Collingwood's model has also been used in a recent study of the Upper Thames Valley in Oxfordshire during the later first millennium BC and earlier first millennium AD.[38] Two areas have been defined in the region of the Upper Thames Valley (*see* Figure 66). In the Oxford Uplands Iron Age sites appear scarce, and this area formed a villa zone. In contrast to this, on the gravel soils of the Oxford Clay Vale settlement is dense throughout the period and villas appear to be absent.

The densely settled Oxford Clay Vale forms a clear contrast to the Uplands in its absence of villas. It would appear that in the Oxford Clay Vale the basis of rural production during the Iron Age, and possibly also in the Roman period, comprised groups of closely associated sites which

130 *Rural Settlement in Roman Britain*

Figure 67 *Settlement development on Park Brow (W Susx), (after Wolseley and Smith 1926–7, figure A), indicating the field system: a. Iron Age settlement; b. Bronze Age settlement; c. Romano-British settlement.*

were integrated into the types of girdle pattern settlement reviewed earlier.[39] It has also been argued that the individual girdle pattern settlement constituted a co-operative association of settlements, encircling an area of arable land on the well-drained gravel terraces which it separated from pasture land on the floodplain and clay soils. These settlement groupings appear to form a division of arable from pasture land at the level of the community rather than the individual settlement, contrasting with the isolated independent farming communities of the Oxford Uplands.

It can also be suggested that, as the basis of production in the valley was co-operative, the villa, as a status symbol, was alien to the community. The development and display of surplus wealth by one family group within the broader property-owning community would have contradicted and damaged the communal basis of property ownership and exploitation. If this argument is correct, it would explain why non-villa settlements occur to the exclusion of villas in the Oxford Clay Vale.[40] These arguments are considered in more detail below.[41]

This is clearly of relevance to the study of the Fenland, where the girdle pattern has also been found to characterize the non-villa settlement pattern. In the Fenland it is likely that the newly drained lowlands were settled by communities based on multiple groups of settlements holding land in common, and that the absence of villas is the result of communal land tenure.

It should be noted that the presence of girdle pattern settlements does not necessarily dismiss the idea that the Fenland and the gravels of the Upper Thames Valley were areas of imperial estate. Many of the leases for imperial land were long-term, and it would appear that some estates in Egypt and Lydia were characterized by the continuation of traditional modes of community organization. Indeed there are suggestions of tenants associated with one area over a long period of time, forming distinct communal groups with some rights over their lands.[42] It is possible that this type of model is also valid for the Fenland and the Upper Thames Valley. In these areas communities with distinctive modes of kinship and land ownership occupied large areas of the landscape and regarded themselves as distinct from others within the province. The Fenland may have represented an imperial estate, and the girdle patterns of settlement a traditional mode of community organization through which the Fens were exploited.[43]

The nature of rural society on Cranborne Chase/Salisbury Plain and on the Sussex Downlands is less certain, as the settlement patterns are not well understood. Further work on the nature and distribution of sites and the organization of land tenure and agricultural regimes will be necessary in these areas if there is to be any attempt to reconstruct the rural economy.

SUMMARY

The evidence for regions of southern Britain typified by villas and for other distinct areas typified by non-villa settlements has been discussed. A number of possible reasons for these patterns have been considered and two particular approaches developed in detail. It has been argued that villas developed in many areas, and that areas not supporting a villa economy may have been either the property of the Emperor or have been characterized by a social structure distinct from those of the villa areas. These suggestions will be assessed further in the concluding chapter.

Chapter 9
The north-south divide

Haverfield divided the Roman province into two regions, cut by a theoretical line extending from the River Tees at Middlesbrough to the Bristol Channel and then to the River Exe at Exeter. The uplands to the north and west of this line were, according to him, occupied by troops and provide little indication of romanization; this region has a scarcity of villas and towns. In contrast to this the lowlands, to the south and east of this line contained, in Haverfield's words, 'nothing but civilian life'.[1] Much of the subsequent literature on the province has followed this division.[2] The north-west region of Britain constitutes the military area of the province, while the south-east region forms the so-called 'civilian zone'.

In this study it is considered that a three-part division is more realistic (*see* Figure 68). First, the southern and eastern areas are characterized by a relatively even distribution of villas and also by the occurrence of local centres although, as noted above, some areas within this broad region do not appear to have supported a villa economy. Second, the northern Midlands and south-eastern Wales were marginal areas in which villas and local centres occur, although not with the same profusion as in the south-eastern region. Finally, in the north of England, in south-west, central and northern Wales, and in the South-West Peninsula villas and local centres are largely absent. The evidence for settlement patterning at this scale will be described, and then some explanations for the variation in patterning considered.

SETTLEMENT PATTERNS IN THE SOUTH AND EAST

The lowlands of the Roman province were conquered swiftly and easily by the Roman army, which was moved on soon afterwards. In this region a civilized urban-based society developed. The region is typified by the creation of *civitas* capitals (one per *civitas* or tribe) and by the development of villas in the countryside. In addition it appears that local market centres occurred in some numbers throughout the civilian zone.

It has been shown above that villas and local centres constituted part of the same integrated, hierarchical system, with villas built with the capital created from surplus agricultural production and the towns providing administration and the market for surplus industrial and

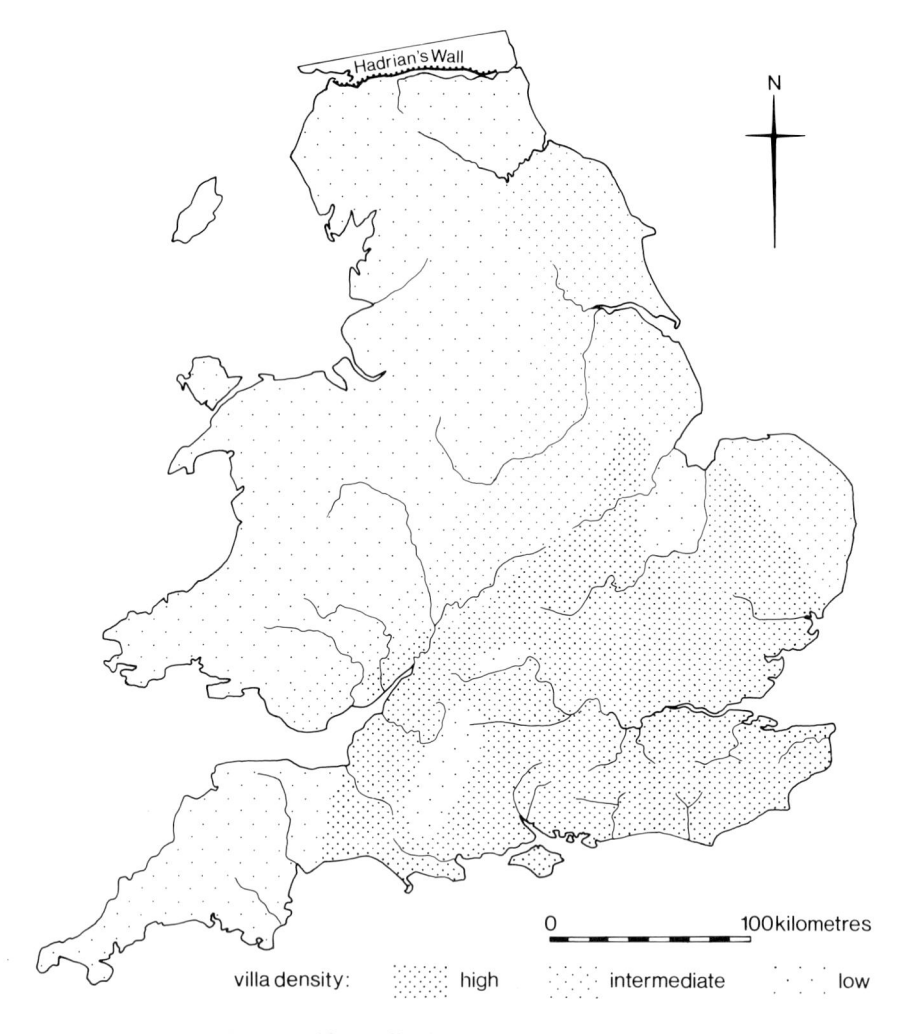

Figure 68 *Villa densities in Roman Britain.*

agricultural goods.³ Villas and local centres were, however, not the only type of rural settlement that occurred in the lowlands. As has been argued, non-villa settlements are also common and in some areas appear to have formed the predominant settlement type.⁴ Non-villa settlements are usually thought of either as the homes of tenants and slaves on estates controlled by those living in the villas, or as the homes of poor land-owning peasants. In other words, non-villa settlements are considered to represent the bottom level of the settlement hierarchy.

The Cantiaci and Regnenses occupied the area that now comprises

Figure 69 *Tribes of Roman Britain. (After Rivet 1970a, figure 9 with alterations).*

south-eastern England (*see* Figure 69). Some of the villas of the Cantiaci and the Regnenses have been studied in detail and they appear to occur in fairly large numbers, particularly along the sides of the North Downs in Kent and on the Sussex Coastal Plain.[5] Cunliffe has suggested that the villas of the Regnenses were clustered in particular areas of the landscape, and that their locations related to the richer, more productive soils from which an agricultural profit could be made with greater ease. In Sussex, villas appear to be clustered on the Upper Greensand Ridge, on the southern edge of the South Downs and on the coastal plain.[6] Clusters of villas also occur in the territory of the Cantiaci, with particularly dense concentrations around the small town of Rochester (Kent) and in the Darenth and Medway valleys.[7]

The local centres of the area are not as well-known as the villas, and on present evidence appear to have been very rare. Known sites and a number of possible sites have been considered by Detsicas.[8] The model for local market centres discussed in this book may suggest that the collection of more information and a modern review of the evidence for local centres is needed for these tribal territories.

Non-villa settlements were particularly common in the territory of the Regnenses and the Cantiaci, as indeed in all of the tribal territories of Roman Britain. It was shown in the last chapter that amongst the Regnenses a distinction occurs between regions in which non-villa settlements predominate and other areas in which villas are common; the Sussex chalk downlands supported a dense distribution of non-villa settlements, while the coastal plain supported villas.

The tribal territories of the Belgae, Durotriges and Atrebates also formed an area in which villas were common.[9] The villas of the region have been discussed in detail by Branigan.[10] Rich early villas are rare in these regions and most of the villas developed gradually from humble beginnings as native farms. By the third to fourth centuries, however, a fairly dense concentration of villas had developed in some parts of the region, particularly around the Roman towns of Ilchester (Somer), Winchester (Hants) and in the area of the tribal boundary between the Belgae and the Dobunni near Bath (Avon). The villas of the Atrebates and Belgae do not appear to have been establishments of the very wealthy, as modest winged corridor buildings are common and true courtyard houses are rare. In areas of Hampshire, amongst the Belgae and Atrebates, aisled houses were particularly common and these occur both as outbuildings to winged corridor houses and as villas in their own right. Contrasting with these are the rich and elaborate villa houses of the area around the local centre and spa of Bath (Avon).

Local centres appear from published evidence to be rather more common than in the south-east of the province, which is especially true in the north-western part of the territory of the Belgae.[11] These sites appear, however, to be very rare in comparison to the areas of the south-eastern Dobunni and the Trinovantes, and there are probably many more sites waiting to be located.

Non-villa settlements are particularly common[12] and, as in south-eastern England, occurred in two types of location. First, these sites lie close to villa settlements; this is clearly demonstrated in the area to the north of Ilchester (Somer). Second, distinct regions within the tribal territories are characterized by the occurrence of non-villa settlements and the absence of villas. Cranborne Chase and Salisbury Plain comprise areas of chalk downland which stretch across the territory of the Durotriges, Belgae and Atrebates from Badbury to Mildenhall, representing an area in which non-villa settlements are very common. This has been discussed above.

In general there appears to be a thinner distribution of villas over the territories of the Iceni, Trinovantes and Catuvellauni than over the lands of the tribes already discussed.[13] Some well-known villas do occur, however, in this area.[14] Concentrations of villas are known, particularly around the Roman towns of *Verulamium* (Herts), Towcester (Northants) and Water Newton (Cambs, *see* Figure 70). A number of villas have been excavated and include the particularly interesting group investigated over a period of years around *Verulamium*.[15]

Local centres are very common over the territory of the Trinovantes.[16] As shown above, these sites appear to occur at approximately ten-kilometre intervals, except to the north and south of the territory where they thin out (*see* Figure 60). Local centres appear on present evidence to be more scarce in the territory of the Iceni and the Catuvellauni.

In some parts of the tribal territory villas and non-villa settlements occur close together. This was the case in the area immediately around Fotheringhay (Northants) in the lower Nene valley. Associations between villa and non-villa settlements also occur in other areas of the Nene, particularly the Welland Valley around the towns of Water Newton (Cambs) and Irchester (Northants) on the boundary between the Catuvellauni and the Coritani (*see* Figure 70). Large areas of the territory of the three tribes appear, however, not to have supported a vigorous villa economy.[17] This is particularly true of the tribal area of the Iceni and also the Fenland, which lay in the territory of the Iceni, Catuvellauni and Coritani. The information for the Fenland as a typical area of peasant settlement has been discussed above.[18]

The territory of the Dobunni is the richest area for villas in the province.[19] Major concentrations of villas occur on the Cotswolds to the north-west of Cirencester and also on the North Oxfordshire Uplands (*see* Figure 66). Local market centres are also common in the south-eastern area of the territory of the Dobunni[20] and, as amongst the Trinovantes, appear to occur at approximately ten-kilometre intervals over the landscape (*see* Figure 61).

As in other parts of the south of the province non-villa settlements are common[21] and again occur in two types of location. In the valley of the Warwickshire Avon, west of Stratford-on-Avon, and in the Thames Valley between Frilford and Abingdon and down-stream to Dorchester-on-Thames, villa and non-villa settlements exist in close proximity. Distinct areas characterized by non-villa settlements also occur. The Thames Valley to the west of Oxford has been discussed above and is an area in which non-villa settlements are common and villas and local centres rare (*see* Figure 66).

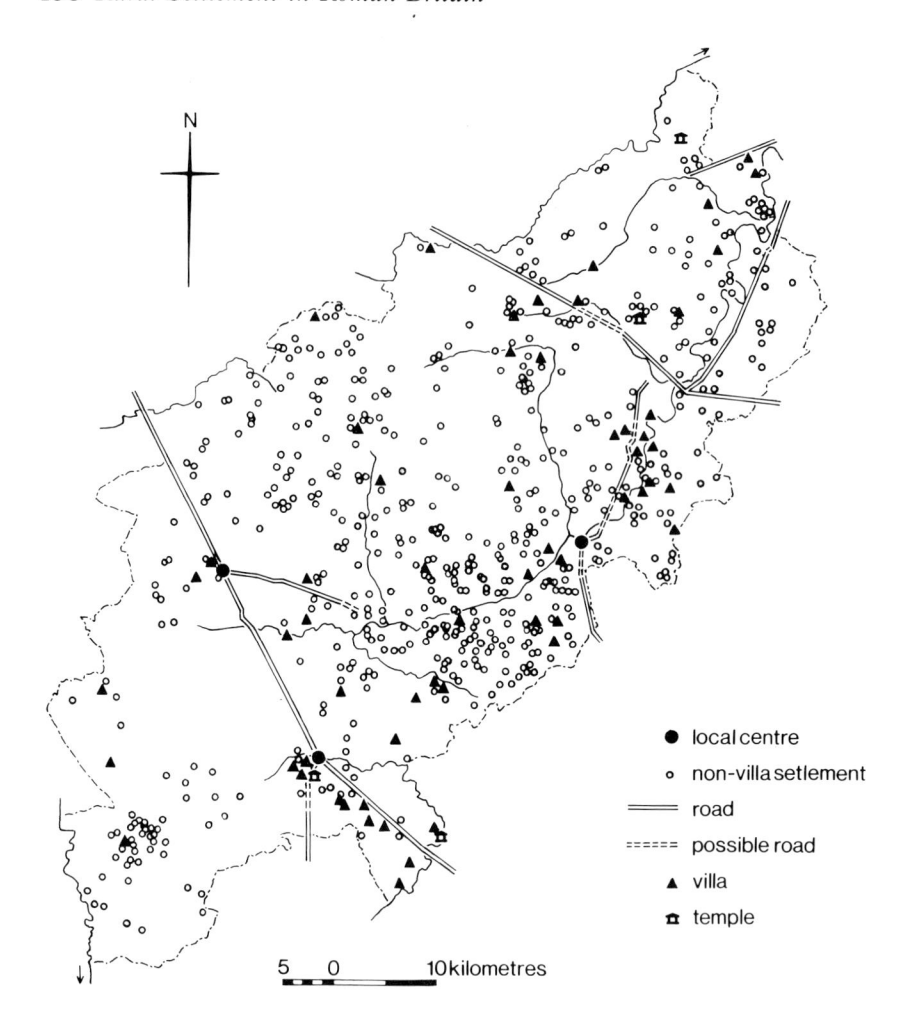

Figure 70 *Roman settlement on the boundary between the Catuvellauni and Coritani (Northants). (After RCHME 1980 and Greene 1986, figure 51).*

AN INTERMEDIATE ZONE

Villas are known in the tribal areas of the Coritani, Cornovii and Parisi [22] although, with the exception of parts of the territory of the Coritani, they are far less common than in the south of the province.[23] Courtyard houses are also very rare, of which only a few possible examples have been recorded.[24] These tribal territories, together with the north-western area of the Dobunni and the territory of the Silures in south-eastern Wales, really form an intermediate area between the southern lowlands in which villas are common and the northern and western uplands where villas are almost totally absent.

Todd's study of the Coritani is of particular interest, as he has attempted to model the density and nature of the settlement evidence and to reconstruct differing modes of settlement organization. It appears that the distribution of villas, as elsewhere in the province, is not evenly spread and that in some areas villas are common, while in other areas they are rare.[25]

Walled local centres are not uncommon in the territories of the Coritani, Cornovii and Parisi. However, few unwalled sites have been located. Local centres do not in fact appear on present evidence to be as common as in the tribal territory of the Trinovantes and Dobunni. Once again, however, the information for distribution requires further investigation.

The predominant settlement type over most of this area is the non-villa settlement. Todd, as mentioned above, has attempted to produce a tentative generalized map of the density of agricultural settlements amongst the Coritani. In some areas, particularly the Trent, Nene and Welland valleys, settlement densities are fairly great, while in other areas the evidence appears to indicate a rather lower density of settlement.[26]

All three tribal areas are characterized by large numbers of non-villa sites which are known from aerial photography and fieldwork. Non-villa settlements defined by small sub-rectangular enclosures appear from the limited evidence to be very common.[27] Again, very few of these sites have been excavated on a large scale. The sub-rectangular enclosure is not the only settlement form.[28]

The south-eastern area of modern Wales was the territory of the Silures, where a number of villas and richer non-villa settlements are known.[29] This territory is comparable to that of the Cornovii, Parisi and Coritani, with a lower villa density than the south and east of England but a higher density than the uplands of the north and west.

SETTLEMENT PATTERNS IN THE NORTH AND WEST

In northern England, in the territory of the Brigantes and Carvetii to the south of Hadrian's Wall, settlements appear to be very common (*see* Figure 10). Villas are, however, almost totally absent, with only a few examples usually in close association with a limited number of towns. *Vici* occur, but are not relevant to the discussion as they were mainly dependent on the demands of the army and probably had very little relevance to the local native population.[30]

In this upland area non-villa settlements are very common. In Northumbria, and more recently in Cumbria and Durham, survey work has provided a fairly detailed understanding of settlement morphology.[31]

140 *Rural Settlement in Roman Britain*

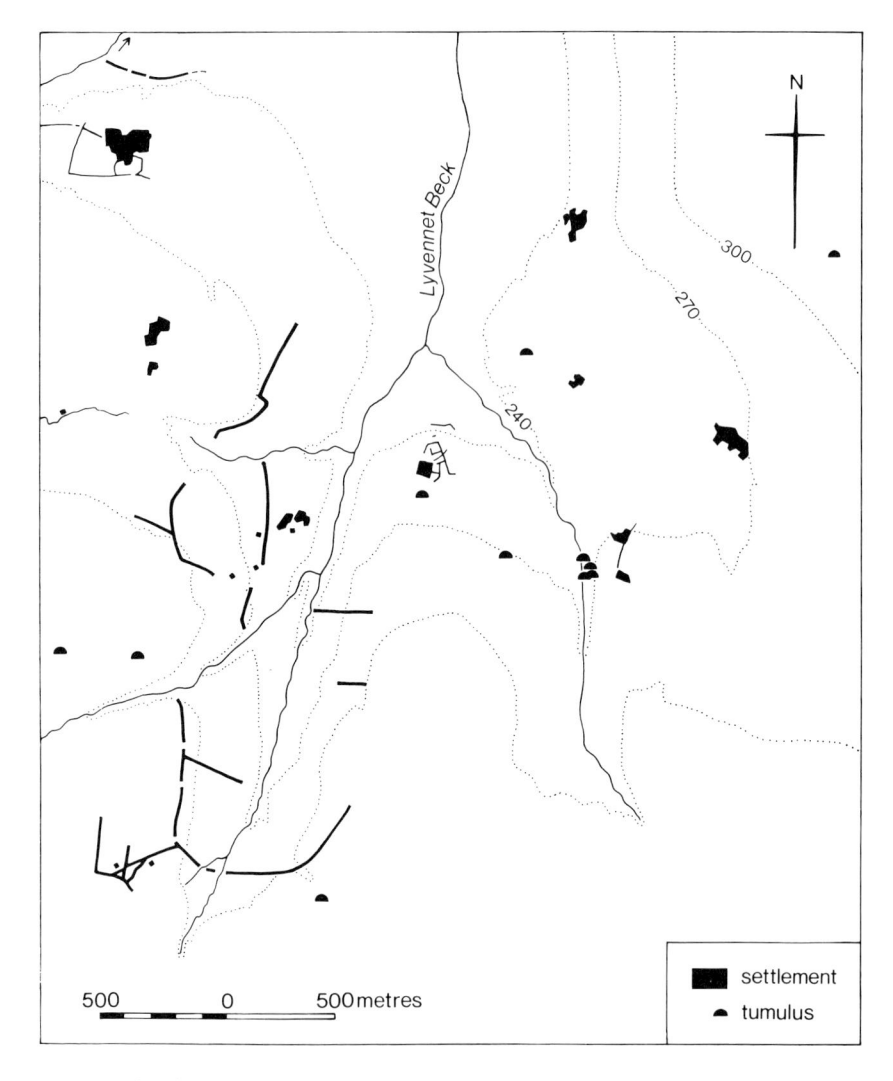

Figure 71 *Settlement patterns in the Crosby Ravensworth area (Cumbr). (After RCHME 1936, figure p 82).*

The picture appears to be one of dispersed settlements distributed, fairly densely in some areas, across the landscape (*see* Figure 71). The typical settlement is enclosed and there appears to be a clear distinction between rectilinear and curvilinear forms, although the significance of this fact is uncertain. Isolated enclosures occurring singly are very common, although in some areas settlements consist of a number of enclosures attached to one another.[32]

In Wales the situation is fairly similar to that of northern England:

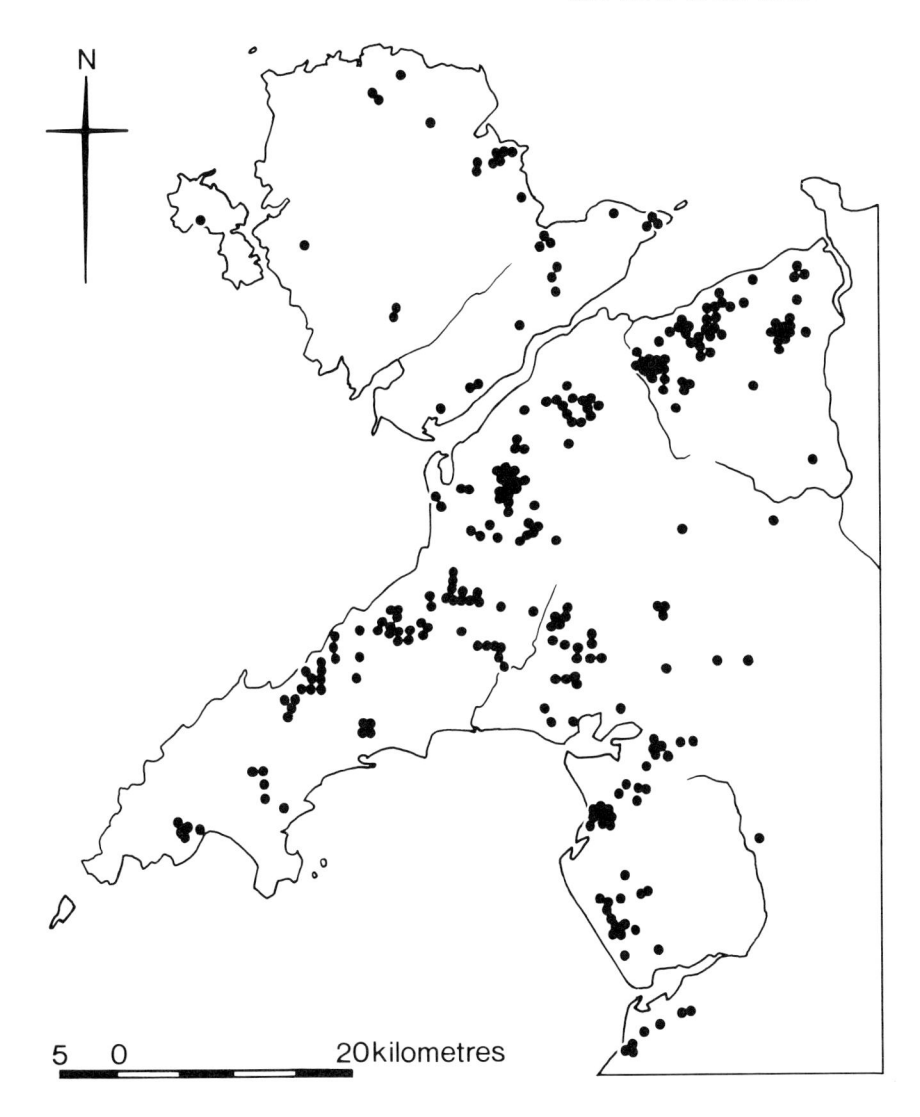

Figure 72 *Settlement in north-western Wales. (After C Smith 1974, figure 1).*

villas and local centres are very rare and non-villa settlements common. There appear, however, to be differences in settlement form across Wales. Hogg has discussed the evidence and distinguished a number of relevant areas.[33] The south-eastern area is part of the intermediate zone and has been discussed above. The south-western area, the territory of the Demetae, has a small number of romanized farms, although villas appear on present evidence to be very rare.[34] More typical is the type of modest defended non-villa farmstead.[35] If the territory of the Silures has

142 *Rural Settlement in Roman Britain*

a similar level of cultural development to that of the Cornovii and Coritani, the south-western territory of the Demetae is more comparable to Cumbria in terms of the level of romanization and to Cornwall in the absence of military installations.

The central and central-western areas of Wales are very poorly known. The north-western area is, however, very rich in settlement remains (*see* Figure 72). The non-villa settlements of north-western Wales are typified once again by the enclosed rectilinear or curvilinear settlement enclosure with a number of internal huts.[36] Many of these stone-built sites survive in good condition and appear to form dispersed but fairly densely settled landscapes. These sites are often associated with small areas of enclosures forming field systems, and mixed farming appears to be represented on many sites.[37]

The south-west of England, the territory of the Dumnoni, is comparable to Wales and northern England in its lack of villas and local centres and in the preponderance of non-villa settlements. Only three villas are known in the area between the River Exe and Land's End. Local centres are also very rare, perhaps non-existent, although a couple

Figure 73 *Enclosed settlements in Cornwall. (After N Johnson and Rose 1982, figure 1).*

of possible sites have been suggested.[38] Even the military *vicus* type of settlements are absent due to the scarcity of military establishments.

As over much of the rest of the north and west of the province, the most common settlement form appears to be small and enclosed (*see* Figure 73), and as many as 1,500 are known to have existed in the south-west. The settlement enclosures are usually round or oval, although sub-rectangular examples do occur, and are called 'rounds'.[39] Large numbers of rounds are known in some areas (*see* Figure 74), some of which have been excavated.[40] Material culture is usually fairly poor, although again mixed farming is indicated by field systems associated with the rounds and by finds from excavations on these sites.

It is clear that in some areas other forms of settlement occur. On the Land's End peninsula a number of settlements with so-called courtyard houses have been located. The type site is Chysauster (Corn), where eight courtyard houses form a hamlet or village settlement. Other isolated and grouped courtyard houses are known. Other settlement

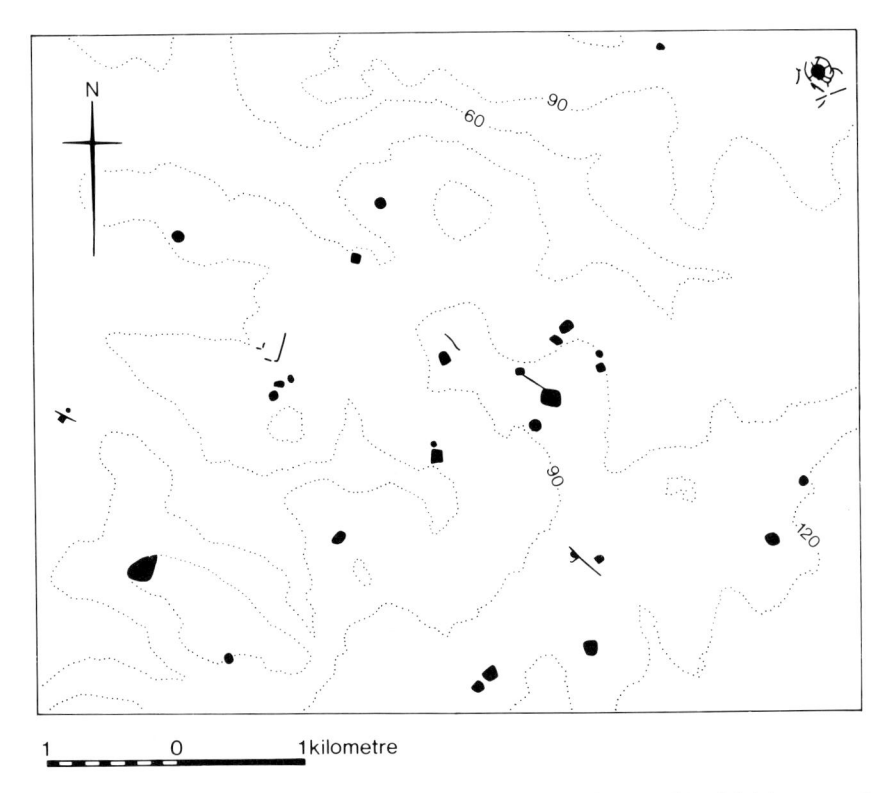

Figure 74 *Settlement patterns in the St Enoder area (Corn). (After N Johnson and Rose 1982, figure 16).*

types include sites that appear to have been unenclosed. At Gwithian (Corn) an isolated oval building was situated within its own field system, and similar sites are known in the west Penwith uplands.[41] Todd has suggested that on some occasions unenclosed groups of round huts could have been dependent on enclosed settlements.[42]

REASONS FOR THE NORTH-SOUTH DIVIDE
Economic poverty and stagnation

In contrast to the civilian lowlands, the uplands or military zone appears to have comprised an area in which economic development was limited. Large areas of Wales, northern and south-western Britain did not support the type of urban 'civilized' society that is evident in the lowlands. An absence of villas and a scarcity of towns exists for most of northern, western and central Wales, Cumbria, Northumbria and Cornwall. In these areas non-villa settlements of a variety of forms predominate. *Vicus* settlements also occur in northern England and Wales.

Vici *and the military market*
Vici developed outside the gates of Roman forts both in the south and in the north and west of Britain. Many local centres in southern Britain continued to be occupied after the army had moved into northern and western Britain. Forts in the north and west continued to be occupied by the military and consequently the *vici* remained in use into the second, third and fourth centuries. The *Vicus* settlements of northern England and Wales developed in order to supply the army with goods and services and were dependent on soldiers' pay.[43] Unlike the local centres of lowland Britain, however, the markets provided by the majority of upland *vici* had little significance for the rural communities in their vicinity.

In 1965 Salway suggested that the *vicus* settlements outside the forts of northern Britain provided markets for the rural civilian settlements in their hinterland, as well as for the soldiers in the fort.[44] The idea was that the *vici* provided a dual service, to the army and to civilian farmers in the immediate vicinity. The evidence of the apparent clustering of non-villa settlements around forts in Cumbria was used to support this model. The tide of opinion has now turned against these suggestions.

Additional information has been collected for the distribution of non-villa settlements and this evidence now indicates that these sites do not cluster around the forts as was originally suggested, but that their distribution is in fact largely independent of them. The bias in the evidence reviewed by Salway resulted from the fact that the initial aerial photographic work was based on the Roman road and fort pattern, and so sites naturally appeared to be centred in the hinterland of forts.[45]

Rural settlements and economic poverty
The non-villa settlements of northern Britain, central and northern Wales and Cornwall often appear to differ little from the pre-Roman Iron Age settlements of the same area. In some areas settlements appear to be quite regularly spaced and a fairly great density of settlement occurs (*see* Figures 10, 72, 73). There is, however, very little indication of the types of settlement hierarchy which exist in southern Britain, and many areas are characterized by the fairly regular repetition of standardized settlement units of the types discussed above.

Settlement types are similar to those of the immediate pre-Roman period and items of material culture are usually very few in number. The absence of large quantities of pottery and coins from the majority of non-villa settlements in northern England and Wales militates against the idea that rural communities were integrated closely into the market economy. The poverty and lack of development of the agricultural and industrial economy in northern England, and the absence of coinage from rural settlements, indicates that the *vici* located outside the forts of northern England and Wales had little economic effect on the farming practices of the native communities. These *vicus* settlements were, in effect, urban islands in a sea of dispersed and decentralized population groupings.[46]

The reasons for poverty

Rivet has suggested that the evidence for the spread of Late Iron Age coinage and continental imports in south-eastern England indicates the area of Britain which at the time of the Roman conquest was economically viable, in the sense that it could support an administrative superstructure as well as a working population. With few minor additions, this is also where Roman villas occur.[47] The areas to the north and west were not economically viable, and this is why the network of Roman towns and villas which spread over the south and east of the province is absent from the north and west. This analysis hints at the idea that the contrasting patterns of economic growth and stagnation are a result of differing patterns of contact with the continental world.

It is possible, therefore, that the inhabitants of the individual upland non-villa settlement were not involved in generating and marketing an agricultural surplus. Two factors should, however, be taken into account. First, those inhabiting these settlements would have been required to pay tax, which would probably have been used to feed the army. Whether this tax was in cash or in kind, its payment would have required the generation of surplus agricultural goods by farmers in these areas. Second, on non-villa settlements in Cornwall, Wales and Cumbria some items of Roman material culture occur, such as coins, wheel-made pottery imported from the south of the province, occasionally Samian, brooches and buckles. If these items were acquired through exchange or trade, possibly at tribal festivals,[48] they must also indicate the creation of some form of agricultural surplus. Some form of restricted exchange or trade network must have existed in these areas.

It appears that items of material culture were obtained while the symbol of the 'Roman' type of house, or villa, was either not desired or was not obtainable. Two explanations seem possible: either that the quantity of surplus created was enough to pay tax and obtain the occasional item of wheel-made pottery and metalwork, but was not great enough to construct a villa or, alternatively, that the inhabitants of western and northern Britain may not actually have wished to construct villa-type buildings.

Some of the relevant factors for Cumbria and Northumbria have been considered, and many of these points may also have been significant for Wales and Cornwall.[49] They can be divided into physical factors, the poverty of soils and the wetness of the climate, and social factors. The relatively poor soils of northern and western Britain may have prevented the creation of a large agricultural surplus by constraining agricultural expansion. The wet and relatively cold climate in upland areas may have increased the difficulties in generating a large surplus. In effect, Roman society in these areas may have been little different from the preceding Iron Age culture. The density of settlement does appear to have increased, but the scale of production and level of wealth at the individual settlement may have remained fairly static.

An alternative model which may be of relevance is that social factors possibly limited the scale of economic expansion. In some of the pre-Roman societies of Britain factors such as the control of a number of clients or followers, or the possession of a large herd of cattle, appear to have constituted sources of status for the wealthy, rather than the ownership of an estate. In the remote upland areas of northern and western Britain the influence of Rome was diluted by distance. Although the rectangular house form appears to have replaced the round form in south-west Wales and Cumbria,[50] the influence of the country houses of the Continent and south-east Britain may not have been very great in the far north and west of the province.

In the north and west the more Roman standards of wealth and status, such as the ownership of land and a romanized house, may have had little or no power as symbols. Traditional symbols of wealth and status, such as the control of followers and ownership of cattle, may have continued to be of greater significance. It is difficult to trace these more traditional modes of status symbolism from the evidence provided by archaeology. However, a limited number of sites in the north and west contain information which is possibly of relevance to this discussion.

Possible evidence for wealth distinction on settlement sites

If the argument for the continuity of social structure is correct, then it is probable that forms of patterning in the north and west should occur which are distinct from those present in the south and east. It is probable that there were wealthy individuals, but that their wealth was invested in items other than elaborate buildings and large quantities of riches. The wealthy amongst the rural communities of western and northern Britain may have controlled either large numbers of cattle and a large following of retainers or kinsmen. Attempts to assess these ideas in relation to the settlement evidence are very rare, probably a result of the fact that it is more difficult to identify these patterns archaeologically than to distinguish the symbols of wealth which were in use in the south of the province.

At Dinorben (Clwyd) a large round hut produced a fairly rich range of small finds, probably indicating a wealthy family group. Nearby were traces of less substantial buildings (*see* Figure 43). Gardner and Savory have suggested that this indicates the existence of a landowner with associated estate workers, in other words an estate which in the more romanized parts of Britain would have been based on a villa.[51] A more likely alternative explanation is that the large round hut was the dwelling of the headman of the lineage and that the other buildings were associated with the kin rather than with estate workers. On this site the houses of dominant and subservient family groups occur. An important point is that the rich individual or family need not have been landowners, but may simply have been the leading family in the community.[52]

Similar patterns may occur on other sites in the north and west of Britain on which a large building, or a building with a rich variety of finds, occurs alongside smaller and poorer dwellings. At Carn Euny (Corn) the settlement appears to be divided into two areas. At the north end of the site three large or major houses are directly associated with the underground passage or *fogou*; at the south end of the site there are at least six smaller houses. It is possible that there is some form of social or economic division between the inhabitants of the two parts of the site. Although the interpretation of this patterning is uncertain, the existence of an economically dominant group and a dependent group may be indicated at Carn Euny.

Elsewhere it is possible that the size of the family group represented within the compound may relate to social standing. Enclosures containing only one small round or rectangular house may have been of low status, while those containing multiple round huts may relate to wealthy households based on polygamous marriages and large numbers of retainers.

Discussions of this type for the northern and western parts of the province are absent. Further work will be necessary to assess the evidence for social hierarchy amongst rural communities in this area. In one region where much excavation and fieldwork has been undertaken, Northumbria, the archaeological evidence does not appear to indicate any clear economic or social divisions within society. In this region the usual pattern appears to be one of repetition of small standardized family units over the whole area. It is possible that both here, and perhaps in other areas of the north and west, social and economic divisions within society were very limited and that family groups were isolated and largely independent of one another.

SUMMARY

The division between villa and non-villa areas introduced in the previous chapter is also of relevance in discussing the relationship of the south and east to the north and west. There is a broad north-south divide, with clear economic growth and wealth display in the south, but general continuity of the Iron Age pattern in the north. Physical factors – poor soil and cold climate – are partly responsible for this situation. It is likely, however, that the attitudes of individuals in the north and west are also relevant to an understanding of this problem. It is possible that any surplus created in these areas was invested in alternative symbols of wealth and status to those adopted over much of the south and east.

Chapter 10
Some themes in the archaeology of rural settlement

THE FAMILY AND THE COMMUNITY

In Chapter 1 a number of points were made about possible continuity in the nature of the family from pre-Roman to Roman Britain. Subsequently the evidence for houses, compounds, settlements and landscapes in the rural areas of Roman Britain has been discussed. How does this evidence help with an understanding of families and communities?

Extended families

Considerable evidence exists to indicate that extended families were typical of the rural areas of the province. It would appear that family structure on many villa and non-villa settlements was broadly similar. The existence of the extended family on rural sites in Britain is indicated by the form of some buidings, and also by the evidence for two or more domestic buildings within compounds on many farm and villa sites.

Buildings
Suggestions have been made that a number of types of Romano-British building were the homes of extended families. The types of buildings for which the evidence may indicate a resident extended family include aisled houses and villa houses consisting of multiple suites of rooms.

Regarding aisled houses, the use of the model for extended families or 'lineage' groups perhaps forces a single rather simplistic social model onto a basic functional type of building. In the case of the aisled houses at North Warnborough and Thruxton (Hants), however, the evidence would appear to indicate extended families.[1]

Copious evidence exists to indicate that many other villas contained two or more suites of rooms. On some sites the two suites occurred within the same villa building, while on other sites the suites of rooms formed two distinct buildings occupying a single compound. At these sites extended families probably comprised a number of nuclear families.[2]

Aisled houses and multiple unit villas appear to provide positive evidence for extended family groupings. An understanding of the nature

150 Rural Settlement in Roman Britain

of families within the other common building types requires further excavation and the recovery of evidence comparable to that uncovered at North Warnborough.

Compounds

A significant number of the excavated farm and villa compounds in the south, west and north of the province have produced two or more dwelling houses of contemporary date. This provides further evidence for the existence of extended families on rural settlement sites. The evidence of these buildings and compounds suggests that extended families were common in the Roman province, but this is not to say that all families were necessarily extended. Compounds with single small dwelling houses occur especially at some local centres[3] and these may represent single nuclear families.

Although it is possible to suggest that many Romano-British families were extended it is difficult to make any further suggestions about the nature of the extended family. For instance, did polygamous marriage regulations exist in the Roman province, or did monogamous marriage replace the presumed Celtic forms?[4] If families of more than one generation existed, how large were they, who was included, and what were the rules of inclusion? There appear to be at least two possibilities which would benefit from further research.

First, some extended families may have formed large communal groups, sometimes divided into distinct male and female sections. This is the model proposed for Glastonbury by D Clarke and appears to fit the evidence from the North Warnborough aisled house. If this type of community existed at North Warnborough, it is possible that other extended families in the province were organized in a similar manner. It is conceivable that the two houses occurring on many farm and villa compounds represent independent dwellings of the men and women of the extended family. The evidence does not exist to assess this proposal. It would require a number of further sites at which large quantities of domestic material survived in living areas, as was the case at North Warnborough, combined with detailed excavation and spatial analysis in order to assess these ideas.

At present, a second possibility appears to explain farm and villa compounds with two or more buildings more convincingly. This suggests that the single extended family was made up of a number of individual nuclear family groups, each of which formed an independent household.

The actual size of the extended family is a very important factor for which there is no certain evidence. Some suggestions have been made for North Warnborough and Bradley Hill on the basis of the living area within the houses and compounds, and the size of the cemetery at

Bradley Hill, but they are no more than hypothetical estimates. They suggest a population of perhaps eight individuals at Bradley Hill and between thirty and fifty at North Warnborough.[5] It is clear that the size and nature of the extended family may have varied greatly between sites and between areas and that the situation across the province as a whole may actually have been extremely complex.

The character of inheritance patterns and descent is uncertain, although the literary sources suggest that land and the position of individuals within the community may have been inherited from the men rather than the women.[6] The existence of a headman in charge of the extended family at Thruxton would support this suggestion, although further research is required.

If extended families were common in Roman Britain, what was the economic basis of the extended family? What held extended families together and prevented the individual constituent family groups from fragmenting? J Smith has explored this topic in a discussion of unit system villas. The development of a compound appears to involve the splitting of one single household, but the new independent households were presumably retaining some form of link. If no link existed, the independent nuclear families would probably have moved into separate compounds, or even have formed new independent settlements. The model that Smith discusses is derived from medieval/post-medieval Wales, where unit system houses occur similar to those of Roman Britain.

In Wales the resource that prevented the division of individual households and the formation of new families appears to have been land. It will be recalled that in early historic Ireland land appears to have been controlled and owned by a three-generation family group descended from a common great-grandfather. It is proposed that the extended family in Roman Britain was derived from joint ownership and/or control of farming land by the family group.[7]

The details of how land was owned and controlled require further research. Garnsey and Saller have observed that in some areas of the empire groupings of adult brothers sometimes united into a 'consortium' and held land in common. This appears to have occurred among the poor and was intended to prevent the splitting up of the small family estate.[8] In Roman Britain, however, it is apparent that the same type of joint control occurred at all levels of society – with the probable exception of slaves – as extended families occur on non-villa settlements as well as on villa sites.

It has been suggested that the inhabitants of both houses on villa compounds were of equal status.[9] The survey of unit system compounds appears to indicate, however, that one house is usually larger or more elaborate than the other (*see* Figures 33 and 34). This is the case at Gayton Thorpe (Norf) and on other villa sites comprising a winged corridor and an aisled house.[10] The family group of the headman on these sites may have been accorded special rights within the compound, and as a consequence was relatively superior to the more distant members of the extended family, housed in the second house. In these cases it is apparent, however, that the occupants of the second house were not downgraded to servants or slaves as they were still housed in relative luxury.

Communities

There are problems in attempting to study the Romano-British community. Too few large-scale excavation projects have been undertaken and the majority of archaeologists still conceive of the settlement as an individual isolated unit. As a result the evidence for the nature of the community is very limited. Nevertheless, a number of suggestions have been made and will now be summarized.

Some communities, particularly in the uplands of the north and west, appear to have consisted of single nuclear or extended households. It is probable, however, that the majority of Romano-British communities in the south of the province consisted of more than a single household. The evidence for communities that consist of a number of extended families exists in at least two forms.

Settlements
A minority of settlements in the uplands of the north and west, and a probable majority of settlements in the south of the province, appear to consist of more than a single farm compound. Each compound formed the home of a nuclear or extended family and, therefore, the nucleated settlement constituted the home of a community made up of a number of extended family groups. The number of family groups within the single settlement can vary from one to as many as twelve families on the largest non-villa settlements, with possibly as many as several hundred at some local centres.

Groups of settlements
In some cases the individual grouping of non-villa settlements forming a girdle pattern of settlement represents the home of a large-scale community which farmed an area of land in common. In many ways these girdle patterns of settlement are similar to nucleated settlements.

It is possible that nucleated non-villa settlements, and girdle pattern settlements, represented communities formed by groups of families which had common rights to an area of land. It has already been suggested that some extended family groups in the province may have owned estates.[11] In some cases, however, an alternative land-owning or holding group may have comprised a community consisting of a number of family groups.[12]

The important principles are that the descent group lived within a single girdle pattern settlement and that some resources within the multiple settlement group were shared.[13] The girdle pattern probably developed through the sharing out of resources between the descendants of an original kin group.[14] This process occurred in the Fenland of Roman Britain and possibly in other areas such as the gravels of the Upper Thames Valley and the sites at Wetwang Slack (Humbs).

An important point in relation to the study of non-villa settlements is that the communities based in nucleated 'hamlet'/'village' and girdle pattern settlements need not have actually owned the land that they cultivated communally. An alternative is that these communities were in fact tenants of the Emperor or other landowners, but that the community had a long-term lease on the land which was divided between sons as if it formed the property of the community.[15]

Status distinctions within the family and community

It has been shown that there is an economic division within some compounds (*see* Figure 75). This is evident in the single aisled house where one end, the upper end, is often partitioned off and given mosaic floors and heated rooms, while the rest of the building retains its rustic character. This indicates the separation and improvement of the rooms belonging to the head of the household, while the rooms of his family or kin were retained in their original state.[16]

This trend is taken further on sites at which a winged corridor villa is built beside an aisled house. In some of these cases the headman appears to have moved out of the aisled house completely and to have built himself a new dwelling of a more romanized type adjacent to the aisled house which continued as the residence of his family. This elevation of the headman and degradation of the family is taken to its logical extreme at Gatcombe (Somer), where a number of houses associated with kin or slaves occur within a large walled compound alongside a villa building (*see* Figure 35).

It appears, however, that the family groups resident within many of the aisled houses on villa compounds were supplied with mosaic floors and hypocausts, and had access to bath-houses. On such sites it seems unlikely that the kin were dispossessed of all rights within the broader community.

It is also evident that the economic divisions between families within the community were often more extreme and more complex than divisions within the family. On villa sites with a separate agricultural compound for farm workers the evidence may, in effect, indicate further

154 *Rural Settlement in Roman Britain*

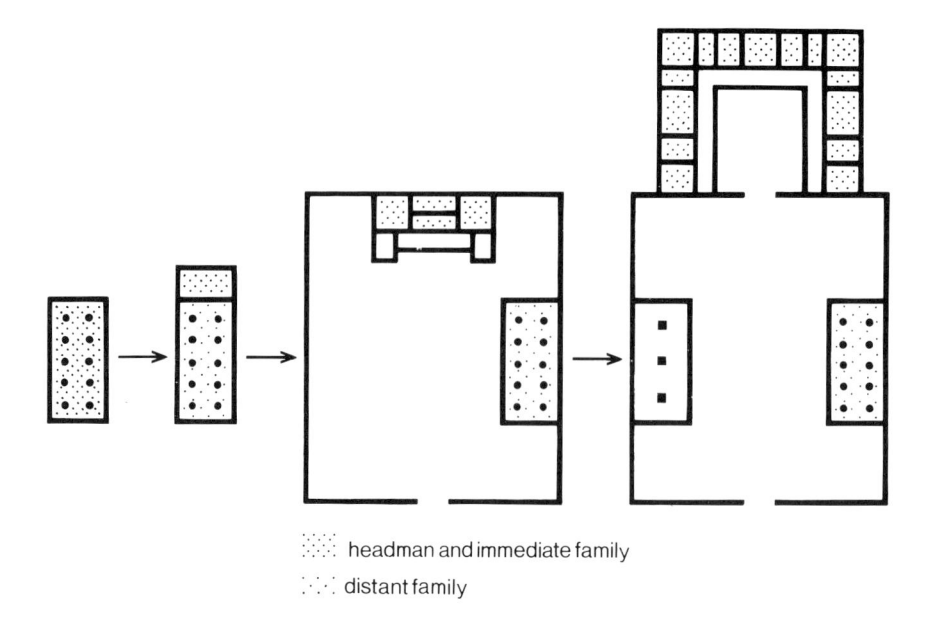

:::: headman and immediate family
:::: distant family

Figure 75 *A model for increased social complexity on Romano-British rural sites.*

degradation of the kin. These sites represent communities in which two family groups existed. The first family lived within the villa compound and had a high standard of living. The second family group lived in the agricultural compound and worked the estate. The *familia* of the owner may still have lived with him on a single settlement, but the lowlier members of the group were segregated into a secondary dependent compound.

At Gorhambury (Herts) this division into two compounds originated in the Late Iron Age and at Claydon Pike (Glos) a similar situation existed on a non-villa settlement during the late first or early second century. At Dinorben (Clwyd) the distinction occurred on the settlement site during the third and fourth centuries. The extent to which the second family of estate workers was dispossessed of all rights is uncertain. At Gorhambury during the second century the workers lived in an aisled house and had access to an elaborate bath-house situated within their own compound. At other larger courtyard villas such as Woodchester, however, the agricultural courtyards demonstrate few signs of status, and it is likely that those who dwelt within the agricultural compound were poor estate workers with no rights to the land of the community.

The alternative situation discussed above is one in which the villa compound and agricultural compound are in effect divided into separate settlements, so that estate owners and estate workers live apart. This situation presumably had a similar significance to that of villas with an additional agricultural compound. In some areas large estates developed, with a villa dominating multiple groups of non-villa settlements.

It can be argued that the evidence for family and community organization demonstrates stages in the degradation of kin, from the status of equals within the headman's family to that of poor estate workers. Applebaum has discussed the evidence for the progressive isolation of agricultural functions from living areas on Roman rural sites.[17] Thus the aisled house is thought to have included storage areas for agricultural products and a byre for cattle (*see* Figure 18). With the construction of simple rectangular buildings, cottage houses and winged corridor villas, the agricultural functions of the building were often confined to outbuildings within a farmyard or compound. During the further development of some villas – represented by the construction of large winged corridor and courtyard buildings – the total segregation of agricultural activities from the residence occurs when an outer agricultural courtyard is built (*see* Figure 75).

It is uncertain, however, to what degree the suggestions regarding the gradual degradation of the kin through time are valid. When the province is considered as a whole it is clear that the process does not occur in all regions. Sites at each stage of development occur in all four centuries of Roman occupation. It has already been shown that the division into two families – an owner family resident within a high status compound and a subservient family of estate workers in an agricultural compound – occurs by the Late Iron Age at Gorhambury and at Claydon Pike during the late first or early second century, while it did not occur until the fourth century at other sites. On many other villa sites where this division eventually develops it would seem to represent a gradual trend which perhaps culminates in the construction of two separate compounds at some stage in the third or fourth centuries.

The comparatively archaic form of the isolated aisled villa house, however, survives into the fourth century. The interesting evidence from North Warnborough, Thruxton and Stroud (Hants) shows that these buildings were still occupied by relatively egalitarian extended family groups at this time. It would appear that, while some rich families were degrading their kin to the status of estate workers, other joint families were still resident within houses symbolizing the equal status of all involved.

That all three of these aisled buildings are in Hampshire may provide a partial solution to this problem. It is possible that the process of the degradation of the kin to the status of estate workers was a regional one and was more advanced in some regions than in others. In this area of Hampshire the process may well have been particularly retarded. It is clear, however, that the simple model of the increasing degradation of the kin through time, until a stage in the late third and fourth centuries when they had become little more than slaves, is too simple to apply indiscriminately to the whole province. This book is not the place to discuss these matters in great detail,[18] although it is clearly important to understand the chronology of the development, if the evidence for rural settlement is ever to be fully comprehended.

REGIONS AND ECONOMIC GROWTH

It has been shown that only some areas of the Romano-British countryside developed economically, while other areas appear to have retained a rather stagnant economy. As has been shown above, these patterns can be distinguished at two levels of scale (see Figure 68). Within southern Britain distinct regions without villas contrast with neighbouring villa zones, while a broad contrast can be drawn between the villa areas of the south and east of Britain and the military northern and western areas.

The estate, the economic basis of many villa owners, has been considered along with the evidence of market landscapes through which agricultural surplus was marketed to create the capital to construct a villa. This is the economic growth that characterizes the richer areas of southern Britain. The contrasting stagnant economy is characterized by a lack of development, an absence of villas and local centres and the prevalence of poor non-villa settlements.

The general causes of contrasting patterns of development and stagnation in the Roman province can be summarized. A range of factors were responsible for the failure of non-villa settlements to develop into villas in some areas of the province, and they have been considered in relation to the evidence from a number of areas in western, northern and southern Britain. The traditional explanation for the situation in the uplands of the north and west is that social groups in these areas were too backward and 'uncivilized' to adopt Roman symbols such as villas. The archaeological evidence for villas and towns indicates that the civilian communities of the lowlands were evidently 'civilized' enough to build villas, and a distinct contrast is therefore drawn between the uplands and the south. Areas in the south without villas must consequently be explained. Farmers evidently wished to build villas, and so communities in areas without villas were obviously constrained from building them by factors outside their control. The most widely used model is that of the imperial estate. Regions in which non-villa settlements predominate at the expense of villas are assumed to represent the property of the Emperor, and the poverty of the inhabitants is taken to indicate that they had the status of poor tenants or slaves.

It has been argued that this view is simplistic. The interpretation of any area as an imperial estate should be considered in a critical manner unless there is epigraphic evidence to support the identification. Even if such evidence does exist it requires thorough analysis, as imperial estates clearly did not constitute a static phenomenon and could be reduced or increased in size by appropriation or sale. An area such as the Fenland or Salisbury Plain may have been an imperial estate during the first and second centuries, and may have been sold off to private landowners later in the Roman period. In addition, even if the various areas of southern Britain formed imperial estates this does not mean that the social and economic organization of these areas is of no interest.

Moreover, the concept that Britain can be neatly divided into a military upland zone where social groups were too traditional and 'uncivilized' to adopt Roman building forms, and a 'civilized' lowland where social groups quickly adopted Roman building standards, is far too simple. Instead of viewing the villa as a building form that was quickly and eagerly adopted by all rich Romano-British farmers an alternative model has been proposed. The villa was clearly a symbol of the adoption of 'Roman' standards, and probably also indicates the expansion and intensification of agricultural production. However, it is necessary to study the adoption of the villa in detail and in a regional perspective.

Social groups will have been organized in varying ways in different areas of the province, and will have responded to the opportunities provided by the Roman invasion differently. Thus it has been shown that some family groups in the south and east of the province adopted villa buildings at a comparatively early stage. In other areas villas were adopted more slowly – over the Gloucestershire Cotswolds as a whole villas are unusual before the late second century, and replace more traditional building types on the sites of non-villa settlements during the third and fourth centuries.[19] This is also the case elsewhere in the province.[20] In other areas villas were never adopted, but this need not always indicate poverty as will now be considered.

NEW DIRECTIONS FOR STUDY

A number of general points have been made in this study and one particular theme will now be considered which may form a basis for future research.

Was the villa a 'normal' development?

A model for the development and stagnation of settlement in two distinct areas of southern Britain has been described. The model indicates an important fact about the villa in Roman Britain. Instead of

158 Rural Settlement in Roman Britain

being seen as a 'normal' development, as another author has suggested,[21] it may be necessary to return to the point of view of Vinogradoff and view the villa as a phenomenon alien to at least some of the communities of northern, western and southern Britain.[22]

The construction of a villa represented the production of a symbol of the wealth of an individual or family group, and in some cases may have demonstrated the dissolution of traditional ties within some of the communities of Britain. An individual or family group living in a community such as those represented by the girdle type patterns of settlement in the Fenland may have possessed the wealth to construct a villa, but may have been constrained from investing their wealth in this way by social ties preventing the demonstration of an individual family's success over other families within the immediate community.[23]

Two contrasting trends may be indicated in the Romano-British countryside. In some areas the first to fourth centuries witnessed the development of a lively and wealthy market economy. In this environment the villa, the concepts of the private estate and the market were adopted swiftly and became tools in a competitive system of increased production and exchange. These regions contrast with those in which the communal organization of society remained important, and here villas were alien to society. In the latter type of region individual families may have been unable, or unwilling, to adopt villa-style buildings because, as a symbol of the status of a single family group, they represented an alien concept.

It has been suggested that an important factor may be the contrast between societies in which the individual extended family was the basic group who controlled or owned land, and those in which land was in effect owned or controlled by a community made up of multiple groupings of extended families. In other words, it may have been the size of the communal, or property-owning, group which was relevant as to whether a villa was built or not. It is possible that a fairly restricted social group, such as a nuclear or extended family, could be defined as an estate owner and was able to construct a villa. The evidence of North Warnborough may indicate that in some cases this group consisted of as many as thirty to fifty individuals. When a community or collection of families constituted the group which had the rights to and which cultivated an estate, however, the villa was not a viable symbol. In this case no one individual or family had the ability to appropriate the estate and to build a wealthy house within it.

This discussion raises a second important topic, which will now be examined.

Was the villa the only way to indicate status?

It is of interest to turn back to an area of non-villa settlements, the Fenland, to consider a further aspect of the settlement record. In this region it would appear that a progressive growth in settlement size and population density was halted during the early third century, probably by marine transgression.[24] Settlement did, however, continue during the third and fourth centuries and the evidence indicates that there was considerable wealth in the hands of some individuals during the fourth century AD. Quantities of bronze, pewter and silver vessels buried in hoards have been discovered, particularly in the central Fenland. Large quantities of third and fourth-century coinage have also been found.[25]

This wealth takes the form of portable material items. Wealth was not invested in obvious and overt symbols of status such as winged corridor buildings, courtyard buildings, mosaics, tessellated floors or bath-houses. Potter has argued that the owners of such wealth may have been free tenants on an imperial estate.[26] In any case the existence of wealth in the hands of some individuals within the fourth-century central Fenlands indicates the falsity of the idea that all wealthy farmers within the Roman province of Britain built villas as symbols of their wealth and status. Clearly some farmers were using their wealth for other purposes, and villas were not the only type of status symbol available to them.

It has been suggested that the investment of wealth in items of material culture such as metalwork and coinage was an expression of peasant mentality, in particular the desire to avoid higher taxation by hiding wealth.[27] In addition it appears likely that the deposition of metalwork and perhaps also coinage had some form of religious significance.[28] Whatever the circumstances of purchase or acquisition and deposition of metalwork and coinage, it seems clear that considerable wealth existed which was not invested in villa-type buildings.

Is it possible that the evidence actually indicates an alternative method of exhibiting status to the construction of villas? One method of obtaining or demonstrating status within Celtic society in the pre-Roman period was the provision of feasts for followers by the head of a lineage or community.[29] This status was afforded to the wealthy individual because he was able to give away some of the surplus which was not required for his everyday needs. The deposition of eating utensils in the Fens during the fourth century may in some way be connected with the creation of status through the feeding of followers. Feasting was a traditional Celtic act of communal generosity, unlike the construction of a villa. The feast was a communal act, while the villa symbolized the success of an individual or single family over others within the community.

The absence of villas from areas such as the Fenland, the gravels of the Upper Thames Valley and Salisbury Plain/Cranborne Chase may have been as much a matter of social constraints on the display of wealth as of actual economic poverty. The situation may not be one of regions of wealth and poverty but of regions in which capital was invested in different ways.

The problem of non-villa settlements which produce items of rich material culture has hardly been touched upon by the standard archaeological works on Roman Britain. This is because excavators usually search for some alternative explanation for exotic or rich items of material culture on non-villa sites. At Wasperton (Warw) an apparently poor first to fourth-century farm has been excavated which produced an unusually early assemblage of Samian pottery. From the evidence available it is difficult to concede that the first-century inhabitants could have afforded to purchase Samian ware during the pre-Flavian period.

The same point has been argued for the first-century settlement at Grandford (Cambs) in the Fens, where pre-Flavian Samian, other imported pottery and first-century coins have led Potter to suggest a military presence. According to him, while there is no specific evidence for military occupation, the early assemblage is uncharacteristically rich for an apparently peasant settlement in an ill-drained and unattractive area of land.[30] When a first-century settlement appears, or is assumed to have been too poor in material terms to have been the home of people who could have afforded imported pottery, a possible military connection is usually argued. It is assumed that the imported pottery was used by the army and that the peasant settlement was associated with a fort.

Claydon Pike provides another example. The evidence for two compounds of apparently differing levels of wealth and status existing alongside one another has already been discussed.[31] The wealthier compound has produced 'unusually large quantities of amphorae sherds',[32] and Miles has suggested that it may have been occupied by a detachment of soldiers who policed the collection of taxation in kind from the surrounding area.[33] The quantity and nature of the supposed military finds from Claydon Pike does not appear, however, to be conclusive in demonstrating military occupation.[34] It has already been remarked that villas appear to have been an alien concept to the inhabitants of the Upper Thames Valley, and the nature of the appearance of a wealthy late first/early second-century farm in the Gloucestershire Thames Valley is uncertain. It seems probable that Claydon Pike actually represented a wealthy native settlement even though a villa building does not occur on the site. Claydon Pike was a high status settlement, with no obvious connections with the military, but was also not a villa site.

Other non-villa settlements have produced indications of wealth. One at Appleford (Oxon) produced a collection of pewter vessels, probably from the fill of a well. The excavation report suggests that these vessels found their way on to the non-villa settlement from a neighbouring villa site one kilometre to the north. The Fenland evidence appears to indicate, however, that the inhabitants of some non-villa settlements were able to afford goods of this sort. The pewter vessels possibly belonged to the inhabitants of the non-villa settlement and constituted an alternative form of wealth investment.[35] Other non-villa settlements which have produced unexpected signs of wealth include Overton Down (Wilts) and Bullock Down (E Susx).[36]

The idea that the villa building need not have been the ideal of all free and wealthy Roman farmers may seem controversial. It is necessary to remember, however, that contemporary views of Roman Britain are constrained by the available literary sources and that the historical approach has given a biased perspective to the study of Romano-British society.[37] It has been argued several times that the indigenous background of social groups in Roman Britain will have had an important influence on the adoption of Roman culture, and that in some cases existing rules and regulations may have constrained the adoption of a full set of Roman standards.

SUMMARY

The need for a more open-minded approach to the analysis of rural settlement patterns should be stressed. The inter-relationship of Roman and Celt in the province of Britain is of particular interest. Provincial history is usually written, however, from the Roman perspective. Britain is seen as a reflection, if a rather pale one, of Rome and the other Mediterranean provinces. The fact that this approach remains dominant is partly a consequence of pessimism over the nature of the archaeological record. It is considered that material evidence can never give a full picture of how people lived, even if the evidence is of the highest quality and studied in great detail.

This view is too pessimistic. What is required is an open mind and the development of new research orientations. Such an approach will open up the field of Romano-British rural archaeology for the creation and assessment of new and useful interpretations. A rigorous analysis of these theories and their comparison with the archaeological evidence is vital. This will enable the subject to break away from the limited and intellectually biased perspective which has characterized research into rural settlement in Roman Britain.

Notes

CHAPTER 1

1. See Potter 1986 and R Jones 1987 for recent discussions of past research.
2. Haverfield 1912, 24.
3. p. 13.
4. Haverfield's book was written in 1905 but not published until 1912.
5. As is indicated by a number of fairly large-scale research projects which were undertaken in the final decade of the nineteenth century and first twenty years of this century (Cunliffe 1984; Potter 1986).
6. Collingwood was succeeded by Richmond and then by Frere, both of whom published influential surveys. The most recent follower of this tradition is Salway, with his recent book *Roman Britain* (Collingwood 1923; Collingwood and Myres 1937; Richmond 1955; Frere 1967; Salway 1981).
7. This conceptual scheme characterizes to a greater or lesser extent all the general surveys of the archaeology of the province and also many studies of more localized areas. National studies include those mentioned in note 6 above, the studies of Rivet 1970a and Liversidge 1973. Local studies include those of Detsicas 1983; Higham and GD Jones 1985; Branigan 1985; Todd 1973; Webster 1975a; Ramm 1978; Cunliffe 1973b; Dunnett 1975.
8. Two broad and distinct types of historical evidence are used to provide this historical framework. The first type of evidence consists of a limited body of writing by classical authors and a comparatively restricted body of inscriptions. Historical sources provide direct evidence for some events in the history of Roman Britain and also a few elements of an administrative framework for the province. Historical sources which discuss Britain are particularly rare and, as a consequence, a second type of historical evidence has been adopted in the study of Roman Britain.

   This second type of source is the historical material – including the work of classical authors, inscriptions and papyri – from other provinces of the empire. These sources are used by analogy to enlighten the Roman archaeologist about the situation in Britain. Rivet has summarized this perspective by likening knowledge of Roman Britain to a jigsaw. The type

Notes 163

of administrative and political picture that should emerge in the case of Roman Britain is evident because, although this particular jigsaw is torn and faded almost beyond recognition, the plans of others in the same series are better preserved. The analogy suggests that the historical and archaeological evidence for Britain is extremely incomplete and can only be understood in relation to other provinces of the Roman Empire for which there is far more literary and epigraphic evidence (Rivet 1970a, 31–2).

9. For accounts see the references in note 6.

10. For criticisms of the traditional approach see Burnham and Johnson 1979; M Jones and D Miles 1979; Reece 1982 and Cunliffe 1984.

11. Research orientations have changed little for three reasons. First, villas and walled small towns can be fitted with greater ease into the historical framework of analytical models than can non-villa settlements and unwalled small towns. In addition, intellectual élitism has doubtlessly continued to play a part. Even if the majority of villas and walled towns are no longer considered to be the homes of actual Romans the archaeologist was able, by studying the homes of the Britons who adopted Roman ways, to excavate evidence for the wealthy élite of the province. The third factor is very simple: these sites usually produce a richer range of finds and structures than the settlements of the poor and backward and are thus more rewarding in material terms.

12. In recent years it has been realized that to view those who did not swiftly adopt Roman culture as unworthy of attention is élitist. It is apparent, however, that if the historical perspective is to be adhered to then those who did not copy Roman manners and standards will be very difficult to study. The inhabitants of Britain who were too poor or obstinate to adopt Roman ways presumably continued to live in a 'British' manner, and there is little historical information to indicate how Iron Age people lived. In addition, very little information exists on the poor peasants of other provinces and what does exist was recorded by the literate classes who did not take part in peasant life and culture (Macmullen 1974, 26). The use of analogies from the Mediterranean provinces of the empire is therefore of limited value. Consequently the poor of the province cannot be studied from the limited historical evidence and their way of life is impossible to understand.

13. The publications listed in note 6 illustrate the bias in attention towards the walled small towns and villas of the province and away from the non-villa settlements and unwalled small towns. This is also illustrated by specific publications that are concerned with villas (Rivet ed. 1969; Percival 1976; Todd ed. 1978; R Smith 1987; Black 1987) as against discussions of non-villa settlements which figure only in general accounts of rural settlements in the province (*eg* C Thomas ed. 1966, D Miles ed. 1982). Indeed very few non-villa settlements and unwalled small towns were excavated on any scale before the 1960s. Exceptions to this rule

include non-villa settlements at Woodcuts (Dorset), Rotherley Down (Wilts), Park Brow (W Susx) and Chysauster (Corn).

14. See Chapter 2.

15. An example of the use of an analogy from another area of the empire which has incorrectly been applied to the villas of Britain is given in Chapter 2 (p. 22). In addition Reece, in a review of Salway's book on Roman Britain, has critically assessed the value of the historical references that exist for Britain in connection with Salway's comments about the barbarian incursion of AD 367 (Salway 1981, 380; Reece 1982, 455). In this case Reece has argued that the archaeological evidence has been distorted to fit into a framework which has been developed in an uncritical fashion from the historical sources (Reece 1982, 456).

   Knowledge of events in the history of Roman Britain is far from complete as major events clearly occurred in the province which were not recorded and consequently gaps occur in the historical narrative. In addition, the evidence that actually exists for dates and events is in itself open to criticism. Reece's comments on the Roman fort at Lympne (Kent) demonstrate this (Reece 1982, 456). Reece has concluded that if historical references in the few cases in which they have been checked do not agree with the archaeological evidence then they are not a source out of which to fashion a history of Roman Britain (Reece 1982, 455).

16. Some examples of population estimates are as follows. C Taylor has suggested that the density of population was probably as great as one settlement per 0.4 to 0.5 square kilometre in some areas of east Northamptonshire and Bedfordshire (C Taylor 1984, 83). Williamson has conducted a very intensive survey of an area of 28 square kilometres in north-west Essex. This is an area of very heavy soils which was formerly thought to be only very lightly settled. The survey has, however, indicated a density of settlement as high as one site per 0.77 square kilometre (Williamson 1984). Similar densities of settlement occur in the Fenland and on the Corallian Ridge of south Oxfordshire around Frilford. For Staffordshire C Smith has suggested that a density of one settlement per 1.5 square kilometres is probably an underestimate of the true figure (C Smith 1977a, 55). In northern England Haselgrove has suggested that a density of one site per 3.3 kilometres occurs in the Wear Lowlands, while Higham has argued that the density of population was considerably greater in the upland margins of Northumberland and some of the better drained areas of Cumbria (Haselgrove 1982, 59; Higham 1986, 198). In Cornwall the density of rounds varies from one site per 2.1 square kilometres to one site per 4.5 square kilometres in a number of areas studied by C Thomas (1966).

17. Salway 1981, 544–5. for other similar estimates see Cunliffe 1978b and C Smith 1977a.

18. For instance Frere's estimate of rather over two million; Frere 1967, 296, 349.

19. Salway 1981, 544–5. It may be of significance that many historians consider that the fourteenth-century population had outrun both the land supply and technological capacity of medieval society. Indeed the devastating effects of the Black Death may have been partly a consequence of this overpopulation and resulting malnutrition (Grigg 1980, 60).

20. Large-scale excavations have recently been conducted on non-villa settlements at Catsgore (Somer), Bradley Hill (Somer), Odell (Beds), Claydon Pike (Glos), Walesland Rath (Dyfed), Whitton (S Glam), Tower Knowe (Northum) and Kennel Hall Knowe (Northum) and on many other sites in the north, west and south,

21. See recent publications including Todd 1970; W Rodwell and Rowley eds. 1975; R Smith 1987. Recent large-scale excavations include Hibaldstow (Humbs), Neatham (Hants), Towcester (Northants), Baldock (Herts), Braughing (Herts), Wanborough (Wilts).

22. Figures for the proportion of villas to non-villa settlements have been calculated for three areas: Northamptonshire (information from figure 70), Warwickshire (information from Warwickshire Sites and Monuments Record) and the Oxfordshire Upper Thames Valley (information from figure 66). These figures indicate that villas form no more than 10–16 per cent of the total villa and non-villa settlements, even in southern Britain.

Region	Villas %	total	Non-villa %	total
Northants	10	(62)	90	(557)
Warwickshire	14	(13)	86	(82)
Oxfordshire Upper Thames	16	(21)	84	(110)

23. Figures for the excavation of villa and non-villa settlements have been calculated by examining sites recorded in the Roman Britain sections of *JRS* and *Britannia*. There are some problems of definition when a small-scale trench or watching brief becomes an excavation, but the figures give a rough indication of the proportion of sites of each type examined. The most clear-cut trend is the increase in the proportion of non-villa settlements excavated during the 1970s and 1980s.

Decade	Villas %	total	Non-villa Settlements %	total
1920s (1925–9)	77.5	(31)	22.5	(9)
1930s	67	(48)	33	(24)
1940s	86	(36)	14	(6)
1950s	70	(71)	30	(30)
1960s	70	(155)	30	(67)
1970s	55	(214)	45	(176)
1980s (1980–6)	61	(115)	39	(72)

166 *Rural Settlement in Roman Britain*

24. p. 22.
25. See Stevens 1966; J Smith 1963, 1978a; I Hodder 1972; Applebaum 1972.
26. In addition these studies are usually dismissed by those who hold to a more traditional view of the history and archaeology of the province (see Rivet 1975; Frere 1975, 1982; Salway 1981, 541).
27. J Smith 1978a, 170.
28. See Keesing 1975 and Fox 1967 for simple introductions to kinship and family structure.
29. Evidence for the Roman family has been discussed by Orsted 1985, 13; Garnsey and Saller 1987, 126–47; Herlihy 1985, 4–6. Macmullen has discussed the probable nucleated nature of the basic family group in other Mediterranean areas of the empire (1974, 27).
30. Charles-Edwards 1972; Powell 1958.
31. Herlihy 1985, 55.
32. Herlihy 1985, 55.
33. Charles-Edwards 1972; Stevens 1966; J Smith 1978a.
34. D Clarke 1972.
35. Vinogradoff 1905; Stevens 1966.
36. J Smith 1978a.
37. It is possible that ownership of some land within the Irish community was by the kin rather than by the individual household or extended family (Powell 1958; Charles-Edwards 1972, but see Herlihy 1985 for an alternative view). The land-owning group might therefore on occasions have represented a community rather than a family.
38. Greene 1986, 124.
39. Hopkins 1980, 1983, xiv-xvi; see also Mann 1986 for economic development within the Roman Empire in a comparative perspective. The discussion in this section is derived primarily from Hopkins 1983.
40. Cunliffe 1978a, 332.
41. Rivet 1969.
42. Although there were occasional rebellions in the first century and barbarian incursions in the third and fourth centuries (see Salway 1981 for details).
43. M Crawford 1970; Hopkins 1980, 1983; Reece 1972, 1973; Mann 1986, 271.
44. See M Crawford 1970, 44. Money acted as a medium of exchange,

although in the first and second centuries the value of coins was rather high and they would only have been used for purchasing or selling valuable goods or large quantities of goods (Reece 1973, 250). Nevertheless some rural farmers would have been introduced to the idea of coinage as a standard of exchange. By the third and fourth centuries the devaluation of the coinage of the empire resulted in coins with a far lower value probably used for fairly small-scale transaction (Reece 1973, 250). At this time coinage also becomes far more common in the Roman countryside and much of the province was probably integrated into the market economy.

45. Hopkins 1980, 105.

46. Hopkins 1983.

47. Industrially-produced pottery is the most obvious local traded good, but large quantities of personal ornaments such as brooches and bracelets are also found.

48. p. 21.

49. See Collingwood and Myres 1937, 212. The term 'capital' may appear to have a rather modern ring. In this book, however, 'capital' refers to the wealth derived from marketing agricultural surplus. It is not important how this wealth was stored, although it is clear that much was invested in items of material culture such as industrially-produced pottery and metalwork and villa-type buildings. The important point is that the Roman invasion provided new ways by which this capital could be stored, invested or consumed.

50. Rivet 1969.

51. p. 123.

CHAPTER 2

1. Early excavations of Roman villas include sites at Woodchester (Glos) excavated in the 1790s, Bignor (W Susx) excavated in the 1810s, a number of villas in the Nene Valley excavated in the early 1800s, and Witcombe (Glos) excavated in the 1820s.

2. Rivet 1969, 201.

3. Webster 1969, 218.

4. A few examples of sites that have recently been the subject of large-scale excavation can be given. Non-villa settlements at Claydon Pike (Glos), Wasperton (Warw), Bradley Hill (Somer), Odell (Beds), Catsgore (Somer), Whitton (S Glam), Walesland Rath (Dyfed), Cefn Graeanog (Gwyn), Silloth Farm (Cumbr), Tower Knowe (Northum) and Trethurgy (Corn). Villas at Gadebridge (Herts), Fishbourne (W Susx), Barton Court (Oxon), Winterton (Humbs), Bancroft (Bucks) and Barnsley Park (Glos).

168 *Rural Settlement in Roman Britain*

Local centres at Stonea (Cambs), Towcester (Northants), Hibaldstow (Humbs), Braintree (Essex), Neatham (Hants) and Tiddington (Warw).

5. Hampton and Palmer 1977; Wilson 1982.
6. A building has been located at Fulbrook (Warw) in an arable field by a fine series of aerial photographs. The photographs show a large rectangular stone-walled building in which individual rooms can be seen. It has been suggested that this is a courtyard villa, but ground inspection and documentary work have indicated that the site is actually a fifteenth-century castle (Hingley 1985b).
7. Hallam 1970.
8. Greene 1986, 122.
9. The archaeological definition uses the evidence derived from archaeological excavation and field work and consists of a description of the range of characteristics that are used to define a villa building. In contrast to this the historical definition utilizes historical sources to define the social and economic significance of the Mediterranean villa.
10. See Haverfield 1912; Collingwood 1923; Collingwood and Richmond 1969; Rivet 1970a; Frere 1967; Todd, ed. 1978; Percival 1976.
11. Thus Collingwood argued that a villa should be a dwelling that was somewhat romanized in manner, while Richmond defined the villa as the establishment of any folk who farmed the land and were able to build upon it a house of 'Roman style' (Collingwood 1923, 113; Richmond 1969, 51).
12. Richmond defined a group of 'cottage houses', simple rectangular stone-built dwellings, and called these villas (Richmond, 1969, 52–3). Others have adopted this definition and have suggested that any farmhouse of rectangular plan with stone-walled foundations that was built in the countryside was a villa (see Wilson 1974 on Britain and Drinkwater 1983 on Gaul).
13. p. 30.
14. p. 39.
15. Richmond 1969; Percival 1976; J Smith 1978b.
16. Rivet 1969; Richmond 1969; Percival 1976; Todd 1978; Detsicas 1983.
17. As was the case in Italy. Rivet 1969; Salway 1981, 600.
18. This is the 'Villa Faustini' of the Antonine Itinerary. Villa Faustini may correspond with either of the known Roman sites at Scole (Norf) or Stoke Ash (Suff). At both places a Roman site is known, although a recognizable villa of the type discussed by Rivet is yet to be found and is perhaps not to be expected (Rivet and Smith 1979, 163, 499).
19. Rivet 1969.

20. For England as a whole see Walthew 1975; for the south-east see Black 1987, 15; for the Catuvellauni see Branigan 1985, 109.

21. Slofstra 1983. Percival, from a review of classical allusions to villas, has argued that a precise definition cannot be derived from the historical sources. Some classical authors evidently used the term to refer to the estate of an individual person – the house, fields and tenants – while in other cases it appears to refer only to the actual dwelling house of the owner or bailiff (Percival 1976, 13–15). There is no coherent historical model for the significance of the villa.

22. p. 8.

23. On a number of villa sites the presence of estate workers is suggested by aisled houses in proximity to the villa house (Richmond 1969), while on other sites estate workers clearly lived in a separate settlement but in relatively close proximity to the villa building (p. 102). The traditional model would suggest that any estate workers were the tenants or slaves of the villa owner. In origin, however, many estate workers may have been the kin of a headman and may gradually have been reduced to tenant or slave status by the rise of an individual villa owner (Applebaum 1972, 231). What appears to be occurring is the degradation of some families to the status of workers by an individual, or dominant land holding family. On many sites, however, the subservient kin may have contined to hold some form of rights over the lands of the settlement. This is discussed in greater detail below (p. 153).

24. In addition, were all villas actually involved primarily in agriculture? Is it always necessary to look to an estate as the source of the wealth that created the villa building? If the villa building was related to surplus wealth and the desire to symbolize this surplus, it is clear that this wealth need not always have been derived from agriculture. Buildings with the archaeological characteristics of villas do not only occur in rural isolation, but also in local market centres and *civitas* capitals.

It is possible that some of the wealth of the owners of villa-type buildings in the *civitas* capitals and local centres of Britain was derived partly from trade and exchange (p. 86–7). In addition, some rural villas appear to be connected directly with industry. At a limited number of villas in Gaul industry may actually have been more important than agriculture (see Percival 1976, 161–2). It is likely that villas in the Nene Valley around Water Newton (Cambs) were connected with the major pottery industry of this area. Other villas were closely associated with industry (*eg* Wiggonholt (W Susx) with pottery, Rapsley (Surrey) with tile production, Creech (Dorset) with shale and Droitwich (Here & Worc) with the winning of salt). It therefore seems possible that some villas were constructed with a surplus derived at least in part from industry and trade rather than agriculture.

25. The term 'native settlement' has been avoided in this study as the majority of villas and local centres were also the homes of natives.

26. This is discussed further on p. 75.

27. p. 160.

28. As direct evidence for the status of the inhabitants of non-villa settlements is absent, the sites are fitted into the villa/estate centre model that was discussed above (p. 22). Literary texts for the Roman Empire refer to tenants and slaves, workers who were evidently commonly part of the agricultural estate of landowners (Ste Croix 1981; MacMullen 1974). It should be noted that these tenants included men of some status and means (Garnsey and Saller 1987, 72). In addition, evidence for peasant landowners of fairly low status exists for some areas of the empire (Ste Croix 1981, 114–15; Garnsey and Saller 1987, 75–7). It is usually assumed that the inhabitants of non-villa settlements fell into one of these three groups: either slaves, tenants or poor land-owning peasants (Rivet 1970a, 117; Salway 1981, 605–7; Potter 1981).

29. Imperial property came in many forms, and these will be discussed in detail below (p. 127).

30. For instance Saint Melania the Younger (AD 383–439) owned land in Italy, Sicily, Africa, Spain and Britain (Applebaum 1972, 23).

31. Todd 1976; R Smith 1987; Todd 1970; articles in W Rodwell and Rowley, ed. 1975; Burnham 1986, 1987.

32. Alchester (Oxon), Alcester (Warw), Ilchester (Somer), Kenchester (Here & Worc) and Water Newton (Cambs) are examples.

33. p. 1.

34. Rivet 1970a, 66.

35. Thus the evidence that Water Newton (Cambs) was a *vicus* in the second century should indicate that this town, while being subservient to a *civitas*, had a degree of local responsibility vested in some form of local council. By inference many of the other local centres of Roman Britain may also have had similar administrative functions (Frere 1967, 209).

36. Todd 1970; Rivet 1975.

37. S Johnson has summarized the work of Festus and Isidore of Seville and has observed that originally the term *vicus* was derived from a type of settlement that had streets but no walls. The term signified a small settlement, generally without any form of self-government and subject to the administration of another larger town nearby. Although Festus mentions magistrates these may well have been officials appointed to watch over the market and need not imply any administrative significance for the *vicus*. The evidence of inscriptions from Gallic *vici* could indicate that some of these sites had an element of self-government (S Johnson 1975, 75–7). Salway has remarked from the writings of Ulpian and other considerations that the term was used indiscriminately of a village, a settlement outside a fort, a ward of a city, or even a sub-division of the

canabae of a legion (Salway 1981, 591). It is even possible that the *civitas* capital was considered a *vicus* and retained this rank unless it was promoted to either colonial or municipal status by the Emperor (S Johnson 1975, 75).

38. See especially Frere 1975.

39. Salway 1965; Sommer 1984.

40. Forts and fortresses with *vicus* settlements in northern Britain and Wales include Corbridge (Northum), Housesteads (Northum), Old Carlisle (Cumbr), Nether Denton (Cumbr), Chester (Ches), Newton Kyme (N Yorks), Piercebridge (Durham) and Trawscoed (Dyfed).

41. Frere 1975, 6.

42. p. 90.

43. Rivet 1975, 112.

44. Frere's analysis of the origin of Romano-British small towns was based on a sample of seventy nine small towns of which the majority, forty eight sites, are known to have had walled circuits. Hodder and Millett used a comparable body of evidence in their analysis of the relationship of villas to small towns. More recently Burnham has included a number of additional sites to bring the total figure for small towns up to ninety seven (Frere 1975; I Hodder and Millett 1980; Burnham 1986).

45. Rivet, in his study *Town and Country in Roman Britain*, only considered walled examples of small towns in any detail. Todd, however, noted that a large number of small towns existed which were never walled although these probably differed very little in character from some of the more humble walled sites. Todd also remarked that the majority of the unwalled sites are very poorly known (Rivet 1970a; Todd 1970, 117; see also Webster 1975b).

46. See Crickmore 1984a for a recent survey of walled towns in Roman Britain.

47. Sites at Kingscote (Glos), Braughing (Herts), Camerton (Avon), Bourton-on-the-Water (Glos), Charterhouse-on-Mendip (Somer) and Springhead (Kent) do not appear to have had defences. Defensive circuits have been claimed for some sites, but the evidence does not appear to be conclusive, *eg* Wycomb (Glos).

48. Rivet 1975, 111; R Smith 1987, 1.

49. Both Todd and Webster consider that a small town should cover a considerable area. Rodwell has defined the minimum area for a small town as around ten hectares (Webster 1975b; W Rodwell and Rowley, ed. 1975, 1; W Rodwell 1975, 87; see also Todd 1970, 117).

50. The site at Catsgore (Somer) which has been subject to large-scale excavation is a fairly extensive road-side settlement. It resembles the local

centres of the province in being located on a road, but the total extent of the site appears to be only around five hectares. In addition the excavated evidence indicates little else than basic agricultural production on the site and it appears that Catsgore may represent a non-villa settlement with a primarily agricultural function (Leech 1982, 34). This indicates that roadside location alone is not enough to identify the status of a site as a local market centre. It is also clear that if densely settled a local centre need not have covered as much as ten hectares.

51. p. 111.

CHAPTER 3

1. For recent discussions of agricultural buildings see Applebaum 1972 and Morris 1979.
2. Leech 1982, 29.
3. p. 33–4.
4. Richmond 1969.
5. Hodson 1964; Harding 1974; Cunliffe 1978a.
6. J Williams 1976, 112.
7. Drury 1980, figure 3:7 and 3:8.
8. See Leech 1982.
9. The conversion of earth and timber round houses into stone is also known at Thorplands (Northants), Kennel Hall Knowe (Northum) and Tower Knowe (Northum).
10. At local centres: Alcester (Warw), Godmanchester (Cambs), Baldock (Herts). On non-villa settlements: Catsgore (Somer), Brockworth (Glos), Atwood (Surrey), Stanstead (Essex), Kennel Hall Knowe (Northum), Tower Knowe (Northum), Carn Euny (Corn), Cefn Graeanog (Gwyn). On sites that were later to be rebuilt as villas: Gorhambury (Herts), Shakenoak (Oxon), Littlecote Park (Wilts), Marshfield (Glos). As outbuildings probably with a domestic function associated with villa buildings: Winterton (Humbs), Kirk Sink (N Yorks), Stanwick (Northants), Bancroft (Bucks).
11. Circular huts also survive into the third/fourth centuries at Somersham (Cambs), Portishead (Avon), Fisherwick (Staffs) and Staunton (Notts).
12. p. 35.
13. Gardner and Savory 1964.
14. W Rodwell 1978a.
15. Insubstantial rectangular houses are known at the local centres: the

Alchester road suburb of Towcester (Northants), at Baldock (Herts), Neatham (Hants), Godmanchester (Cambs). Similar buildings occur on non-villa settlements at Park Brow (W Susx) and at Old Brampton, Risehow and Penrith (Cumbr) and Walesland Rath (Dyfed).

16. Leech 1982, 31.

17. Timber, daub and thatch houses of this type are known at Chelmsford (Essex) and Godmanchester (Cambs). Examples with stone foundations and timber and daub walls occur at Catsgore phase 2 (Somer) and Studland (Dorset). Examples built of stone up to the eaves with heavy slate roofs are known at Catsgore phase 3.

18. Houses of this type occur at local centres: Chelmsford (Essex), Great Chesterford (Essex), Hibaldstow (Humbs), East Bridgeford (Notts), Scole (Norf), Baldock (Herts). On non-villa settlements: Catsgore (Somer), Bradley Hill (Somer), Collyweston (Northants), Quinton (Northants), Iwerne (Dorset), Studland (Dorset). As outbuildings on villa sites: Gadebridge (Herts), Gatcombe (Glos).

19. Buildings of this type develop into villas at Clear Cupboard (Glos) and Cox Green (Berks).

20. p. 48.

21. Leech's estimate of the population of the houses at Bradley Hill is based on analysis of cemetery data. Some possible supporting evidence can be obtained from an examination of the living area of the two houses. The total areas of the two main living rooms at Bradley Hill are approximately 56 and 35 square metres. Cook and Heizer have suggested a formula for estimating population from the living area within houses. They suggest an area of 10 square metres per head of population (Cook and Heizer 1968). This would give figures of five to six and three to four people for each house at Bradley Hill and these figures are close to the estimate proposed by Leech. Both types of estimate are hypothetical but they do support the suggestion that houses of this type contained nuclear family groups (Leech 1981, 197).

22. Richmond 1969, 52–3.

23. Buildings of this type develop into winged corridor villa houses at Hambleden (Bucks), Park Street (Herts), Frocester Court (Glos), Ditches (Glos). Examples at Carsington (Derby) and Whitwell (Leics) never developed beyond the cottage phase.

24. R Brown 1982, 76.

25. Richmond 1969, 50.

26. Todd 1981.

27. J Smith 1963; Richmond 1969; Applebaum 1972.

28. Applebaum 1972, 227.

29. At Claydon Pike (Glos), Somerford Keynes (Glos) and Bancroft (Beds).
30. Morris 1979.
31. Morris 1979.
32. Morris 1979; Hadmann 1978.
33. Aisled houses appear to represent villa buildings at North Warnborough (Hants), Stroud (Hants), Combley (I of W) and Holcombe (Devon). They occur as outbuildings or additional villa buildings on a range of villa sites: Winterton (Humbs), Norton Disney (Lincs), Mansfield Woodhouse (Notts), Carisbrooke (I of W), Brading (I of W), West Dean (Wilts). At local centres: Alcester (Warw), Tiddington (Warw), Dorchester-on-Thames (Oxon), Neatham (Hants) and Water Newton (Cambs). On non-villa settlements: Claydon Pike (Glos), Roystone Grange (Derby), Whitwell (Leics) and Shirebrook (Derby).
34. J Smith 1963, 4.
35. Richmond 1969, 65.
36. p. 67.
37. J Smith 1963, 12–7. Applebaum has proposed a model which differs slightly from that of J Smith. Utilising the Laws of ancient Wales Applebaum has argued that the aisled house was the abode of the extended family, the kindred occupying the aisles and the chief the upper end (Applebaum 1972, 134). This supports J Smith's model and suggests that the aisled house was the abode of the extended family, or the 'kindred' of the lord. Applebaum, however, also proposed that the Roman aisled hall was at the centre of a manor, with the kin of the lord living outside the aisled house but meeting and feasting in his hall.
38. Applebaum 1963, 4.
39. p. 48.
40. Undivided, or unpartitioned aisled houses occur at Claydon Pike (Glos), Stroud early phase (Hants), Sparsholt early phase (Hants), Roystone Grange (Derby).
41. Developed examples of aisled houses occur at Norton Disney (Lincs), Mansfield Woodhouse (Notts), Carisbrooke (I of W), West Dean (Wilts), Stroud (Hants), North Warnborough (Hants), Acton Scott (Salop), Combley (I of W), East Grimstead (Wilts), Lippen Wood (Hants) and Winterton (Humbs); see J Smith 1963 and Morris 1979.
42. J Smith 1963, 4.
43. R Brown 1982.
44. J Smith 1963.
45. Black 1987.

46. Aisled houses with multiple residential suites have been discussed by Black, 1987, 79 and include Clanville (Hants), Sparsholt (Hants), Stroud (Hants), North Warnborough (Hants), Brading (I of W), Carisbrooke (I of W). In addition multiple suites of rooms may occur within more northerley aisled houses, for instance at Mansfield Woodhouse (Notts), Norton Disney (Lincs) and Winterton (Humbs).

47. Black 1987, 80–1.

48. Neal 1982, 164.

49. Applebaum 1972, 136.

50. Liddell 1931; Applebaum 1972, 135–6.

51. p. 8.

52. An attempt can be made to assess the potential population of the North Warnborough aisled house using the formula proposed by Cook and Heizer (see note 21, above). Two figures will be estimated; the first figure is for the whole of the aisled house excluding the byres, the second includes only the areas that produced occupation debris during excavation. The area of the whole building is 568 square metres, which would give an estimated population of 57 individuals. The lower figure is 300 square metres, and the estimated population is 30 individuals.

53. In some cases male and female slaves were kept apart in separate accommodation, and it could be suggested that the evidence indicates that the house v. occupied by slaves employed on an agricultural estate. The wing or tower rooms and the hypocaust at North Warnborough do not, however, support the idea that the building was the home of slaves. Wing/tower rooms were added to many types of Romano-British houses and appear to have been used as indicators of status (see p.   ). It seems unlikely that an estate owner would add wing/tower rooms or a hypocaust to a slave house. In addition the spearheads, which were among the distinctively male artefacts from the building, do not suggest a slave population.

54. p. 37.

55. For instance Feltwell (Norf), Star (Somer), Clay Lane (Northants), Wymbush (Bucks).

56. Star (Somer); Marshfield (Glos).

57. Lockleys (Herts) and Brixworth (Northants).

58. Clay Lane (Northants) and Feltwell (Norf).

59. D Smith 1978, 117.

60. D Smith 1978.

61. p. 22.

62. D Smith 1978.

176 *Rural Settlement in Roman Britain*

63. Winged corridor buildings occur on the local centres at Tiddington (Warw), Alcester (Warw), Hibaldstow (Humbs), Camerton (Avon) and probably at Chelmsford (Essex). Winged corridor buildings have also been excavated in *civitas* capitals (*eg* building XII.2 at Cirencester, Glos).
64. p. 22.
65. J Smith 1978b, 358.
66. North Warnborough (Hants), Stroud (Hants), Tiddington (Warw), Mansfield Woodhouse (Notts) and possibly at Thruxton (Hants).
67. p. 37.
68. Great Staughton (Cambs), Barnsley Park (Glos) and Kingsweston (Glos).
69. See especially J Smith 1978a and D Smith 1978.
70. See Branigan 1976; D Smith 1978, 141.
71. See J Smith 1978b, 358.
72. J Smith 1978a, 170.
73. p. 41.
74. J Smith 1985.
75. In fact Webster and L Smith have dismissed J Smith's suggestions and have argued that the social model which fits the Barnsley Park villa best is that of an 'important occupier' living with his family in the large central room, with 'menials' living in the rooms to the south of the villa (Webster and L Smith 1987).
76. Richmond 1969, 50; D Smith 1978.
77. Applebaum 1972, 132.
78. p. 8.
79. Symmetrical winged corridor unit system villas have been identified at Boxmoor (Herts), Ditchley (Oxon), Hambleden (Bucks); see J Smith 1978a, 174–178.
80. J Smith 1978a.
81. Richmond 1969, 142.
82. Stroud (Hants), Sparsholt (Hants), Combley (I of W), Winterton (Humbs), Brading (I of W).
83. p. 83.
84. Woodchester (Glos), North Leigh (Oxon), Bignor (W Susx), and Spoonley Wood (Glos).
85. Richmond 1969, 64.

86. Since J Smith's article was published Webster has proposed an alternative interpretation of the Chedworth villa as a guest house associated with a nearby temple (Webster 1983). Webster's suggestion appears to be based on the nature of the villa plan as a series of separate units rather than a single 'splendid house', and also on the unusual location of the site, on a steep slope and the discovery of a shrine and religious objects from the site. Webster's argument is not fully conclusive as Smith's model also provides an interpretation for the presence of several house units on the site and the absence of a single great house. Religious objects and shrines are known on other villa sites: shrines at Darenth (Kent), Rapsley (Surrey), Bancroft (Bucks) and possibly Downton (Wilts). The suggestion that the site of the villa is unsuitable for agriculture is based on the idea that villas are invariably the centres of agricultural estates and this has already been dismissed (p. 22).

CHAPTER 4

1. p. 8.
2. Possible examples include Feltwell (Norf), Gayton Thorpe (Norf), Beadlam (N Yorks) and perhaps Littlecote Park (Wilts).
3. For a review see Cunliffe 1978a.
4. p. 80.
5. Hallam 1970, 49.
6. The Bristol region (Fowler 1978a), Sussex (Drewett 1978), the Upper Thames Valley (D Miles 1978), Essex (W Rodwell 1978b), south Yorkshire/north Nottinghamshire (Riley 1978, 1980).
7. p. 75.
8. Excavated examples include Grambla (Corn), Trethurgy (Corn), Trelissy (Dyfed), Whitton (S Glam), Cefn Graeanog (Gwyn), Cae Metta (Gwyn), Penrith (Cumbr), Silloth Farm (Cumbr), Tower Knowe (Northum), Kennel Hall Knowe (Northum).
9. Barton Court (Oxon), Langton (N Yorks), Callow Hill (Oxon), Norton Disney (Lincs), the earlier phase of Frocester Court (Glos).
10. Winterton (Humbs), the later phase at Frocester Court (Glos), Halstock (Dorset), Tarrant Hinton (Dorset), Stroud (Hants), Combley (Hants), Brading (I of W), Clanville (Hants), Hambleden (Bucks), Llantwit Major (S Glam).
11. p. 83.
12. Wacher 1974.

13. Areas in which enclosures are marked out at least partly by ditches have been excavated at Dragonby (Humbs), Hibaldstow (Humbs), at the Alchester road suburb of Towcester (Northants) in two areas of the settlement at Tiddington (Warw) and at Neatham (Hants).

14. At Braughing (Herts), Alchester (Oxon), Kenchester (Here & Worc), Irchester (Northants), Wanborough (Wilts) and Water Newton (Cambs); see the evidence of aerial photography for these sites which has been discussed by Wilson 1975.

15. Hingley 1984a, 1984b; Bowden and Mcormish 1987.

16. Leech 1982, 38.

17. Multiple dwelling houses at Catsgore by phase:

Compound	Period 1 (c. 100/120 to AD 150/180)	Period 2 (c. 150/180 to early 4th)	Period 3 (early 4th to c. 360)
1	1 or 2	2	1
2	?1	?1	?1
3	?2	1	2
4	–	?	2 or 3
5	–	?2	?1

(information from Leech 1982).

18. p. 37.

19. At Park Brow (W Susx) a group of five buildings of simple rectangular type existed within a compound defined by lynchets and ditches. Two of these buildings were larger than the others, and a compound with two dwelling houses and three ancillary buildings may be indicated (although see Black 1987, 21 for an alternative interpretation). This reconstruction is hypothetical as the excavation was undertaken in the 1920s and the chronology of this site is not known in detail. At Odell (Beds) the first-century BC farm consisted of a group of fields and one ditched settlement enclosure on either side of a trackway. Within the settlement compound there were two round dwellings each of which had been rebuilt three times. This compound was occupied until the end of the first century AD, when it was replaced by a new settlement area within the fields of the original farm. It is possible to identify other farm compounds at Garden Hill (E Susx), Claydon Pike (Glos), Upton St Leonards (Glos), Atwood (Surrey), Dunston's Clump (Notts), Kelvedon (Essex) and Overton Down (Wilts), although most of these sites are not fully published and detailed discussion must await full publication.

20. At Whitton (S Glam) in Period X the north and west ranges of buildings appear to represent a pair of rectangular dwellings (J Smith 1987, 247). Other sites include Carn Euny (Corn), Trethurgy (Corn), Grambla (Corn), Walesland Rath (Dyfed), Cefn Graeanog (Gwyn), Roystone Grange I (Derby), Tower Knowe (Northum), Kennel Hall Knowe (Northum), Doubstead (Northum), Forcegarth Pasture North (Durham)

and on numerous other unexcavated crop mark and earthwork sites in northern and western Britain.

21. At Trethurgy (Corn), Whitton (S Glam), Cefn Graeanog (Gwyn), Tower Knowe and Kennel Hall Knowe (Northum) two or more houses occur during the occupation of each site.
22. Farm compounds with single houses occur at Catsgore (Somer), at Dunston's Clump (Notts) and at Chysauster (Corn).
23. Applebaum 1972, 151–205; J Smith 1978a.
24. Applebaum 1972, 155.
25. p. 8.
26. See especially J Smith 1978a and Black 1987.
27. J Smith 1978a, 153.
28. J Smith 1987.
29. RCHME 1983.
30. p. 59.
31. J Smith 1978a.
32. p. 41.
33. p. 41.
34. J Smith 1963, 12–3.
35. D Johnston 1978; Black 1987, 77.
36. Winterton (Humbs), Hambleden (Bucks), Littlecote Park (Wilts), Llantwit Major (S Glam), Bancroft (Beds), Spoonley Wood (Glos) and Woodchester (Glos).
37. Applebaum 1972, 45.
38. p. 155.
39. See Percival on Anthee (Belgium) and Koln-Mungersdorf (Germany); Percival 1976, figures 21 and 24.
40. see p. 102.
41. At Towcester (Northants), Dorchester-on-Thames (Oxon), Scole (Norf), East Bridgeford (Notts), Brampton (Norf), Kenchester (Here & Worc), Chelmsford (Essex), Sea Mills (Glos), Irchester (Northants) and elsewhere.
42. Wanborough (Wilts), Baldock (Herts).
43. Although see Burnham 1987, 176 for further discussion.
44. At Godmanchester (Cambs), Cambridge (Cambs) and Great Dunmow (Essex); Burnham 1987, 176.

180 *Rural Settlement in Roman Britain*

CHAPTER 5

1. In this study a distance of about 150 metres will be used as an interval between settlements. Hallam uses an approximately equivalent measure for the same purpose (1970, 31). If the compounds are within 150 metres of each other they are taken to indicate a single settlement, while if they are spread out across the landscape at distances greater than 150 metres a series of distinct settlements are represented.

2. p. 16.

3. Hallam 1970, Table A.

4. Hallam 1970, 61.

5. p. 59–60.

6. Studland (Dorset), Clay Lane (Northants), Topsham (Devon), Whitwell (Leics), Atwood (Surrey) and Park Brow (W Susx).

7. Also Ditchley (Oxon), Ditches (Glos), Holcombe (Devon).

8. Settlements with two to three compounds include Claydon Pike (Glos), where the two compounds had differing levels of wealth (see p. 80), and Staunton (Notts) which had at least two clusters of huts, although the evidence for this site is incomplete. Chisenbury Warren (Wilts) consists of at least four separate farm compounds and therefore represents a site of this type (Leech 1982). Bullock Down (E Susx) appears to have four pairs of house platforms which may represent four house compounds. Roystone Grange I (Derby) consisted of five farm compounds, although it is uncertain whether they are all contemporary. At Greaves Ash (Northum) thirty or more houses occur both inside and outside a large double ditched sub-rectangular enclosure. This site is known from surface survey and has not been excavated, and consequently the chronology of its development is not understood. It seems likely, however, that more than one compound occurred at any period. This is also the case at the Ewe Close and Ewe Locks sites at Crosby Ravensworth and sites at Crosby Garrett appear to consist of multiple joined enclosures located on the limestone fells and differing significantly from the usual enclosed settlements of Cumbria. These sites are also unexcavated and known only from surface survey. The closest parallels, however, are the river valley settlements of southern Britain, some of which probably represent the homes of more than a single family group (see p. 80).

9. Millett and Graham 1986, 154.

10. 150 compounds, if each contained an extended family of twenty persons; and 600 compounds, if the average family had five members.

11. Alcester (Warw), Alchester (Oxon), Water Newton (Cambs) and Kenchester (Here & Worc).

12. 500 compounds of twenty persons each, or 2,000 compounds of five people on each site.
13. Other estimates include 1,450–2,600 people for Towcester (Northants) and around 950–1,700 for Dropshort (Bucks).
14. Farm compounds on both sides of a track exist at Catsgore (Somer), Claydon Pike (Glos), Chisenbury Warren (Wilts), Chitterne Down (Wilts) and on a range of other excavated and crop mark sites.
15. Miles has noted the occurrence of items of military origin at Claydon Pike, including a gilded vine leaf, a bronze mount in the form of a symbolic shield and vulva, and several bronze studs. In addition two intaglios, an amphora sherd inscribed LEGIIA and a silver Republican coin (D Miles 1984a, 199, 202). On the basis of the evidence for large-scale reorganization of the settlement in the late first/early second centuries and taking these finds into account Miles has suggested some form of military presence; perhaps a small number of soldiers policing an agricultural settlement where tax was collected in the form of produce from a surrounding area (D Miles 1984a, 208).

    In this study the site is interpreted as being civilian. The military connection is not demonstrated by the small quantity of military finds that have been made. First/second century military objects are fairly common on a number of other civilian villa and non-villa settlements and local centres that have been excavated on a far smaller scale than the Claydon Pike site (see especially Griffiths 1982). Non-villa settlements at Catsgore (Somer), Stanstead (Essex), Rotherley Down (Wilts), villas at Rockbourne (Hants), Atworth (Wilts), Box (Wilts) and numerous local centres including Towcester (Northants), Kingscote (Glos), Dorn (Glos) and Braughing (Herts) have produced military objects, but no certain evidence of the presence of the military. It is uncertain how the military objects got to these sites, but an official military link for these sites need not always be indicated.
16. D Miles 1984a.
17. Leech 1982, figure 5; Ellis 1984.
18. Leech 1982, 38.
19. p. 21.
20. p. 147.
21. Percival 1976; Leday 1980.
22. At North Wraxhall (Wilts) a corridor house has been excavated within a walled yard with associated farm buildings within a second yard outside the entrance to the villa compound. At Brading (I of W) the villa building is flanked on two sides of its walled courtyard by aisled buildings and there are traces, only partly excavated, of an outer courtyard which presumably contained agricultural buildings. The situation appears to

have been very similar at the Norfolk Street villa, close to the centre of Roman Leicester. At Darenth (Kent) a large corridor villa was associated with an agricultural compound and beyond this a third outer agricultural compound. At Rapsley (Surrey) two compounds are also known with the villa house in one and aisled houses in the other. Rivenhall (Essex) was probably also divided in this way.

At a number of other villa sites a group of buildings is situated in close proximity to a villa compound but apparently are not integrated into a second compound. These sites include Bancroft (Bucks) and Stanwick (Northants).

23. At Spoonley Wood (Glos) an aisled house occurs to one side of the courtyard house, possibly representing part of a second agricultural compound. Bignor (W Susx) has an inner residential courtyard and an outer agricultural yard. Chedworth (Glos) appears to have traces of two courtyards, although the outer courtyard was probably residential. North Leigh (Oxon) does not seem to have two courtyards as such, but the agricultural buildings are situated adjacent to the main villa buildings just to the north-west.

24. Selkirk 1983.

25. p. 28.

26. At Neatham (Hants), Towcester (Northants), Hibaldstow (Humbs).

27. p. 35.

28. At Tiddington (Warw), Alcester (Warw), Hibaldstow (Humbs), Braughing (Herts), Camerton (Avon), and Ilchester (Somer). Large, wealthy houses of uncertain plan also existed in the south-eastern part of the walled areas at Water Newton (Cambs) and Kenchester (Here & Worc).

29. See Rivet 1970a, 119; Todd 1970, 207; Todd 1978, 207.

30. Todd 1970; W Rodwell 1975; Webster 1975b; R Smith 1987.

31. p. 71.

32. Frere 1986, xv-xvi.

33. Frere 1986, xv-xvi.

34. R Smith 1987, 33.

35. Frere 1986, xvi.

36. See Burnham 1987 for a fuller discussion.

37. Alcester (Warw), Irchester (Northants), Kenchester (Here & Worc), Wycomb (Glos), Baldock (Herts), Chesterton-on-Fosse (Warw) and Water Newton (Cambs); see also Wilson 1975.

38. Alchester (Oxon), Wanborough (Wilts), Stonea (Cambs). Burnham is willing to include a wider range of sites in this category (1987, 167–71), although many of these sites show only a very limited degree of planning.

Notes

39. This follows on from the arguments of Wacher 1974, 21.
40. Braughing (Herts), Scole (Norf), Ashton (Northants), Braintree (Essex). It should be noted, however, that excavations on the majority of these sites have been small-scale and further discoveries may indicate the existence of public or administrative buildings.
41. The rich Late Iron Age burials at Baldock (Herts) are an exception to this.
42. Wacher 1974.
43. Burnham 1987, 179.
44. Catterick (N Yorks), Wall (Staffs), Godmanchester (Cambs), Wanborough (Wilts), Chelmsford (Essex) and possibly Water Newton (Cambs).
45. Burnham 1987.
46. For Godmanchester see H Green 1975, Dorchester-on-Thames see Branigan 1985, 92 and for Towcester Branigan 1985, 83.
47. Burnham 1987, 180.
48. Irchester (Northants). Springhead (Kent), Wycomb (Glos), Kenchester (Here & Worc), Great Chesterford (Essex), Chelmsford (Essex), Godmanchester (Cambs), Frilford (Oxon) and many other local centres.
49. Henig 1984; Hingley 1985a.
50. Examples include ironworking at Ashton (Northants), Baldock (Herts), Braughing (Herts), Chelmsford (Essex), Towcester (Northants) and Tiddington (Warw); potting at Tiddington (Warw) and Chelmsford (Essex); manufacture of pewter at Camerton (Avon) and Towcester (Northants).

CHAPTER 6

1. p. 3–4.
2. At Long Wittenham (Oxon), Claydon Pike (Glos), Church Lawford (Warw) and on a number of other sites known to the author in Oxfordshire, Warwickshire and Gloucestershire (see for instance Benson and D Miles 1974; Webster and Hobley 1964).
3. Some clusters of two or three small enclosed settlements occur in Cornwall and north-western Wales, although none of these groups of sites has been subject to intensive excavation and they are not necessarily contemporary (N Johnson and Rose 1982, 172; RCAHMWM 1956). At Forcegarth Pasture (Durham) two enclosed settlements lie within about 150 metres from each other and are probably at least partly contemporary. In addition possible groups of settlements occur at Roystone Grange I and II (Derby), Wetwang/Garton Slack (Humbs), Silloth Farm (Cumbr) Aughertree Fell (Cumbr).

184 *Rural Settlement in Roman Britain*

4. Two enclosed sites at Forcegarth Pasture (Durham) have been tested by excavation, as have a group of closely associated Roman non-villa settlements at Wetwang/Garton Slack (Humbs) and a pair of neighbouring non-villa settlements at Claydon Pike and Thornhill Farm (Glos). Excavation indicates that at Forcegarth Pasture the settlements may be successive, although their phases of occupation probably overlap. The sites at Wetwang/Garton Slack are discussed in the main text. The Thornhill Farm site is probably at least in part contemporary with the neighbouring settlement at Claydon Pike. Miles' preliminary suggestion based on morphology, that Thornhill Farm was possibly rather poorer and less romanized than Claydon Pike (D Miles 1984a, 208), is now being tested by excavation.

5. p. 24.

6. p. 152.

7. Hallam 1970, 54–55.

8. GR Jones 1985, 163–4.

9. Hingley 1987a, 1988.

10. p. 152.

11. p. 95.

12. Todd 1978, 205.

13. Applebaum 1963.

14. Todd 1970, 126; 1978, 207; Percival 1976.

15. At Lockington (Leics) aerial photography and fieldwork has produced evidence for a villa and non-villa settlement within 100 metres of one another, although it is uncertain in this case that the two settlements were contemporary and it is possible that the non-villa settlement is actually Late Iron Age. A second possible site is Whitminster (Glos), where a probable villa located through field work is situated about 100 metres from a non-villa settlement known from fieldwork and limited excavation. At Great Lemhill Farm on the Oxfordshire/Gloucestershire county boundary a villa is known from small-scale excavation about 150 metres and on the opposite side of a stream from an extensive non-villa settlement at Langford, which is known from aerial photography and fieldwork. At Fotheringhay (Northants) a villa and extensive non-villa settlement about 250 metres apart are known from aerial photography and excavation. Villa and non-villa settlements also occur in close association but rather further apart. At Hockwold-cum-Wilton (Norf) a probable villa is known from aerial photography and fieldwork and is situated about 700 metres from a non-villa settlement known from aerial photography, fieldwork and limited excavation.

16. Applebaum has argued that the land unit exploited by the villa at Ditchley

(Oxon) had the same boundaries on three sides as the medieval parish in which the villa is situated (Applebaum 1972, Appendix 1). The distribution of villas at one per parish or township has been recognised in other areas.

Fowler has argued that in the Vale of Wrington (Somer) the pattern of Saxon estates correlates remarkably well with the distribution of villas, with one villa per parish (Fowler 1975, 132). At Kings Sutton, Newbottle and Farthinghoe (Northants) it has been suggested that '... in Roman times the basic outline of the medieval land units was already in existence...' (F Brown and C Taylor 1978, 87).

In other areas villas appear to occur approximately one per parish. In south Oxfordshire detailed field survey of a number of medieval parishes and townships around Frilford and Garford appears to have established this type of pattern fairly conclusively. General observations concerning continuity in parish/township boundaries from the Roman to medieval periods have also been made for Somerset and Warwickshire (Leech 1976; Hooke 1985). Therefore, it is possible that in some areas land units, at least at the parish or township level, survived into the Saxon and medieval periods.

This apparent continuity of land units from the Roman to the medieval period does not, however, appear to occur in all areas of Britain. Detailed field survey of some areas indicates litle correlation between the Roman and medieval settlement patterns. At Chalton (Hants) and also in south-east Northamptonshire (see C Taylor 1984, figure 30) there is little evidence to support the idea of continuity of land holdings. It is quite possible that this approach, the tracing of medieval land units back into the Roman period, may work for some areas and not for others and is a topic requiring further research.

17. Fowler 1975.
18. Percival 1976, 123–4.
19. Percival 1976, 31–2.
20. Applebaum 1963, 2–3.
21. Webster 1969, 234; Applebaum 1972, 249.
22. Applebaum 1963, 2.
23. Applebaum 1963.
24. Applebaum 1975.
25. Applebaum 1963, 7.
26. Branigan 1977a, 206.
27. G Clarke 1982, figure 5.
28. Duncan-Jones 1976, 12; Salway 1981, 628; Macmullen 1974, 5; Garnsey and Saller 1987, 68.

186 *Rural Settlement in Roman Britain*

29. Applebaum 1972, 19–25; Salway 1981, 599–600.
30. Hingley 1988.

CHAPTER 7

1. p. 144.
2. p. 26.
3. p. 28.
4. W Rodwell 1975. Well-known sites include Braughing (Herts), Great Chesterford (Essex), Braintree (Essex), Chelmsford (Essex), Kelvedon (Essex); less well known sites include (according to Rodwell) Radwinter (Essex), Halstead (Essex), Billericay (Essex) and Ipswich (Suff).
5. W Rodwell 1975.
6. K Rodwell ed., 1975; D Miles 1982, 58 and figure 1; Young 1986, 59–60. The local centres of the south-eastern Dobunni include some fairly well-known sites, such as Alcester (Warw), Tiddington (Warw), Astall (Oxon), Frilford (Oxon), Alchester (Oxon), Bourton-on-the-Water (Glos), Dorchester-on-Thames (Oxon), Dorn (Glos), Chesterton-on-Fosse (Warw). Probable but less well-known sites: Abingdon (Oxon), Wantage (Oxon), Sansom's Plat (Oxon), Brailes (Warw), Highworth (Wilts), Swalcliffe (Oxon).
7. See B Hodder and Ukwu 1969; I Hodder 1972; Hoskins 1954; Brush and Bracey 1955.
8. p. 133–9.
9. p. 144.
10. p. 128.
11. Rivet 1975, 112.
12. Of the sixteen fairly definite and eleven possible local centres in the South Midlands shown on Figure 62, only four have clear military origins, or between 16 percent and 28 per cent. Only the seven best known of these sites were considered in Frere's analysis, in which he argued that 55 per cent of small towns exhibited military origins (above p. 26). Rodwell's analysis of the Trinovantian sites indicates that a larger proportion appear to have Iron Age origins than evidence for associated Roman forts (W Rodwell 1975, Table on p. 92). The proportion of local centres with military origins may therefore have been overestimated due to the concentration on walled sites.

In addition, care should be exercised over the identification of a military presence on local centres from the discovery of one or a few small items of military metalwork. In note 15 for Chapter 5 it was argued that military objects are common from non-villa settlements and probably had no significant connection with the Roman military; the same may be true of some local centres. A military origin cannot be suggested convincingly unless large quantities of military finds or military structures have been found.

Analysis of Frere's figures demonstrates that thirty five (81 per cent) walled sites considered had military origins, in contrast to only eleven (33 per cent) unwalled sites. If it is true, as Rivet has argued, that the walled local centres had an important imposed administrative function, is it possible that sites originally associated with the army during the first century were chosen as stations of the Imperial Post and as tax collection centres? If so, it would appear that by concentrating on walled sites romanists have created the apparent pattern of military origins for local centres, as walled sites are those most likely to have first-century military associations, while comparatively poorly known undefended sites are less likely to demonstrate military origins.

13. Compare Hoskins 1954, figure 34 with figure 63.
14. Reynolds 1977, 46.
15. Shaw 1979.
16. Davies 1984.
17. Hingley, work in progress.
18. Hingley 1985a, 211; Henig 1984, 39.
19. Local centres with temples have been reviewed in note 48 for Chapter 5; however, some local centres appear to have been associated with very significant major temple complexes. Frilford (Oxon) is discussed in the text. Other comparable sites probably exist. The temple-theatre complex and associated settlement at Gosbecks (Essex) covers a comparable area to the Frilford settlement, although its proximity to Colchester may indicate that a market function is improbable for this site except on feast days. The local centre at Wycomb (Glos), with its associated temple, and possible theatre/amphitheatre is a second possibility. Charterhouse-on-Mendip (Avon) has an amphitheatre in close proximity, which may cast doubt on the suggestion that it was a settlement of slaves associated with the mining of lead; a temple has yet to be located.
20. Henig 1984, 39.
21. p. 11.
22. Todd 1970, 1978.
23. Branigan 1985; W Rodwell 1975; I Hodder and Millett 1980.
24. Some examples of local centres with villas in close association are Great Casterton (Leic), East Bridgeford (Notts), Ancaster (Lincs), Godmanchester (Cambs), Great Chesterford (Essex), Water Newton

188 *Rural Settlement in Roman Britain*

(Cambs), Braughing (Herts), Towcester (Northants), Chesterton-on-Fosse (Warw), Frilford (Oxon), Abingdon (Oxon).

25. Todd 1970, 126.
26. p. 102.
27. Todd 1970; exceptions include studies in W Rodwell and Rowley ed., 1975 and R Smith 1987.
28. Rivet 1969; W Rodwell 1975; I Hodder and Millett 1980; Branigan 1985.
29. p. 28.
30. W Rodwell 1975, 96.
31. p. 105

CHAPTER 8

1. Todd in attempting to describe the density of settlement and different types of settlement within the territory of the Coritani, works towards this type of approach (Todd 1973, 69–105). The quality and quantity of information for the area discussed by Todd is clearly not sufficient to enable a fuller description of the pattern of settlement, which is also the case regarding most other areas of the province.
2. Rivet 1970a, 101.
3. p. 4.
4. p. 102.
5. Collingwood and Myres 1937, 212–3.
6. Black 1987, 70–1.
7. Cunliffe 1973b, 103. The nature of Iron Age settlement on the Sussex Coastal Plain has been discussed more recently by Bedwin (Bedwin 1978 and Bedwin and Pitts 1978).
8. Hingley 1987a, 1988.
9. It is important, however, to stress that this will not have been the case in all regions. In some parts of Britain villas appear to occur in areas which were fairly intensively exploited during the Iron Age. Some areas that were not exploited intensively did not witness the development of a villa economy in the Roman period. The Fenland, which was only very sparsely occupied prior to the Roman occupation having dense concentrations of non-villa settlements, is a case in point.
10. p. 116.
11. p. 16.

12. Excavated settlements in the Fenland are very few in number. Small trenches have been excavated on the extensive non-villa settlements at Hockwold-Cum-Wilton (Norf) and Grandford (Cambs). A large area of the local centre at Stonea (Cambs) has recently been excavated with interesting results. For small trenches in other sites see C Phillips ed., 1970 and Potter 1981.

13. Collingwood and Myres 1937, 209-10; see also Bowen and Fowler 1966.

14. Very little excavation has been undertaken on non-villa settlement in the Salisbury Plain/Cranborne Chase area, although something is known of sites at Woodcuts, Rotherley and Overton Down. A range of settlement types from farmsteads to villages occur. Sites at Woodcuts (Dorset) and Rotherley Down (Wilts) appear to consist of single farmsteads, Overton Down (Wilts) appears to consist of two compounds, while Chisenbury Warren (Wilts) is rather larger in size. The site at Overton Down survives as an earthwork, and two apparent compounds can be distinguished which fit into a pre-existing pattern of Celtic fields. Two small rectangular houses of fourth-century date have been excavated from which a collection of 40 coins, roof tile and painted plaster indicate in the words of the excavator a degree of romanization somewhat surprising in a remote upland settlement (Fowler 1967, 30).

15. M Taylor 1939a, 268-9; Young 1986, 60.

16. Excavated sites on the gravels of the Upper Thames Valley west of Oxford include Claydon Pike (Glos), which has been discussed above (p. 80). Neighbouring sites at Thornhill Farm (Glos) and Somerford Keynes (Glos) are currently under excavation.

17. Park Brow (W Susx), one of the few excavated sites of this region, consists of a group of five simple rectangular houses which Black has recently suggested fall into two chronological phases, with three houses in each phase. These houses were probably of timber and daub construction, although roof tiles and painted plaster show some sophistication (Black 1987, figure 40). Little else is known of the non-villa settlements of the Sussex Downs. Other excavated non-villa settlements in this general area include Bullock Down (E Susx) and Chalton (Hants). Bullock Down consisted of four pairs of possible huts indicated by earthwork survey. Limited excavation was undertaken on one of these house platforms, and the evidence for the structure of the house was inconclusive. This site has produced a fairly rich collection of artefactual material, including exotic metalwork and at least five coin hoards. At Chalton a settlement consisting of a number of earthwork enclosures has been investigated and two house platforms partly excavated. Very few non-villa settlements have been excavated on any scale, although enough information exists to indicate that a variety of sites ranging from single farms to nucleated hamlets and village-type settlements are represented.

190 *Rural Settlement in Roman Britain*

18. One further example of a region characterized by non-villa settlements occurs to the south of Chelmsford in the territory of the Trinovantes (W Rodwell 1975, 96).

19. D Crawford 1976, 40.

20. Applebaum 1972, 28–33.

21. Rivet 1970a, 102–3.

22. A Jones 1964, 416.

23. Rivet 1970a, 102; D Crawford 1976, 44.

24. D Crawford 1976.

25. Rivet 1970a, 102.

26. D Crawford 1976, 36.

27. Applebaum 1972, 27–9.

28. Collingwood and Myres 1937, 224.

29. Stevens 1966, 120.

30. Authors who have suggested that the Fenland was an area of imperial property include Salway (1970, 1981, 604); Frere (1967, 275–7) and Rivet (1970a).

31. Salway 1970, 9.

32. Collingwood and Myres 1937, 212–3.

33. p. 122.

34. Collingwood and Myres 1937, 213.

35. Collingwood interpreted pits on Iron Age and Roman settlements which had been excavated on Salisbury Plain and Cranborne Chase as sunken dwellings. Pits occur in hundreds on many of these sites, and Collingwood argued that these represented extensive 'villages' (*eg* Collingwood 1923, 87). The excavation of the Iron Age settlement at Little Woodbury (Wilts) clearly demonstrated that these supposed pit dwellings were in fact storage and rubbish disposal pits (Bersu 1940). At Little Woodbury only a single, or perhaps two contemporary round houses were located. Little Woodbury became a site-type for Iron Age studies in Wessex, and the dominant interpretation therefore switched from characterizing of the area in terms of village-type settlements to the isolated farmstead with a single family group (*eg* Rivet 1970a, 104).

Rivet argued that Collingwood's distinction between villas and villages, and the suggestion that they formed two distinct types of social organization existing side by side, is a myth. Collingwood's supposed myth is, according to Rivet, undermined at its base by the archaeological demonstration that most of Collingwood's villages were in fact single farms (Rivet 1970a, 30). In other words, Collingwood's model does not work because his villages were actually isolated settlements similar in all but wealth to the villa settlements of the periphery of Cranborne Chase; and therefore as a minute subdivision of land did not occur on these sites this cannot have been the cause of the rigid and unprogressive nature of the economy.

It is clear from recent work, however, that village type settlements do occur on Cranborne Chase/Salisbury Plain – the site at Chisenbury Warren (Wilts) is a well known example. The situation would now appear to be that villages and isolated farmsteads occurred throughout the area during the Iron Age and Roman periods (see Bowen and Fowler 1966).

36. Rivet 1970a, 117.

37. p. 122.

38. p. 122.

39. p. 98.

40. Hingley 1987a, 1988.

41. p. 158.

42. D Crawford 1976, 45–7.

43. p. 158.

CHAPTER 9

1. Haverfield 1912, 24.

2. Collingwood 1923; Rivet 1970a; Frere 1967; Salway 1981.

3. Rivet 1969.

4. p. 23.

5. Villas at Fishbourne (W Susx), Southwick (W Susx), Folkestone (Kent), Faversham (Kent), Darenth (Kent), Lullingstone (Kent). Rich early villas occur in both of these areas, and include the first-century villas of the Sussex Coastal Plain – the most remarkable of which is Fishbourne – and the early villas of Kent, which include Eccles. Later villas are also known in some numbers in both areas and these include rich extensive houses such as Darenth and Folkestone.

6. Cunliffe 1973b, 74.

7. Detsicas 1983, figure 3.

8. Detsicas 1983. Large areas of the sites at Neatham (Hants) and Springhead (Kent) have been excavated in recent years providing some information on the chronology and organization of the local centres of

192 *Rural Settlement in Roman Britain*

south-eastern England. Few other local centres have been investigated on a large-scale.

9. Sparsholt (Hants), Rockbourne (Hants), North Warnborough (Hants), Gatcombe (Somer), Holcombe (Devon), Halstock (Dorset).

10. Branigan 1976.

11. Substantial areas of some local centres have recently been excavated, at Ilchester (Somer) and Wanborough (Wilts).

12. Non-villa settlements on Cranborne Chase and Salisbury Plain have been discussed above (p. 124). Non-villa settlements elsewhere in the south of England are comparable to these examples. Bradley Hill (Somer) and Studland (Dorset) are single isolated farmsteads, while Catsgore (Somer) is a village of as many as twelve farms. These three non-villa settlements lie close to known villas and may have been part of their estates.

13. Branigan 1985, 129–30; Dunnett 1975, 94–101.

14. Gayton Thorpe (Norf), Feltwell (Norf), Park Street (Herts), Boxmoor (Herts), Lockleys (Herts), Gadebridge (Herts), Hambleden (Bucks). An early villa at Rivenhall (Essex), comparable to the early villas of Sussex and Kent, has been recently excavated. Some of the other villas of the region appear to begin to develop during the first century, such as some of those that cluster around *Verulamium* (Percival 1976, 98–9). Large, wealthy third/fourth-century villas are rare, however, with courtyard villas hardly represented at all (the so-called 'courtyard villas' around Water Newton are actually fairly modest villas with outbuildings set around a courtyard; Branigan 1985, 129–30).

15. Neal 1978.

16. Excavated examples include Towcester (Northants), Ashton (Northants), Baldock (Herts) and Braughing (Herts) which have been excavated on a large scale.

17. Salway 1981, 604; Gregory 1982, 355.

18. p. 124.

19. Examples include Frocester Court (Glos), Woodchester (Glos), Chedworth (Glos), Barnsley Park (Glos), North Leigh (Oxon), Ditchley (Oxon), Shakenoak (Oxon), Barton Court (Oxon). Villas at Ditches (Glos) and Shakenoak (Oxon) have origins as early as many of the villas in the south and east, in the late first century. The majority of the villas of the region, however, have modest beginnings in the second century or later. Some of these villas grew into rich courtyard establishments during the third and fourth centuries, including some of the richest and best known villas of southern Britain. As in every other Romano-British tribe, however, winged corridor houses are far more common than the large and elaborate types of houses.

20. Sites at Alcester (Warw), Tiddington (Warw) and Dorchester-on-Thames (Oxon) have recently been subject to relatively large-scale excavation.

21. Wasperton (Warw) and Beckford (Here & Worc) in the Avon Valley and Appleford (Oxon) in the Thames Valley. The majority of the non-villa settlements in this region have been located and examined using aerial photography and limited fieldwork. The recently excavated sites in the Gloucestershire Thames Valley have been discussed above (p. 126).

22. Langton (N Yorks), Winterton (Humbs), Norton Disney (Lincs), Rudston (Humbs).

23. Webster 1975a, Ramm 1978, Todd 1973, 76.

24. Todd 1973, 76.

25. Todd 1973, 78.

26. Todd 1973, figure 17.

27. Excavated examples include Dunston's Clump (Notts) Breaston (Derby) and Sharpstones Hill (Salop) (see also Ramm 1978, figures 25–8). The Dunston's Clump enclosure contains a number of rectangular houses and other structures, forming part of an extensive complex of fields which contain additional settlement sites (Riley 1980).

28. At Roystone Grange (Derby) on the White Peak an interesting group of sites have recently been studied through excavation and earthwork survey. Roystone Grange I includes at least five house platforms, one of which has been excavated and has produced an aisled building. The surrounding field system has also been investigated. Although too little excavation has been conducted to demonstrate this point it is possible that Roystone Grange I may represent a hamlet or village rather than a farmstead.

    The excavated site at Staunton (Notts) also has at least two clusters of round houses of third/fourth-century date, and may represent a hamlet rather than an isolated farm. At Wetwang/Garton Slack (Humbs) a number of settlements consisting of groups of enclosures of first-century BC to fourth-century date constitute a large-scale division of the landscape, and both Staunton and Wetwang/Garton Slack appear to represent larger groupings of settlement rather than single isolated enclosure.

    In addition to these farmsteads and hamlets it appears that a number of caves were occupied in this area during the Roman period, such as Poole's Cavern (Derby) and others (discussion in Bramwell et al, 1983). Traces of second-century occupation also appear in some of the hillforts of the region indicating that they may not have been given up immediately after the Roman conquest of the territories (Todd 1973, 102).

29. The large villa at Llantwit Major (S Glam) is often quoted, although the majority of villas in this area are probably rather less extensive and

wealthy. The non-villa settlement at Whitton (S Glam) may be rather more representative of the typical site of this area.

30. p. 144.

31. G Jobey 1966, 1982a, 1982b; Higham and GD Jones 1983, 1985; Haselgrove 1982; Higham 1982.

32. p. 76.

33. Hogg 1966, 1979.

34. Examples include Llys Brychan (Dyfed) and Abercyfar (Dyfed); see Lloyd Jones 1984, 52.

35. Castle Flemish (Dyfed), Llangynog II (Dyfed), Cwmbrwyn (Dyfed), Trelissy (Dyfed) and Walesland Rath (Dyfed). Wainwright and Lloyd Jones have suggested that these sites represent the romanization of a pre-existing Iron Age form (Wainwright 1972; Lloyd Jones 1984, 52).

36. C Smith 1974, 1977b, figures 1–2.

37. A site of this type has recently been excavated at Cefn Graeanog (Gwyn), where a second-century oval homstead was enlarged and reconstructed as a rectangular enclosure with a number of internal round huts.

38. Sites that have been said to represent small towns or trading centres occur at Seaton (Devon) and Carvossa (Corn), although the nature of both sites is uncertain.

39. Todd 1987, 224.

40. C Thomas 1966; N Johnson and Rose 1982; see Todd 1987 for a recent discussion.

41. Todd 1987, 226.

42. Todd 1987, 224.

43. GD Jones and Walker 1983; GD Jones 1984.

44. Salway 1965, 117–9.

45. Higham and GD Jones 1975, 19.

46. See GD Jones and Walker 1983; GD Jones 1984 and Higham 1986, 177–8 on northern England; and for Wales see Davies 1984.

47. Rivet 1969, 186.

48. p. 116.

49. GD Jones 1984, 89.

50. p. 35.

51. p. 82.

52. Gardner and Savory 1964, 97–8.

CHAPTER 10

1. p. 43–5.
2. p. 50.
3. p. 74.
4. p. 7.
5. p. 37, 45.
6. See p. 8, although for the importance of maternal ties see Herlihy 1985, 36.
7. A small area of land was owned by each individual household, but groups of plots were owned by the extended family as a whole and were regularly redistributed (J Smith 1978a, 172).
8. Garnsey and Saller 1987, 129.
9. J Smith 1978a, 1982.
10. p. 69.
11. p. 22.
12. Macmullen has discussed the apparent evidence for joint ownership and inheritance of property in Roman Syria (1974, 24).
13. In medieval Wales the girdle pattern of settlement appears to have been associated with what GR Jones has titled 'hereditary lands'. The principle of hereditary land involves rights to land passing to male descendants in equal shares. In some areas of south Wales during the medieval period these rights appear to have become invested in a large descent group formed of the male descendants of an ancestor, known as a *gwely*. Within the *gwely* a hereditary owner's share consisted of personal holdings of land probably comprising scattered arable plots, some meadow land and a homestead, and an undivided share of joint land comprising common pasture, waste and woodland (GR Jones 1985, 156).
14. p. 100.
15. p. 131.
16. p. 42.
17. Applebaum 1972, 231.
18. It has been suggested that the slave mode and the subsequent *colonate* system were not dominant to the same degree in Britain as in Italy, Spain and Southern Gaul (Hingley 1984c, based on P Anderson 1974).
19. At Barnsley Park (Glos); Clear Cupboard (Glos); Kingsweston (Glos).
20. Barton Court (Oxon); Holcombe (Devon); Feltwell (Norf); Great Staughton (Cambs); Langton (N Yorks); see DJ Smith 1978.

21. p. 121.
22. Vinogradoff 1905.
23. Hingley 1988.
24. Hallam 1970, 47–8.
25. Salway 1970, 16 and Potter 1981, 129.
26. Potter 1981.
27. Salway 1970, 16.
28. Manning 1972, 239.
29. p. 146.
30. Potter 1981, 85.
31. p. 80.
32. D Miles 1984a, 202.
33. D Miles 1984a, 208.
34. p. 80.
35. The hoard of pewter vessels from the probable aisled house at Weyhill (Hants) (see D Johnston 1978, 74) may also be of relevance to this discussion of feasting and the communal nature of the extended family. It should be noted that a building closely associated with hoards of pewter and bronze bowls at Weeting (Norf) appears from the interim report to represent a rather unusual type of winged hall of only one room.
36. The simple buildings on the two-compound settlement at Overton Down (Wilts) produced painted plaster and a number of bronze objects and coins. The non-villa settlement of Bullock Down (E Susx) has produced quantities of metalwork and coinage.
37. p. 3.

Abbreviations

List of abbreviations used in the Site Index and Bibliography

Agric.Hist.Rev.	Agricultural History Review
Ant.J.	Antiquaries Journal
Arch.Ael.	Archaeologia Aeliana
Arch.Camb.	Archaeologia Cambrensis
Arch.Cant.	Archaeologia Cantiana
Arch.J.	Archaeological Journal
Aufs.Nied.Rom.Welt	Aufstieg und Niedergang der Romischen Welt
BAR	British Archaeological Reports
Berks.Arch.J.	Berkshire Archaeological Journal
Bull.Inst.Arch.Lond.	Bulletin of the Institute of Archaeology of London
Bull.Board Celtic Stud.	Bulletin of the Board of Celtic Studies
Carm.Ant.	The Carmarthen Antiquary
CBA	Council for British Archaeology
Cornish Arch.	Cornish Archaeology
Derby.Arch.J.	Derbyshire Archaeological Journal
Devon Arch.J.	Devon Archaeological Journal
Dorset Nat.Hist.Arch.Soc.	Dorset Natural History and Archaeological Society
Durham Arch.J.	Durham Archaeological Journal
East Anglian Arch.	East Anglian Archaeological Report
East Riding Arch.	East Riding Archaeologist
Essex Arch.	Essex Archaeology
Essex Arch.Hist.	Essex Archaeology and History
HBMC	Historic Buildings and Monuments Commission
HMSO	Her Majesty's Stationery Office
JBAA	Journal of the British Archaeological Association
JRS	Journal of Roman Studies
Med.Arch.	Medieval Archaeology
Norfolk Arch.	Norfolk Archaeology
Northants.Arch.	Northamptonshire Archaeology
OJA	Oxford Journal of Archaeology
OS	Ordnance Survey

Proc.Devon Arch.Soc.	Proceedings of the Devon Archaeological Society
Proc.Prehist.Soc.	Proceedings of the Prehistoric Society
Proc.Hants.Field Club	Proceedings of the Hampshire Field Club
Proc.Somer.Arch.Nat.Hist.Soc.	Proceedings of the Somersetshire Archaeological and Natural History Society
Rom. Brit.	*See* Britannia
RCAMCE	Royal Commission on the Ancient Monuments and Constructions of England
RCAHMWM	Royal Commission on Ancient and Historical Monuments in Wales and Monmouth
RCHME	Royal Commission on Historical Monuments of England
Records Bucks.	Records of Buckinghamshire
SMR	Sites and Monuments Record for given county
Staffs.Rec.Soc.	Staffordshire Records Society
Surrey Arch.Coll.	Surrey Archaeological Collection
Susx.Arch.Coll.	Sussex Archaeological Collection
Trans.Archit.Arch.Soc.Durham Northum	Transactions of the Architectural and Archaeological Society of Durham and Northumberland
Trans.Birmingham Warw.Arch.Soc.	Transactions of the Birmingham and Warwickshire Archaeological Society
Trans.Bristol Glos.Arch.Soc.	Transactions of the Bristol and Gloucestershire Archaeological Society
Trans.Leic.Arch.Hist.Soc.	Transactions of the Leicestershire Archaeological and Historical Society
Trans.Royal Hist.Soc.	Transactions of the Royal Historical Society
Trans.South Staffs.Arch.Hist.Soc.	Transactions of the South Staffordshire Archaeology and History Society
Trans.Thornton Soc.Notts.	Transactions of the Thornton Society of Nottinghamshire
Trans.Wool.Nat.Field Club	Transactions of the Woolhope Naturalists' Field Club
VCH	Victoria County History
Wilts.Arch.Mag.	Wiltshire Archaeological and Natural History Society

Index of Romano-British sites mentioned in the text

The references that are given in this index are to the sources that were consulted and are not all to primary reports on sites.

List of abbreviations used for counties of England and Wales:

BEDS	Bedfordshire	LEIC	Leicestershire
BERKS	Berkshire	LINCS	Lincolnshire
BUCKS	Buckinghamshire	NORTHANTS	Northamptonshire
CAMBS	Cambridgeshire	NORF	Norfolk
CHES	Cheshire	NORTHUM	Northumberland
CORN	Cornwall	NOTTS	Nottinghamshire
CUMBR	Cumbria	N YORKS	North Yorkshire
DERBY	Derbyshire	OXON	Oxfordshire
E SUSX	East Sussex	SALOP	Shropshire
GLOS	Gloucestershire	S GLAM	South Glamorgan
GWYN	Gwynedd	SOMER	Somerset
HANTS	Hampshire	STAFFS	Staffordshire
HERE & WORC	Hereford and Worcestershire	SUFF	Suffolk
		WARW	Warwickshire
HERTS	Hertfordshire	WILTS	Wiltshire
HUMBS	Humberside	W SUSX	West Sussex
I of W	Isle of Wight		

Site	County	Reference
ABERCYFAR	(DYFED)	Lloyd Jones 1984, 52.
ABINGDON	(OXON)	R Thomas unpublished.
ACTON SCOTT	(SALOP)	Acton 1845.
ALCESTER	(WARW)	Booth 1980; R Brit in 1985, 393–5.
ALCHESTER	(OXON)	Rowley 1975.
ANCASTER	(LINCS)	Todd 1973.
ANGMERING	(W SUSX)	Black 1987.
APPLEFORD	(OXON)	Hinchliffe and R Thomas 1980.
ASHTON	(NORTHANTS)	Hadman and Upex 1975; Hadman 1984.
ASTHALL	(OXON)	K Rodwell (ed) 1975, 13.
ATWOOD	(SURREY)	Little 1964.
ATWORTH	(WILTS)	Griffiths 1982, 49–51.
AUGHERTREE FELL	(CUMBR)	Higham 1978, figure 16.6.
BALDOCK	(HERTS)	Stead and Rigby 1986.
BANCROFT	(BUCKS)	Mynard 1987; R Brit in 1986, 327.
BARNSLEY PARK	(GLOS)	Webster and L Smith 1982; J Smith 1985; Webster and L Smith 1987.

Site	County	Reference
BARTON COURT	(OXON)	D Miles 1984b.
BATH	(AVON)	Cunliffe and Davenport 1985.
BEADLAM	(N YORKS)	R Brit in 1969, 277–9.
BECKFORD	(HERE & WORC)	Britnell 1974.
BELLING LAW	(NORTHUM)	G Jobey 1977.
BIGNOR	(W SUSX)	Frere 1982; Applebaum 1975.
BILLERICAY	(ESSEX)	W Rodwell 1975, figure 3.
BINCHESTER	(DURHAM)	R Jones pers com.
BOURTON GROUNDS	(BUCKS)	A Johnson 1975.
BOURTON-ON-THE-WATER	(GLOS)	RCHME 1976, 17–9.
BOX	(WILTS)	Griffiths 1982, 51.
BOXMOOR	(HERTS)	Neal 1970.
BRADING	(I of W)	Haverfield 1900, 313–6.
BRADLEY HILL	(SOMER)	Leech 1981.
BRAILES	(WARW)	Hingley 1987b.
BRAINTREE	(ESSEX)	Drury 1976.
BRAMPTON	(NORF)	Knowles 1977.
BRAUGHING	(HERTS)	Partridge 1975; 1981.
BREASTON	(DERBY)	Todd 1973, figure 26.
BRIXWORTH	(NORTHANTS)	R Brit in 1971, 322–3.
BROCKWORTH	(GLOS)	Rawes 1981.
BULLOCK DOWN	(E SUSX)	Rudling 1982.
CAE METTA	(GWYN)	R Brit in 1973, 398.
CALLOW HILL	(OXON)	N Thomas 1957.
CAMBRIDGE	(CAMBS)	Burnham 1987, 176.
CAMERTON	(AVON)	Todd 1976, 108–12.
CARISBROOKE	(I of W)	Haverfield 1900, 316–7.
CARLISLE	(CUMBR)	Higham and GD Jones 1985.
CARN EUNY	(CORN)	Christie 1978.
CARSINGTON	(DERBY)	Ling and Courtney 1981.
CARVOSSA	(CORN)	Carlyton 1987.
CASTLE FLEMISH	(DYFED)	Wheeler 1923.
CASTLE GOTHA	(CORN)	Saunders and Harris 1982.
CATSGORE	(SOMER)	Leech 1982.
CATTERICK	(N YORKS)	Burnham 1987, figure 7.
CEFN GRAEANOG	(GWYN)	R Brit in 1977, 406–7.
CHALTON	(HANTS)	Cunliffe 1973a.
CHARLBURY	(OXON)	Copeland 1982.
CHARTERHOUSE-ON-MENDIP	(AVON)	Elkington 1976.
CHEDWORTH	(GLOS)	J Smith 1978a, figure 54; Webster 1983.
CHELMSFORD	(ESSEX)	Drury 1975.
CHESTER	(CHES)	Mason 1987.
CHESTERHOLM	(NORTHUM)	Bidwell 1985.
CHESTERTON-ON-FOSSE	(WARW)	Crickmore 1984b.
CHEW STOKE	(AVON)	Applebaum 1972, 27.

Index of Romano-British sites mentioned in the text

Site	County	Reference
CHIGNALL ST JAMES	(ESSEX)	Potter 1986, figure 54.
CHISENBURY WARREN	(WILTS)	Bowen and Fowler 1966, 50–2.
CHITTERNE DOWN	(WILTS)	R Brit in 1983, 322.
CHURCH LAWFORD	(WARW)	Warwickshire SMR PRN 4972.
CHURCHOVER	(WARW)	Crickmore 1984b.
CHYSAUSTER	(CORN)	Hencken 1933.
CLANVILLE	(HANTS)	Haverfield 1900, 295–7.
CLAYDON PIKE	(GLOS)	D Miles 1984a.
CLAY LANE	(NORTHANTS)	Windell 1983.
CLEAR CUPBOARD	(GLOS)	Gascoigne 1969.
COLLYWESTON	(NORTHANTS)	Knocker 1965.
COMBE DOWN	(AVON)	Applebaum 1972, 29.
COMBLEY	(I of W)	R Brit in 1975, 364–6.
CORBRIDGE	(NORTHUM)	Salway 1965, figure 5.
COX GREEN	(BERKS)	Bennett 1963.
CREECH	(DORSET)	Todd 1978, 203.
CROSBY GARRETT	(CUMBR)	RCHME 1936, 75.
CROSBY RAVENSWORTH	(CUMBR)	RCHME 1936, 84–5.
CWMBRWYN	(DYFED)	Ward 1907.
DARENTH	(KENT)	Philp 1984.
DEANSHANGER	(NORTHANTS)	R Brit in 1972, 294.
DIN LLIGWY	(GWYN)	Hogg 1975.
DINORBEN	(CLWYD)	Gardner and Savory 1964.
DITCHES	(GLOS)	Trow and James 1985.
DITCHLEY	(OXON)	Radford 1936; Broadribb, Hands and Walker 1968–78.
DORCHESTER-ON-THAMES	(OXON)	Rowley 1975; Frere 1984a.
DORN	(GLOS)	RCHME 1976, 12–13.
DOUBSTEAD	(NORTHUM)	G Jobey 1982b.
DOWNTON	(WILTS)	Rahtz 1963.
DRAGONBY	(HUMBS)	May 1970.
DROITWICH	(HERE & WORC)	Crickmore 1984b.
DROPSHORT	(BUCKS)	Mynard 1987, 10–11.
DUNSTON'S CLUMP	(NOTTS)	R Brit in 1981, 356–8.
EASTBOURNE	(E SUSX)	Black 1987.
EAST BRIDGEFORD	(NOTTS)	Todd 1969.
EAST GRIMSTEAD	(WILTS)	J Smith 1963, 29.
ECCLES	(KENT)	Detsicas 1983, 120–6.
ENGLETON	(STAFFS)	Ashcroft 1938.
FARNINGHAM	(KENT)	Meates 1973.
FAVERSHAM	(KENT)	Philp 1968.
FAWLER	(OXON)	M Taylor 1939b, 318–9.

Site	County	Reference
FELTWELL	(NORF)	Gurney 1986.
FISHBOURNE	(W SUSX)	Cunliffe 1971.
FISHERWICK	(STAFFS)	H Miles 1969.
FOLKESTONE	(KENT)	Winbolt 1926.
FORCEGARTH PASTURE	(DURHAM)	Fairless and Coggins 1980, 1986.
FOTHERINGHAY	(NORTHANTS)	Branigan 1985, figure 34.
FRILFORD	(OXON)	Hingley 1985a.
FRILFORD VILLA	(OXON)	Hingley, work in progress.
FROCESTER COURT	(GLOS)	Gracie 1970.
GADEBRIDGE	(HERTS)	Neal 1974.
GARDEN HILL	(E SUSX)	Money 1977.
GARFORD VILLA	(OXON)	Hingley, work in progress.
GATCOMBE	(SOMER)	Branigan 1977a.
GAYTON THORPE	(NORF)	Atkinson 1926.
GODMANCHESTER	(CAMBS)	H Green 1975.
GOLDHERRING	(CORN)	Guthrie 1969.
GORHAMBURY	(HERTS)	Neal 1978; Selkirk 1983.
GOSBECK	(ESSEX)	Crummy 1980.
GRAMBLA	(CORN)	Saunders 1972.
GRANDFORD	(CAMBS)	Potter 1981.
GREAT CASTERTON	(LEIC)	Todd 1973, 68–9.
GREAT CHESTERFORD	(ESSEX)	R Brit in 1980, 348–50.
GREAT DUNMOW	(ESSEX)	Burnham 1987, 176.
GREAT LEMHILL FARM	(GLOS)	RCHME 1976, 75.
GREAT STAUGHTON	(CAMBS)	R Brit in 1959, 224–5.
GREAVES ASH	(NORTHUM)	G Jobey 1964, figure 6.
GWITHIAN	(CORN)	Fowler 1962.
HALSTEAD	(ESSEX)	W Rodwell 1975, figure 1.
HALSTOCK	(DORSET)	R Brit in 1982, 326–8.
HAMBLEDEN	(BUCKS)	Cocks 1921.
HAM HILL	(SOMER)	Branigan 1977b, 39–40.
HIBALDSTOW	(HUMBS)	R Brit in 1976, 389; RF Smith 1987.
HIGHWORTH	(WILTS)	Unpublished information.
HOCKWOLD-CUM-WILTON	(NORF)	C Phillips (ed) 1970, 244; Gurney 1986.
HOLCOMBE	(DEVON)	Pollard 1974.
HOLME HOUSE	(N YORKS)	R Brit in 1970, 251–2.
HOUSESTEADS	(NORTHUM)	Salway 1965, 84–91.
HUNTSHAM	(HERE & WORC)	Bridgewater 1962; R Brit in 1964, 208.
ILCHESTER	(SOMER)	Leech 1982.
INGLEBY BARWICK	(DURHAM)	Heslop 1984.

Index of Romano-British sites mentioned in the text 203

Site	County	Reference
IPSWICH	(SUFF)	R Rodwell (ed) 1975, figure 1.
IRCHESTER	(NORTHANTS)	Branigan 1985, 89.
ISLIP	(OXON)	D Miles 1982, figure 8.
IWERNE	(DORSET)	Hawkes 1947.
KELVEDON	(ESSEX)	R Brit in 1973, 442; 1981, 372.
KENCHESTER	(HERE & WORC)	Wilmott 1980.
KENNEL HALL KNOWE	(NORTHUM)	G Jobey 1978.
KEYNSHAM	(AVON)	Bulleid and Horne 1926.
KINGSCOTE	(GLOS)	RCHME 1976, 70–3.
KINGSWESTON	(GLOS)	Boon 1950.
KIRK SINK	(N YORKS)	R Brit in 1975, 317–8.
LANGFORD	(OXON)	Oxfordshire SMR PRN 3120.
LANGTON	(N YORKS)	Corder and Kirk 1932.
LIPPEN WOOD	(HANTS)	J Smith 1963, 30.
LITTLEBURY GREEN	(ESSEX)	Williamson 1984.
LITTLECOTE PARK	(WILTS)	R Brit in 1981, 387–8.
LLANGYNOG II	(DYFED)	Avent 1973.
LLANTWIT MAJOR	(S GLAM)	Hogg 1974.
LLYS BRYCHAN	(DYFED)	Jarrett 1963.
LOCKINGTON	(LEIC)	Clay 1984.
LOCKLEYS	(HERTS)	Ward Perkins 1938.
LONG WITTENHAM	(OXON)	Gray 1977.
LULLINGSTONE	(KENT)	Meates 1979.
LYE HOLE	(SOMER)	Fowler 1975, figure 8:4.
LYMPNE	(KENT)	Cunliffe 1980.
MADDLE FARM	(BERKS)	Gaffney, Gaffney and Tingle 1985.
MANCETTER	(WARW)	Crickmore 1984b.
MANSFIELD WOODHOUSE	(NOTTS)	Oswald 1949.
MARSHFIELD	(GLOS)	R Brit in 1982, 317; J Smith 1987.
MIDDLE GUNNAR PEAK	(NORTHUM)	I Jobey 1981.
MILEOAK	(NORTHANTS)	C Green and Draper 1978.
NEATHAM	(HANTS)	Millett and Graham 1986.
NETHER DENTON	(CUMBR)	Maxwell and Wilson 1987, figure 4.
NEWTON KYME	(N YORKS)	GD Jones 1984, figure 2.
NORFOLK STREET	(LEIC)	R Brit in 1980, 337–8.
NORTH LEIGH	(OXON)	Richmond 1969, figure 2:4.
NORTH WARNBOROUGH	(HANTS)	Liddell 1931; J Smith 1963; Neal 1982.
NORTH WRAXHALL	(WILTS)	J Jackson 1862.
NORTON DISNEY	(LINCS)	Oswald and Buxton 1937.

Site	County	Reference
OAKLANDS FARM	(OXON)	Hingley unpublished.
ODELL	(BEDS)	Simco 1984, 24–5.
OLD BRAMPTON	(CUMBR)	Higham 1982, figure 17.
OLD CARLISLE	(CUMBR)	GD Jones 1984, figure 1.
OVERSTONE	(NORTHANTS)	J Williams 1976.
OVERTON DOWN	(WILTS)	Fowler 1967.
PARC GELLI	(GWYN)	RCAHMWM 1956, figure 107.
PARK BROW	(W SUSX)	Wolseley and RA Smith 1926–7.
PARK STREET	(HERTS)	O'Neil 1945.
PENRITH	(CUMBR)	Higham and GD Jones 1983.
PIERCEBRIDGE	(DURHAM)	GD Jones 1984, plate III.
PITNEY	(SOMER)	Haverfield 1906, 326–8.
POOLE'S CAVERN	(DERBY)	Bramwell et al 1983.
PORTISHEAD	(AVON)	R Brit in 1971, 343–4.
QUINTON	(NORTHANTS)	R Brit in 1971, 322, 4.
RADWINTER	(ESSEX)	W Rodwell 1975, figure 1.
RAPSLEY	(SURREY)	Hanworth 1968.
RINGSTEAD	(NORTHANTS)	D Jackson 1980.
RISEHOW	(CUMBR)	Higham 1982, figure 17.
RIVENHALL	(ESSEX)	W Rodwell and K Rodwell 1985.
ROCHESTER	(KENT)	Detsicas 1983.
ROCK	(I of W)	R Brit in 1975, 369.
ROCKBOURNE	(HANTS)	RCHME 1983.
RODMARTON	(GLOS)	RCHME 1976, 98–9.
ROTHERLEY DOWN	(WILTS)	Grinsell 1957, 38–40.
ROYSTONE GRANGE	(DERBY)	Hodges and Wildgoose 1981.
RUDSTON	(HUMBS)	Stead 1980.
SANSOM'S PLATT	(OXON)	Chambers 1978.
SCARS FARM	(SOMER)	Fowler 1975, figure 8:3.
SCOLE	(NORF)	Rogerson 1977.
SEA MILLS	(AVON)	Ellis 1987.
SEATON	(DEVON)	H Miles 1977; Silvester 1984.
SHAKENOAK	(OXON)	Broadribb, Hands and Walker 1968–1978.
SHARPSTONES HILL	(SALOP)	Webster 1975a, figure 39.
SHIREBROOK	(DERBY)	Kay 1951.
SILLOTH FARM	(CUMBR)	Higham and GD Jones 1983.
SOMERFORD KEYNES	(GLOS)	S Palmer unpublished.
SOMERSHAM	(CAMBS)	R Brit in 1977, 447–8.
SOUTHWICK	(W SUSX)	Black 1987, figure 43.
SPARSHOLT	(HANTS)	D Johnston 1978, figure 25.
SPOONLEY WOOD	(GLOS)	RCHME 1976, 113–4.

Index of Romano-British sites mentioned in the text

Site	County	Reference
SPRINGHEAD	(KENT)	Harker 1980.
STANSTEAD	(ESSEX)	Essex Archaeology 1987, no 4.
STANWICK	(NORTHANTS)	R Brit in 1985, 396–8.
STAR	(SOMER)	Barton 1963.
STAUNTON	(NOTTS)	Todd 1975.
STONEA	(CAMBS)	Potter and D Jackson 1984.
STOKE ASH	(SUFF)	Applebaum 1972, 276.
STOKE GABRIEL	(DEVON)	Masson Phillips 1966.
STONESFIELD	(OXON)	M Taylor 1939b, 315–6.
STROUD	(HANTS)	A Williams 1909.
STUDLAND	(DORSET)	Field 1965.
SWALCLIFFE	(OXON)	K Rodwell (ed) 1975, 14.
TARRANT HINTON	(DORSET)	R Brit in 1981, 386–7.
THORNHILL FARM	(GLOS)	D Miles unpublished.
THORPLANDS	(NORTHANTS)	Hunter and Mynard 1977.
THRUXTON	(HANTS)	Black 1987, 80–81.
TIDDINGTON	(WARW)	N Palmer 1982.
TOLLARD ROYAL	(WILTS)	Wainwright 1968.
TOPSHAM	(DEVON)	Jarvis and Maxfield 1975.
TOWCESTER	(NORTHANTS)	A Brown and Alexander 1982; A Brown, Woodfield and Mynard 1983.
TOWER KNOWE	(NORTHUM)	G Jobey 1973.
TRAWSCOED	(DYFED)	Davies 1984, figure 2.
TREGONNING	(CORN)	N Johnson and Rose 1982, figure 12:10.
TRELISSEY	(DYFED)	W Thomas and Walker 1953.
TRETHURGY	(CORN)	H Miles and T Miles 1973.
TY MAWR	(GWYN)	C Smith 1984.
UPTON ST LEONARDS	(GLOS)	R Brit in 1977, 457–8.
WALESLAND RATH	(DYFED)	Wainwright 1971.
WALL	(STAFFS)	Crickmore 1984b.
WANBOROUGH	(WILTS)	A Anderson and Wacher 1980.
WANTAGE	(OXON)	K Rodwell (ed) 1975.
WASPERTON	(WARW)	G Crawford unpublished.
WATER NEWTON/ CASTOR	(CAMBS)	Wild 1974; Dannell 1974; Mackreth 1979.
WEETING	(NORF)	R Brit in 1979, 375; Gregory 1982.
WEST DEAN	(WILTS)	J Smith 1963, 30.
WETWANG/ GARTON SLACK	(HUMBS)	Dent 1983a, 1983b.
WEYHILL	(HANTS)	D Johnston 1978, 74.
WHARRAM GRANGE	(N YORKS)	Hayfield 1987.
WHITMINSTER	(GLOS)	Leech 1976, 156.
WHITTON	(S GLAM)	Jarrett and Wrathmell 1981.
WHITWELL	(LEIC)	Todd 1981.

Site	County	Reference
WIGGONHOLT	(W SUSX)	Applebaum 1972, 277; Black 1987, 63.
WINGHAM	(KENT)	Applebaum 1972, 277.
WINTERTON	(HUMBS)	Goodburn 1978.
WITCOMBE	(GLOS)	Clifford 1954; RCHME 1976, 60–1.
WITHINGTON	(GLOS)	Finberg 1964.
WOODCHESTER	(GLOS)	G Clarke 1982.
WOODCUTS	(DORSET)	Hawkes 1947.
WYCOMB	(GLOS)	RCHME 1976, 125–6.
WYMBUSH	(BUCKS)	Mynard 1987.

Bibliography

ACTON, F.S. 1846: 'Description of a Roman Villa discovered at Acton Scott, near Church Stretton, in Shropshire, in 1817 . . .', *Archaeologia*, 31, 339–45.

ANDERSON, A.S. and WACHER, J.S. 1980: 'Excavations at Wanborough, Wiltshire: An Interim Report', *Britannia*, 11, 115–26.

ANDERSON, P. 1974: *Passages from Antiquity to Feudalism* (London).

APPLEBAUM, S. 1963: 'The Pattern of Settlement in Roman Britain', *Agric.Hist.Rev.*, 11, 1–14.

APPLEBAUM, S. 1972: 'Roman Britain', in Finberg, H. (eds.) 1972, 3–270.

APPLEBAUM, S. 1975: 'Some observations on the Economy of the Roman Villa at Bignor, Sussex', *Britannia*, 6, 118–32.

ASHCROFT, D. 1938: 'Report on the Roman villa at Engleton, near Brewood', *Staffs.Rec.Soc.*, 1938, 267–93.

ATKINSON, D. 1926: 'The Roman Villa of Gayton Thorpe', *Norfolk Arch.*, 23, 166–209.

AVENT, R. 1973: 'Excavations at Llangynog II 1972', *Carm.Ant.*, 9, 33–52.

BARTON, K.J. 1963: 'Star Roman Villa, Shipham, Somerset', *Proc.Somer.Arch. Nat.Hist.Soc.*, 108, 45–93.

BEDWIN, O.R. 1978: 'Iron Age Sussex – The Downs and the Coastal Plain', in Drewett, P. (ed.) 1978, 41–51.

BEDWIN, O.R. and PITTS, M.W. 1978: 'The Excavation of an Iron Age Settlement at North Bersted, Bognor Regis, West Sussex', *Sussex Arch.Coll.*, 116, 293–346.

BENNETT, C.M. 1963: 'Cox Green Roman Villa', *Berks.Arch.J.*, 60, 62–91.

BENSON, D. and MILES, D. 1974: *The Upper Thames Valley: An Archaeological Survey of the River Gravels* (Oxford).

BERSU, G. 1940: 'Excavations at Little Woodbury, Wiltshire, Part 1: The Settlement as revealed by excavation', *Proc.Prehist.Soc.*, 6, 30–111.

BIDWELL, P.T. 1985: *The Roman Fort of Vindolanda* (Gloucester).

BLACK, E.W. 1987: *The Roman Villas of South-East England* (Oxford).

BLAGG, T.F.C. and KING, A.C. (eds.) 1984: *Military and Civilian in Roman Britain: Cultural Relationships in a Frontier Province* (Oxford).

BOON, G.C. 1950: 'The Roman Villa in Kingsweston Park (Lawrence Weston Estate), Gloucestershire', *Trans.Bristol.Glos.Arch.Soc.*, 69, 5–58.

BOOTH, P.M. 1980: *Roman Alcester* (Warwick).

BOWDEN, M. and MCOMISH, D. 1987: 'The Required Barrier', *Scottish Archaeological Review*, 4, 76–84.

BOWEN, H.C. and FOWLER, P.J. 1966: 'Romano-British Rural Settlements in Dorset and Wiltshire', in Thomas, C. (ed.) 1966, 43–67.

BOWEN, H.C. and FOWLER, P.J. (eds.) 1978: *Early Land Allotment in the British Isles* (Oxford).

BRAMWELL D., DALTON, K., DRINKWATER, J.F., LORIMER, K.L. and MACKRETH, D.F. 1983: 'Excavations at Poole's Cavern, Buxton: An Interim Report', *Derby.Arch.J.*, 103, 47–74.

BRANDT, R. and SLOFSTRA, J. (eds.) 1983: *Roman and Native in the Low Countries* (Oxford).

BRANIGAN, K. 1976: 'Villa Settlement in the West Country', in Branigan, K. and Fowler P. (eds.) 1976, 120–41.

BRANIGAN, K. 1977a: *Gatcombe Roman Villa* (Oxford).

BRANIGAN, K 1977b: *The Roman Villa in South-West England* (Bradford-on-Avon).

BRANIGAN, K. 1985: *The Catuvellauni* (Gloucester).

BRANIGAN, K. and FOWLER, P.J. (eds.) 1976: *The Roman West Country: Classical Culture and Celtic Society* (London).

BRIDGEWATER, N.P. 1962: 'The Huntsham Roman Villa: First Report', *Trans.Wool.Nat.Field Club*, 37, 179–91.

BRIGGS, G., COOK, J. and ROWLEY, T. (eds.) 1986: *The Archaeology of the Oxford Region* (Oxford).

BRITNELL, W. 1974: 'Beckford', *Current Archaeology*, 4, 293–7.

BRODRIBB, A.C.C., HANDS, A.R. and WALKER, D.R. 1968–78: *Excavations at Shakenoak Farm, Near Wilcote, Oxon, Parts 1–5* (Oxford).

BROWN, A.E. and ALEXANDER, J.A. 1982: 'Excavations at Towcester 1954: the Grammar School site', *Northants.Arch.*, 17, 24–59.

BROWN, A.E., WOODFIELD, C. and MAYNARD, D.C. 1983: 'Excavations at Towcester, Northamptonshire: the Alchester road suburb', *Northants.Arch.*, 18, 43–140.

BROWN, F. and TAYLOR, C.C. 1978: 'Settlement and Land Use in Northamptonshire: a comparison between the Iron Age and the Middle Ages', in Cunliffe, B. and Rowley, T. (eds.) 1978, 77–90.

BROWN, R.J. 1982: *English Farmhouses* (London).

BRUSH, J.E. and BRACEY, H.E. 1955: 'Rural service centres in southwestern Wisconsin and southern England', *Geographical Review*, 45, 559–69.

BULLEID, A. and HORNE, D.E. 1926: 'The Roman House at Keynsham, Somerset', *Archaeologia*, 75, 109–38.

BURNHAM, B. 1986: 'The Origins of Romano-British Small Towns', *OJA*, 5, 185–203.

BURNHAM, B. 1987: 'The Morphology of Romano-British "Small Towns"', *Arch.J.*, 144, 156–90.

BURNHAM, B. and JOHNSON, H. 1979: 'Introduction', in Burnham, B. and Johnson, H. (eds.) 1979, 1–8.

BURNHAM, B. and JOHNSON, H. (eds.) 1979: *Invasion and Response: The Case of Roman Britain* (Oxford).

CARLYTON, P.M. 1987: 'Finds from the Earthwork at Carvossa, Probus', *Cornish Arch.*, 26, 103–43.

CHAMBERS, R.A. 1978: 'The Archaeology of the Charlbury to Arncott Gas Pipeline, 1972', *Oxoniensia*, 43, 40–47.

CHANG, K.C. (ed.) 1968: *Settlement Archaeology* (California).

CHAPMAN, J.C. and MYTUM, H.C. (eds.) 1983: *Settlement in Northern Britain 100 BC – AD 1000* (Oxford).

CHARLES-EDWARDS, T.M. 1972: 'Kinship, Status and the origin of the Hide', *Past and Present*, 56, 3–33.

CHERRY, J.F., GAMBLE, C. and SHENNAN, S. (eds.) 1978: *Sampling in Contemporary British Archaeology* (Oxford).

CHRISTIE, P.M.L. 1978: 'The excavations of an Iron Age souterrain and settlement at Carn Euny, Sancreed, Cornwall', *Proc.Prehist.Soc.*, 44, 309–433.

CLACK, P. and HASELGROVE, S. (eds.) 1982: *Rural Settlement in the Roman North* (Durham).

CLARKE, D.L. 1972: 'A provisional model of an Iron Age society and its settlement system', in Clarke, D.L. (ed.) 1972, 801–69.

CLARKE, D.L. (ed.) 1972: *Models in Archaeology* (London).

CLARKE, G. 1982: 'The Roman Villa at Woodchester', *Britannia*, 13, 197–228.

CLAY, P. 1984: 'A Survey of two Cropmark Sites in Lockington-Hemington Parish, Leicestershire', *Trans.Leic.Arch.Hist.Soc.*, 59, 17–26.

CLIFFORD, E.M. 1954: 'The Roman Villa, Witcombe', *Trans.Bristol Glos.Arch.Soc.*, 73, 5–69.

COCKS, A.H. 1921: 'A Romano-British Homestead, in the Hambleden Valley, Bucks', *Archaeologia*, 71, 141–98.

COLLINGWOOD, R.G. 1923: *Roman Britain* (Oxford).

COLLINGWOOD, R.G. and MYRES, J.N.L. 1937: *Roman Britain and the English Settlements* (Oxford).

COLLINGWOOD, R.G. and RICHMOND, I. 1969: *The Archaeology of Roman Britain* (London).

COLLIS, J. (ed.) 1977: *The Iron Age in Britain: A Review* (Sheffield).

COOK, S.F. and HEIZER, R.F. 1968: 'Relationships among houses, settlement areas and population in aboriginal California', in Chang, K.C. (ed.) 1968, 79–116.

COPELAND, T. 1982: 'Charlbury with Shorthampton', *CBA Group 9 Newsletter*, 12, 120–5.

CORDER, P. and KIRK, J.L. 1932: *A Roman Villa at Langton, near Malton, East Yorkshire* (Oxford).

CRAWFORD, D.J. 1976: 'Imperial Estates', in Finley, M.I. (ed.) 1976, 35–70.

CRAWFORD, M. 1970: 'Money and Exchange in the Roman World', *JRS*, 60, 40–8.

CRICKMORE, J. 1984a: *Romano-British Urban Defences* (Oxford).

CRICKMORE, J. 1984b: *Romano-British Urban Settlement in the West Midlands* (Oxford).

CRUMMY, P. 1980: 'The Temples of Roman Colchester', in Rodwell, W. (ed.) 1980, 243–83.

CUNLIFFE, B.W. 1971: *Excavations at Fishbourne, 1961–69* (Oxford).

CUNLIFFE, B.W. 1973a: 'Chalton, Hants: The Evolution of a Landscape', *Ant. J.*, 53, 173–90.

CUNLIFFE, B.W. 1973b: *The Regni* (London).

CUNLIFFE, B.W. 1976a: 'A Romano-British village at Chalton, Hants', *Proc.Hants.Field Club*, 33, 45–67.

CUNLIFFE, B.W. 1978a: *Iron Age Communities in Britain* (London).

CUNLIFFE, B.W. 1978b: 'Settlement and Population in the British Iron Age: some facts, figures and fantasies', in Cunliffe, B.W. and Rowley, T. (eds.) 1978, 3–24.

CUNLIFFE, B.W. 1980: 'Excavations at the Roman Fort at Lympne, Kent 1976–78', *Britannia*, 11, 227–88.

CUNLIFFE, B.W. 1984: 'Images of Britannia', *Antiquity*, 58, 175–8.

CUNLIFFE, B.W. and DAVENPORT, P. 1985: *The Temple of Sulis Minerva at Bath: Volume 1 The Site* (Oxford).

CUNLIFFE, B.W. and MILES, D. (eds.) 1984: *Aspects of the Iron Age in Central Southern Britain* (Oxford).

CUNLIFFE, B.W. and ROWLEY, T. (eds.) 1978: *Lowland Iron Age Communities in Europe* (Oxford).

DALTON, G. (ed.) 1979: *Research in Economic Anthropology, Volume 2* (London).

DANNELL, G. 1974: 'Roman Industry in Normangate Field, Castor', *Durobrivae*, 2, 7-9.

DAVIES, J.L. 1984: 'Soldiers, peasants and markets in Wales and the Marches', in Blagg, T.F.C. and King, A.C. (eds.) 1984, 93-127.

DENT, J.S. 1983a: 'The Impact of Roman Rule on Native Society in the Territory of the Parisi', *Britannia*, 14, 35-44.

DENT, J.S. 1983b: 'A Summary of the excavations carried out in Garton Slack and Wetwang Slack 1964-80', *East Riding Arch.*, 7, 1-13.

DETSICAS, A. 1983: *The Cantiaci* (Gloucester).

DREWETT, P.L. 1978? 'Field Systems and Land Allotment in Sussex, 3rd Millennium BC to 4th century AD', in Bowen, H.C. and Fowler, P.J. (eds.) 1978, 67-80.

DREWETT, P.L. (ed.) 1978: *Archaeology in Sussex to AD 1500* (London).

DRINKWATER, J.F. 1983: *Roman Gaul* (London).

DRURY, P.J. 1975: 'Chelmsford', in Rodwell, W. and Rowley, T. (eds.) 1975, 159-74.

DRURY, P.J. 1976: 'Braintree: Excavations and Research 1971-76', *Essex Arch.Hist.*, 8, 1-143.

DRURY, P.J. 1980: 'Non-Classical Religious Buildings in Iron Age and Roman Britain: A Review', in Rodwell, W. (ed.) 1980, 45-78.

DRURY, P.J. (ed.) 1982: *Structural Reconstruction: Approaches to the interpretation of the excavated remains of buildings* (Oxford).

DUNCAN-JONES, R. 1974: *The Economy of the Roman Empire* (Cambridge).

DUNCAN-JONES, R. 1976: 'Some Configurations of Landholding in the Roman Empire', in Finley, M.I. (ed.) 1976, 7-24.

DUNNETT, R. 1975: *The Trinovantes* (London).

ELKINGTON, H.D.H. 1976: 'The Mendip Lead Industry', in Branigan, K. and Fowler, P.J. (eds.) 1976, 183-97.

ELLIS, P.J. 1984: *Catsgore 1979, Further Excavation of the Romano-British Village* (Gloucester).

ELLIS, P.J. 1987: 'Sea Mills, Bristol: The 1965-1968 excavations in the Roman Town of Abonae', *Trans.Bristol Glos.Arch.Soc.*, 105, 15-108.

ESSEX ARCHAEOLOGY 1987: 'Stanstead Airport Catering Building', in *Essex Arch.*, 4, p. iv (Essex County Council Pamphlet).

FAIRLESS, K.G. and COGGINS, D. 1980: 'Excavations at the Early Settlement Site of Forcegarth Pasture North, 1972–74', *Trans.Archit.Arch.Soc.Durham Northum*, 5, 31–8.

FAIRLESS, K.G. and COGGINS, D. 1986: 'Excavations at the Early Settlement Site of Forcegarth Pasture South, 1974–5', *Durham Arch.J.*, 2, 25–39.

FIELD, N.H. 1965: 'Romano-British Settlement at Studland, Dorset', *Dorset Nat.Hist.Arch.Soc.*, 87, 142–207.

FINBERG, H.P.R. 1964: *Lucerna. Studies of some problems in the early history of England* (London).

FINBERG, H.P.R. (ed.) 1972: *The Agrarian History of England and Wales I:II (AD 43–1042)* (Cambridge).

FINLEY, M.I. (ed.) 1976: *Studies in Roman Property* (London).

FOWLER, P.J. 1962: 'A Native Homestead of the Roman Period at Porth Godrevy, Gwithian', *Cornish Arch.*, 1, 17–60.

FOWLER, P.J. 1967: 'The Archaeology of Fyfield and Overton Downs, Wiltshire: Third interim report', *Wilts.Arch.Mag.*, 62, 16–33.

FOWLER, P.J. 1975: 'Continuity in the Landscape? Some local archaeology in Wiltshire, Somerset and Gloucestershire', in Fowler, P.J. (ed.) 1975, 121–37.

FOWLER, P.J. 1976: 'Farms and Fields in the Roman West Country', in Branigan, K. and Fowler, P.J. (eds.) 1976, 162–82.

FOWLER, P.J. 1978a: 'Pre-Medieval Fields in the Bristol Region', in Bowen, H.C. and Fowler, P.J. (eds.) 1978, 29–48.

FOWLER, P.J. 1978b: 'Lowland landscapes: culture, time and personality', in Limbrey, S. and Evans, J.G. (eds.) 1978, 1–11.

FOWLER, P.J. (ed.) 1975: *Recent Work in Rural Archaeology* (Bradford-on-Avon).

FOX, R. 1967: *Kinship and Marriage* (Harmondsworth).

FRERE, S.S. 1967: *Britannia* (London).

FRERE, S.S. 1975: 'The Origin of "Small Towns"', in Rodwell, W. and Rowley, T. (eds.) 1975, 4–8.

FRERE, S.S. 1982: 'The Bignor Villa', *Britannia*, 13, 135–96.

FRERE, S.S. 1984a: 'Excavations at Dorchester on Thames, 1963', *Arch.J.*, 141, 91–174.

FRERE, S.S. 1986: 'Foreword', in Millett, M. and Graham, D. 1986, xv-xvi.

GAFFNEY, C.F., GAFFNEY, V. and TINGLE, M. 1985: 'Settlement, Economy or Behaviour? Micro-regional Land Use Models and the Interpretation of Surface Artefact Patterning', in Haselgrove, C., Millett, M. and Smith, I. (eds.) 1985, 95–107.

GAFFNEY, C.F. and GAFFNEY, V.L. (eds.) 1987: *Pragmatic Archaeology Theory in Crisis?* (Oxford).

GARDNER, W. and SAVORY, H.N. 1964: *Dinorben: A Hill-Fort Occupied in Early Iron Age and Roman Times* (Cardiff).

GARNSEY, P., HOPKINS, K. and WHITTAKER, C.R. (eds.) 1983: *Trade in the Ancient Economy* (London).

GARNSEY, P. and SALLER, R. 1987: *The Roman Empire: Economy, Society and Culture* (London).

GASCOIGNE, P.E. 1969: 'Clear Cupboard Villa, Farmington, Gloucestershire', *Trans.Bristol Glos.Arch.Soc.*, 88, 34–67.

GOODBURN, R. 1978: 'Winterton: Some villa problems', in Todd, M. (ed.) 1978, 93–102.

GRACIE, H.S. 1970: 'Frocester Court Roman Villa: First Report', *Trans.Bristol Glos.Arch.Soc.*, 89, 15–86.

GRAY, M. 1977: 'Northfield Farm, Long Wittenham', *Oxoniensia*, 42, 1–29.

GREEN, C. and DRAPER, J. 1978: 'The Mileoak Roman Villa, Handley, Towcester, Northamptonshire: Report on the excavations of 1955 and 1956', *Northants.Arch.*, 13, 28–66.

GREEN, H.J.M. 1975: 'Godmanchester', in Rodwell, W. and Rowley, T. (eds.) 1975, 183–210.

GREENE, K. 1986: *The Archaeology of the Roman Economy* (London).

GREGORY, T. 1982: 'Romano-British Settlement in West Norfolk and on the Norfolk Fen Edge', in Miles, D. (ed.) 1982, 351–76.

GRIFFITHS, N. 1982: 'Early Roman Military Metalwork from Wiltshire', *Wilts.Arch.Mag.*, 77, 49–54.

GRIGG, D.B. 1980: *Population growth and agrarian change: An historical perspective* (Cambridge).

GRINSELL, L.V. 1957: 'Archaeological Gazetteer', in *VCH*, 1957, 21–273.

GURNEY, D. 1986: *Settlement, Religion and Industry on the Fen-edge: Three Romano-British Sites in Norfolk* (Hunstanton).

GUTHRIE, A. 1969: 'Excavation of a Settlement at Goldherring, Sancreed, 1958–61', *Cornish Arch.*, 8, 5–39.

HADMAN, J. 1978? 'Aisled buildings in Roman Britain', in Todd, M. (ed.) 1978, 187–96.

HADMAN, J. 1984: 'Ashton, 1979–82', *Durobrivae*, 9, 28–30.

HADMAN, J. and UPEX, S. 1975: 'The Roman Settlement at Ashton near Oundle', *Durobrivae*, 3, 12–5.

HALLAM, S.J. 1970: 'Settlement round the Wash', in Phillips, C.W. (ed.) 1970, 22–113.

HAMPTON, J. and PALMER, R. 1977: 'Implications of Aerial Photography for Archaeology', *Arch.J.*, 134, 157–93.

HANWORTH, R. 1968: 'The Roman Villa at Rapsley, Ewhurst', *Surrey Arch.Coll.*, 65, 1–70.

HARDING, D.W. 1974: *The Iron Age In Lowland Britain* (London).

HARKER, S. 1980: 'Springhead: A Brief Re-Appraisal', in Rodwell, W. (ed.) 1980, 285–8.

HASELGROVE, C.C. 1982: 'Indigenous Settlement Patterns in the Tyne-Tees Lowlands', in Clack, P. and Haselgrove S. (eds.) 1982, 57–103.

HASELGROVE, C.C., MILLETT, M. and SMITH, I. (eds.) 1985: *Archaeology from the Ploughsoil* (Sheffield).

HAVERFIELD, F. 1900: 'Romano-British Remains', in *VCH*, 1900, 265–348.

HAVERFIELD, F. 1906: 'Romano-British Somerset', in *VCH*, 1906, 207–372.

HAVERFIELD, F. 1912: *The Romanization of Roman Britain* (Oxford).

HAWKES, C.F.C. 1947: 'Britons, Romans and Saxons round Salisbury and Cranborne Chase', *Arch.J.*, 104, 27–81.

HAYFIELD, C. 1987: *An Archaeological Survey of the Parish of Wharram Percy, East Yorkshire: 1. The Evolution of the Roman Landscape* (Oxford).

HENCKEN, H. O'NEILL, H.E. 1933: 'An Excavation by H.M. Office of Works at Chysauster, Cornwall, 1931', *Archaeologia*, 83, 237–84.

HENIG, M. 1984: Religion in Roman Britain (London).

HERLIHY, D. 1985: *Medieval Households* (London).

HESLOP, D.H. 1984: 'Initial excavations at Ingleby Barwick, Cleveland', *Durham Arch.J.*, 1, 23–34.

HIGHAM, N.J. 1978: 'Early Field Survival in North Cumbria', in Bowen, H.C., and Fowler, P.J. (eds.) 1978, 119–26.

HIGHAM, N.J. 1982: 'The Roman Impact upon Rural Settlement in Cumbria', in Clack, P. and Haselgrove, S. (eds.) 1982, 105–22.

HIGHAM, N.J. 1986: *The Northern Counties to AD 1000* (London).

HIGHAM, N.J. and JONES, G.D.B. 1975: 'Frontier, Forts and Farmers: Cumbrian Aerial Survey 1974–5', *Arch.J.*, 132, 16–53.

HIGHAM, N.J. and JONES, G.D.B. 1983: 'The Excavation of two Romano-British Farm Sites in North Cumbria', *Britannia*, 14, 45–72.

HIGHAM, N.J. and JONES, G.D.B. 1985: *The Carvetii* (Gloucester).

HINCHLIFFE, J. and THOMAS, R. 1980: 'Archaeological Investigations at Appleford', *Oxoniensia*, 45, 9–111.

HINGLEY, R. 1984a: 'The Archaeology of Settlement and the Social Significance of Space', *Scottish Archaeological Review*, 3, 22–26.

HINGLEY, R. 1984b: 'Towards Social Analysis in Archaeology: Celtic Society in the Iron Age of the Upper Thames Valley', in Cunliffe B.W. and Miles, D. (eds.) 1984, 72–88.

HINGLEY, R. 1984c: 'Towns, Trade and Social Organisation in Later Roman Britain', *Scottish Archaeological Review*, 3, 87–91.

HINGLEY, R. 1985a: 'Location, Function and Status: A Romano-British "Religious-Complex" at the Noah's Ark Inn, Frilford (Oxfordshire)', *OJA*, 4, 201–14.

HINGLEY, R. 1985b: 'Fulbrook; Fulbrook Castle', *West Midlands Archaeology*, No 28, 57–8.

HINGLEY, R. 1987a: 'Can we have a Pragmatic Integrated Archaeology', in Gaffney, C.F. and Gaffney, V.L. (eds.) 1987, 89–106.

HINGLEY, R. 1987b: 'Brailes', *West Midlands Archaeology*, 30, 44.

HINGLEY, R. 1988: 'The influence of Rome on indigenous social groups in the Upper Thames valley', in Jones, R.F., Bloemers, J.H.F., Dyson, S.L. and Biddle, M. (eds.) 1988, 73–98.

HODDER, B.W. and UKWU, U.I. 1969: *Markets in West Africa* (Ibadan).

HODDER, I.R. 1972: 'Locational models and the study of Romano-British Settlement', in Clarke, D. (ed.) 1972, 887–907.

HODDER, I.R. and MILLETT, M. 1980: 'Romano-British Villas and Towns: A systematic analysis', *World Archaeology*, 12, 69–76.

HODGES, R. and WILDGOOSE, M. 1981: 'Roman or Native in the White Peak: The Roystone Grange Project and its Regional Implications', *Derby Arch.J.*, 101, 42–57.

HODSON, F.R. 1964: 'Cultural Groupings within the British Pre-Roman Iron Age', *Proc.Prehist.Soc.*, 30, 99–110.

HOGG, A.H.A. 1966: 'Native Settlement in Wales', in Thomas, C. (ed.) 1966, 28–38.

HOGG, A.H.A. 1974: 'The Llantwit Major Villa: A reconsideration of the evidence', *Britannia*, 5, 225–50.

HOGG, A.H.A. 1975: 'Din Lligwy', *Arch.J.*, 132, 285–6.

HOGG, A.H.A. 1979: 'Invasion and Response: The Problem in Wales', in Burnham, B. and Johnson, H. (eds.) 1979, 285–98.

HOOKE, D. 1985: 'Village Development in the West Midlands', in Hooke, D. (ed.) 1985, 125–54.

HOOKE, D. (ed.) 1985: *Medieval Villages* (Oxford).

HOPKINS, K. 1980: 'Taxes and Trade in the Roman Empire (200 BC-AD 400)', *JRS*, 70, 101–25.

HOPKINS, K. 1983: 'Introduction', in Garnsey, P., Hopkins, K. and Whittaker, C.R. (eds.) 1983, ix-xxv.

HOSKINS, W.G. 1954: 'The Medieval Period', in Martin, A.F. and Steel, R.W. (eds.) 1954, 103–20.

HUNTER, R. and MYNARD, D. 1977: 'Excavations at Thorplands near Northampton, 1970 and 1974', *Northants.Arch.*, 12, 97–154.

JACKSON, D.A. 1980: 'Roman Buildings at Ringstead, Northants', *Northants.Arch.*, 15, 12–34.

JACKSON, J.E. 1862: 'On a Roman Villa discovered at North Wraxhall', *Wilts.Arch.Mag.*, 7, 59–80.

JARRETT, M.G. 1963: 'Excavations at Llys Brychan, Llangadog, 1961', *Carm.Ant.*, 4, 2–8.

JARRETT, M.G. and WRATHMELL, S. 1981: *Whitton: An Iron Age and Roman Farmstead in South Glamorgan* (Cardiff).

JARVIS, K. and MAXFIELD, V. 1975: 'The Excavation of a First-Century Roman Farmstead and a Late Neolithic Settlement, Topsham, Devon', *Proc.Devon Arch.Soc.*, 33, 209–66.

JOBEY, G. 1964: 'Enclosed Stone Built Settlements in North Northumberland', *Arch.Ael.*, 42, 41–64.

JOBEY, G. 1966: 'Homesteads and Settlement of the Frontier Area', in Thomas, C. (ed.) 1966, 1–14.

JOBEY, G. 1973: 'A Romano-British Settlement at Tower Knowe, Wellhaugh, Northumberland, 1972', *Arch.Ael.*, 1, 55–80.

JOBEY, G. 1977: 'Iron Age and later farmsteads on Belling Law, Northumberland', *Arch.Ael.*, 5, 1–38.

JOBEY, G. 1978: 'Iron Age and Romano-British settlements on Kennel Hall Knowe, North Tynedale, Northumberland (1976)', *Arch.Ael.*, 6, 1–28.

JOBEY, G. 1982a: 'Between Tyne and Forth: Some Problems', in Clack, P. and Haselgrove, S. (ed.) 1982, 7–20.

JOBEY, G. 1982b: 'The Settlement at Doubstead and Romano-British Settlement on the coastal plain between Tyne and Forth', *Arch.Ael.*, 10, 1–23.

JOBEY, I. 1981: 'Excavations on the Romano-British Settlement at Middle Gunnar Peak, Barrasford, Northumberland', *Arch.Ael.*, 9, 51–74.

JOHNSON, A. 1975: 'Excavations at Bourton Grounds, Thornborough, 1973', *Records Bucks*, 20, 3–56.

JOHNSON, N. and ROSE, P. 1982: 'Defended Settlement in Cornwall – an Illustrated Discussion', in Miles, D. (ed.) 1982, 151–208.

JOHNSON, S. 1975: 'Vici in Lowland Britain', Rodwell, W. and Rowley, T. (ed.) 1975, 75–84.

JOHNSTON, D.E. 1978: 'Villas of Hampshire and the Isle of Wight', in Todd, M. (ed.) 1978, 71–92.

JONES, A.H.M. 1964: *The Later Roman Empire 284–602* (Oxford).

JONES, G.D.B. 1984: '"Becoming different without knowing it: The role and development of *vici*', in Blagg, T.F.C. and King A.C. (eds.) 1984, 75–91.

JONES, G.D.B. and WALKER, J. 1983: 'Either side of Solway: Towards a minimalist view of Romano-British agricultural settlement in the North-West', in Chapman, J.C. and Mytum, H.C. (eds.) 1983, 185–204.

JONES, G.R.J. 1985: 'Forms and Patterns of Medieval Settlements in Welsh Wales', in Hooke, D. (ed.) 1985, 155–70.

JONES, M. and MILES, D. 1979: 'Celt and Roman in the Thames Valley: approaches to culture change', in Burnham, B.C. and Johnston, H.C. (eds.) 1979, 315–25.

JONES, R.F.J. 1987: 'The Archaeologists of Roman Britain', *Bull.Inst.Arch.Lond.*, 24, 85–97.

JONES, R.F.J., BLOEMERS, J.H.F., DYSON, S.L. and BIDDLE, M. (eds.) 1988: *First Millennium Papers: Western Europe in the First Millennium AD* (Oxford).

KAY, S.O. 1951: 'A Romano-British Site at Shirebrook', *Derby.Arch.J.*, 24, 79–80.

KEESING, R.M. 1975: *Kin Groups and Social Structure* (London).

KNOCKER, G.M. 1965: 'Excavations in Collyweston Great Wood, Northamptonshire', *Arch.J.*, 122, 52–72.

KNOWLES, A.K. 1977: 'The Roman Settlement at Brampton, Norfolk: Interim report', *Britannia*, 8, 209–22.

LEACH, P. 1982: *Ilchester: Volume 1 Excavations 1974–1975* (Bristol).

LEDAY, A. 1980: *La Campagne à l'époque romaine dans le Centre de la Gaule* (Oxford).

LEECH, R. 1976: 'Larger Agricultural Settlements in the West Country', in Branigan, K. and Fowler, P.J. (eds.) 1976, 142–61.

LEECH, R. 1981: 'The Excavation of a Romano-British Farmstead and Cemetery on Bradley Hill, Somerton, Somerset', *Britannia*, 12, 177–252.

LEECH, R. 1982: *Excavations at Catsgore, 1970–3* (Bristol).

LIDDELL, D.M. 1931: 'Notes on two excavations in Hampshire', *Proc.Hants.Field Club*, 10, 224–36.

LIMBREY, S. and EVANS, J.G. 1978: *The effect of man on the landscape: the lowland zone* (London).

LING, R. and COURTNEY, T. 1981: 'Excavations at Carsington, 1979–80', *Derby.Arch.J.*, 101, 58–87.

LITTLE, R.I. 1964: 'The Atwood Iron Age and Romano-British Site, Sanderstead, 1960', *Surrey Arch.Coll.*, 61, 29–38.

LIVERSIDGE, J. 1973: *Britain in the Roman Empire* (London).

LLOYD-JONES, M. 1984: *Society and Settlement in Wales and the Marches: 500 BC to AD 1100* (Oxford).

LONGWORTH, I. and CHERRY, J. (eds.) 1986: *Archaeology in Britain since 1945* (London).

LUCAS, J. 1981: 'Tripontium, Third Interim Report', *Trans.Birmingham.Warw. Arch.Soc.*, 91, 25–54.

MACKRETH, D. 1979: 'Durobrivae', *Durobrivae*, 7, 19–21.

MACMULLEN, R. 1974: *Roman Social Relations* (London).

MANNING, W.H. 1972: 'Ironwork Hoards in Iron Age and Roman Britain', *Britannia*, 3, 224–50.

MANN, M. 1986: *The Sources of Social Power, Volume 1* (Cambridge).

MARTIN, A.F. and STEEL, R.W. (eds.) 1954: *The Oxford Region: A Scientific and Historical Survey* (Oxford).

MASON, D.J.P. 1987: 'Chester, The Canabae Legionis', *Britannia*, 18, 143–68.

MASSON PHILLIPS, E.N. 1966: 'Excavation of a Romano-British Site at Lower Well Farm, Stoke Gabriel, Devon', *Devon Arch.J.*, 23, 3–34.

MAXWELL, G.S. and WILSON, D.R. 1987: 'Aerial Reconnaissance in Roman Britain 1977–84', *Britannia*, 18, 1–48.

MAY, J. 1970: 'Dragonby, An Interim Report on Excavations on an Iron Age and Romano-British site near Scunthorp, Lincs', *Ant.J.*, 50, 222–45.

MEATES, G.W. 1973: 'Farningham Roman Villa II', *Arch.Cant.*, 88, 1–21.

MEATES, G.W. 1979: *The Roman Villa at Lullingstone, Kent. 1: The Site* (London).

MILES, D. 1978: 'The Upper Thames Valley', in Bowen, H.C. and Fowler, P.J. (eds.) 1978, 81–8.

MILES, D. 1982: 'Confusion in the Countryside: Some Comments from the Upper Thames Region', in Miles, D. (ed.) 1982, 53–79.

MILES, D. 1984a: 'Romano-British Settlement in the Gloucestershire Thames Valley', in Saville, A. (ed.) 1984, 191–212.

MILES, D. 1984b: *Archaeology at Barton Court Farm, Abingdon, Oxon* (Dorchester).

MILES, D. (ed.) 1982: *The Romano-British Countryside: Studies in Rural Settlement and Economy* (Oxford).

MILES, H. 1969: 'Excavations at Fisherwick, Staffs, 1968 – A Romano-British Farm-stead and a Neolithic Occupation Site', *Trans.South Staffs.Arch.Hist.Soc.*, 10, 1–22.

MILES, H. 1977: 'The Honeyditches Roman Villa, Seaton, Devon', *Britannia*, 8, 107–48.

MILES, H. and MILES, T. 1973: 'Excavations at Trethurgy, St Austell: Interim Report', *Cornish Arch.*, 12, 25–9.

MILLETT, M. and GRAHAM, D. 1986: *Excavations on the Romano-British Small Town at Neatham, Hampshire, 1969–1979* (Gloucester).

MONEY, J.H. 1977: 'The Iron-Age Hill-fort and Romano-British Iron-working Settlement at Garden Hill, Sussex: Interim Report on Excavations, 1968–76', *Britannia*, 8, 339–50.

MORRIS, P. 1979: *Agricultural Buildings in Roman Britain* (Oxford).

MYNARD, D.C. 1987: *Roman Milton Keynes: Excavations and Fieldwork 1971–82* (Aylesbury).

NEAL, D.S. 1970: 'The Roman Villa at Boxmoor: Interim Report', *Britannia*, 1, 156–62.

NEAL, D.S. 1974: *The Excavation of the Roman Villa in Gadebridge Park, Hemel Hempstead, 1963–8* (London).

NEAL, D.S. 1978: 'The growth and decline of villas in the Verulamium area', in Todd, M. (ed.) 1978, 33–58.

NEAL, D.S. 1982: 'Romano-British villas: one or two storied?', in Drury, P.J. (ed.) 1982, 153–71.

O'NEIL, H.E. 1945: 'The Roman Villa at Park Street, near St Albans, Hertfordshire: Report on the Excavations of 1943–45', *Arch.J.*, 102, 21–110.

ØRSTED, P. 1985: *Roman Imperial Economy and Romanization* (Copenhagen).

OSWALD, A. and BUXTON, L.H.D. 1937: 'A Roman Fortified Villa at Norton Disney, Lincs', *Ant.J.*, 17, 138–78.

OSWALD, A. 1949: 'A Re-Excavation of the Roman Villa at Mansfield Woodhouse, Nottinghamshire, 1936–9', *Trans.Thornton Soc.Notts.*, 53, 1–14.

PALMER, N. 1982: *Roman Stratford* (Warwick).

PARTRIDGE, C.R. 1975: 'Braughing', in Rodwell, W. and Rowley, T. (eds.) 1975, 139–58.

PARTRIDGE, C.R. 1981: *Skeleton Green: A Late Iron Age and Romano-British Site* (Gloucester).

PERCIVAL, J. 1976: *The Roman Villa* (London).

PHILLIPS, C.W. (ed.) 1970: *The Fenland in Roman Times: Studies of a major area of peasant colonization* (London).

PHILP, B. 1968: *Excavations at Faversham 1965. The Royal Abbey, Roman Villa and Belgic Farmstead* (London).

PHILP, B. 1984: *Excavations in the Darent Valley, Kent* (Gloucester).

POLLARD, S. 1974: 'A Late Iron Age Settlement and a Romano-British Villa at Holcombe, near Uplyme, Devon', *Devon Arch.*, 32, 59–161.

POTTER, T.W. 1981: 'The Roman Occupation of the Central Fenland', *Britannia*, 12, 79–133.

POTTER, T.W. 1986: 'A Roman Province: Britain AD 43–410', in Longworth, I. and Cherry, J. (eds.) 1986, 73–118.

POTTER, T.W. and JACKSON, R.P.J. 1984: 'British Museum Excavations at Stonea, 1983', *Fenland Research*, 1, 27–31.

POWELL, T.G.E. 1958: *The Celts* (London).

RADFORD, C.A.R. 1936: 'The Roman Villa at Ditchley, Oxon', *Oxoniensia*, 1, 24–69.

RAHTZ, P. 1963: 'A Roman Villa at Downton', *Wilts.Arch.Mag.*, 58, 303–41.

RAMM, H. 1978: *The Parisi* (London).

RAWES, B. 1981: 'The Romano-British site at Brockworth, Gloucestershire', *Britannia*, 12, 45–78.

RCAHMWM 1956: *An Inventory of the Ancient Monuments in Caernarvonshire: Volume 1: East* (London).

RCAHMWM 1964: *An Inventory of the Ancient Monuments in Caernarvonshire: Volume 3, West* (London).

RCHME 1936: *An Inventory of the Historical Monuments in Westmorland* (London).

RCHME 1976: *Iron Age and Romano-British Monuments in the Gloucestershire Cotswolds* (London).

RCHME 1980: *Northamptonshire: An Archaeological Atlas* (London).

RCHME 1983: 'West Park Roman Villa, Rockbourne, Hampshire', *Arch.J.*, 140, 129–50.

REECE, R. 1972: 'A Short Survey of the Roman Coins Found on Fourteen Sites in Britain', *Britannia*, 3, 269–76.

REECE, R. 1973: 'Roman Coinage in the Western Empire', *Britannia*, 4, 227–52.

REECE, R. 1982: 'Review of Roman Britain by P. Salway', *Arch.J.*, 139, 453–6.

REYNOLDS, S. 1977: *An Introduction to the History of the English Medieval Towns* (Oxford).

RICHMOND, I.R. 1955: *Roman Britain* (Oxford).

RICHMOND, I.R. 1969: 'The Plans of Roman Villas in Britain', in Rivet, A.L.F. (ed.) 1969, 49–70.

RILEY, D. 1978: 'An Early System of Land Division in South Yorkshire and North Nottinghamshire', in Bowen, H.C. and Fowler, P.J. (eds.) 1978, 103–8.

RILEY, D. 1980: *Early Landscapes from the Air: Studies of Crop Marks in South Yorkshire and North Nottinghamshire* (Sheffield).

RIVET, A.L.F. 1969: 'Social and Economic Aspects', in Rivet, A.L.F. (ed.) 1969, 173–216.

RIVET, A.L.F. 1970a: *Town and Country in Roman Britain* (London).

RIVET, A.L.F. 1970b: 'The British Section of the Antonine Itinerary', *Britannia*, 1, 34–82.

RIVET, A.L.F. 1975: 'Summing Up: The Classification of Minor Towns and Related Settlements', in Rodwell, W. and Rowley, T. (eds.) 1975, 111–14.

RIVET, A.L.F. (ed.) 1969: *The Roman Villa in Britain* (London).

RIVET, A.L.F. and SMITH, C. 1979: *The Place-Names of Roman Britain* (London).

RODWELL, K. (ed.) 1975: *Historic Towns in Oxfordshire: A Survey of the New County* (Oxford).

RODWELL, W. 1975: 'Trinovantian Towns and their Setting', in Rodwell, W. and Rowley, T. (eds.) 1975, 85–102.

RODWELL, W. 1978a: 'Buildings and Settlements in South-East Britain in the Late Iron Age', in Cunliffe, B.W. and Rowley, T. (eds.) 1978, 25–42.

RODWELL, W. 1978b: 'Relict Landscapes in Essex', in Bowen, H.C. and Fowler, P.J. (eds.) 1978, 89–98.

RODWELL, W. (ed.) 1980: *Temples, Churches and Religion: Recent Research in Roman Britain* (Oxford).

RODWELL, W. and RODWELL, K. 1985: *Rivenhall: investigations of a villa, church and village, 1950–1977* (London).

RODWELL, W. and ROWLEY, T. (eds.) 1975: *Small Towns of Roman Britain* (Oxford).

ROGERSON, A. 1977: 'Excavations at Scole, 1973', *East Anglian Arch.*, no. 5, p. 97–222 (Dereham).

ROWLEY, T. 1975: 'Alchester and Dorchester on Thames', in Rodwell, W. and Rowley, T. (eds.) 1975, 115–24.

RUDLING, D.R. 1982: 'Rural Settlement in Late Iron Age and Roman Sussex', in Miles, D. (ed.) 1982, 269–88.

SALWAY, P. 1965: *The Frontier People of Roman Britain* (London).

SALWAY, P. 1970: 'The Roman Fenland', in Phillips, C.W. (ed.) 1970, 1–21.

SALWAY, P. 1981: *Roman Britain* (Oxford).

SAUNDERS, A. 1972: 'The Excavations at Grambla, Wendron, 1972: Interim Report', *Cornish Arch.*, 11, 50–2.

SAUNDERS, A. and HARRIS, D. 1982: 'Excavation at Castle Gotha, St Austell', *Cornish Arch.*, 21, 109–53.

SAVILLE, A. (ed.) 1984: *Archaeology in Gloucestershire* (Gloucester).

SELKIRK, A. 1983: 'Gorhambury', *Current Archaeology*, 8:4, 115–21.

SHAW, B.D. 1979: 'Rural Periodic Markets in Roman North Africa as Mechanisms of Social Integration and Control', in Dalton, G. (ed.) 1979, 91–117.

SILVESTER, B. 1984: 'Roman Seaton and the Axe', *Devon Arch.*, 2, 25–8.

SIMCO, A. 1984: *Survey of Bedfordshire: The Roman Period* (Bedford).

SLOFSTRA, J. 1983: 'An anthropological approach to the study of romanization Processes', in Brandt, R. and Slofstra, J. (ed.) 1983, 71–104.

SMITH, C. 1974: 'A Morphological Analysis of Late Prehistoric and Romano-British Settlements in North-West Wales', *Proc.Prehist.Soc.*, 40, 157–69.

SMITH, C. 1977a: 'The valleys of the Tame and middle Trent – their populations and ecology during the late first millennium BC', in Collis, J. (ed.) 1977, 51–61.

SMITH, C. 1977b: 'Later Prehistoric and Romano-British Enclosed Homesteads in North-West Wales', *Arch.Camb.*, 126, 38–52.

SMITH, C. 1984: 'Excavations at the Ty Mawr Hut-Circles, Holyhead, Anglesey', *Arch.Camb.*, 133, 64–82.

SMITH, D.J. 1978: 'Regional aspects of the winged corridor villa in Britain', in Todd, M. (ed.) 1978, 117–48.

SMITH, J.T. 1963: 'Romano-British Aisled Houses', *Arch.J.*, 120, 1–30.

SMITH, J.T. 1978a: 'Villas as a key to social structure', in Todd, M. (ed.) 1978, 149–56.

SMITH, J.T. 1978b: 'Halls or Yards? A problem of villa-interpretation', *Britannia*, 9, 349–56.

SMITH, J.T. 1982: 'Villa Plans and Social Structure in Britain and Gaul', *Caesarodunum*, 17, 321–51.

SMITH, J.T. 1985: 'Barnsley Park Villa: Its Interpretation and Implications', *OJA*, 4, 341–51.

SMITH, J.T. 1987: 'The Social Structure of a Roman Villa: Marshfield – Ironmongers Piece', *OJA*, 6, 243–55.

SMITH, R.F. 1987: *Roadside Settlements in Lowland Roman Britain: A Gazetteer and Study of their Origins, Growth and Decline, Property Boundaries and Cemeteries* (Oxford).

SOMMER, C.S. 1984: *The Military Vici in Roman Britain* (Oxford).

STEAD, I.M. 1980: *Rudston Roman Villa* (Leeds).

STEAD, I.M. and RIGBY, V. 1986: *Baldock: the excavation of a Roman and pre-Roman settlement, 1968–72* (Gloucester).

STE CROIX, G.E.M. DE 1981: *The Class Struggle in the Ancient Greek World* (London).

STEVENS, C.E. 1947: 'A Possible Conflict of Laws in Roman Britain', *JRS*, 37, 132–4.

STEVENS, C.E. 1966: 'The Social and Economic Aspects of Rural Settlement', in Thomas, C. (ed.) 1966, 108–28.

TAYLOR, C.C. 1984: *Village and Farmstead: a history of rural settlement in England* (London).

TAYLOR, M.V. 1939a: 'Introduction', in *VCH, 1939*, 267–71.

TAYLOR, M.V. 1939b: 'Country Houses', in *VCH, 1939*, 306–23.

THOMAS, C. 1966: 'The Character and Origins of Roman Dumnonia', in Thomas, C. (ed.) 1966, 74–98.

THOMAS C. (ed.) 1966: *Rural Settlement in Roman Britain* (London).

THOMAS, N. 1957: 'Excavations at Callow Hill, Glympton and Stonesfield, Oxon', *Oxoniensia*, 22, 11–53.

THOMAS, R. unpublished: *Roman Abingdon: An Assessment of the Evidence* (Unpublished Dissertation, University of Southampton).

THOMAS, W.G. and WALKER, R.F. 1953: 'Excavations at Trelissey, Pembrokeshire, 1950–1', *Bull.Board Celtic Stud.*, 18, 295–303.

TODD, M. 1969: 'The Roman Settlement at Margidunum: The Excavations of 1966–8', *Trans.Thornton Soc.Notts.*, 73.

TODD, M. 1970: 'The Small Towns of Roman Britain', *Britannia*, 1, 114–30.

TODD, M. 1973: *The Coritani* (London).

TODD, M. 1975: 'The Romano-British Rural Settlement at Staunton, Nottinghamshire', *Trans.Thornton Soc.Notts.*, 79, 29–39.

TODD, M. 1976: 'The *Vici* of Western England', in Branigan, K. and Fowler, P.J. (eds.) 1976, 99–119.

TODD, M. 1978: 'Villas and Romano-British society', in Todd, M. (ed.) 1978, 197–208.

TODD, M. 1981: *The Iron Age and Roman settlement at Whitwell, Leicestershire* (Leicester).

TODD, M. 1987: *The South West to AD 1000* (London).

TODD, M. (ed.) 1978: *Studies in the Romano-British Villa* (Leicester).

TROW, S. and JAMES, S. 1985: *Ditches Villa 1985* (Privately circulated.)

VCH 1900: *A History of Hampshire and the Isle of Wight, Volume 1* (London).

VCH 1906: *A History of Somerset, Volume 1* (London).

VCH 1939: *A History of Oxfordshire, Volume 1* (London).

VCH 1957: *A History of Wiltshire, Volume 1: Part 1* (London).

VCH 1973: *A History of Wiltshire, Volume 1: Part 2* (London).

VINOGRADOFF, P. 1905: *The Growth of the Manor* (London).

WACHER, J. 1974: *The Towns of Roman Britain* (London).

WAINWRIGHT, G. 1968: 'The Excavation of a Durotrigian Farmstead near Tollard Royal in Cranbourne Chase, Southern England', *Proc.Prehist.Soc.*, 34, 102–47.

WAINWRIGHT, G. 1971: 'The Excavation of a Fortified Settlement at Walesland Rath, Pembrokeshire', *Britannia*, 2, 48–116.

WALTHEW, C.V. 1975: 'The Town House and Villa House in Roman Britain', *Britannia*, 6, 189–205.

WARD, J. 1907: 'Roman Remains at Cwmbrwyn, Carmarthenshire', *Arch.Camb.*, 7, 175–212.

WARD PERKINS, J.B. 1938: 'The Roman Villa at Lockleys, Welwyn', *Ant.J.*, 18, 339–76.

WEBSTER, G. 1969: 'The Future of Villa Studies', in Rivet, A.L.F. (ed.) 1969, 217–49.

WEBSTER, G. 1975a: *The Cornovii* (London).

WEBSTER, G. 1975b: 'Small Towns without Defences', in Rodwell, W. and Rowley, T. (eds.) 1975, 53–66.

WEBSTER, G. 1983: 'The Function of Chedworth Roman "Villa"', *Trans.Bristol Glos.Arch.Soc.*, 101, 5–20.

WEBSTER, G. and HOBLEY, B. 1964: 'Aerial Reconnaissance over the Warwickshire Avon', *Arch.J.*, 121, 1–22.

WEBSTER, G. and SMITH, L. 1982: 'The Excavation of a Romano-British Rural Settlement at Barnsley Park: Part II', *Trans.Bristol Glos.Arch.Soc.*, 100, 65–190.

WEBSTER, G. and SMITH, L. 1987: 'Reply to JT Smith's suggested re-interpretation of Barnsley Park Villa', *OAJ*, 6, 69–89.

WHEELER, R.E.M. 1923: 'A Roman Site in Pembrokeshire', *Arch.Camb.*, 3, 211–24.

WILD, J.P. 1974: 'Roman Settlement in the Lower Nene Valley', *Arch.J.*, 131, 140–70.

WILLIAMS, A.M. 1909: 'The Romano-British Establishment at Stroud, near Petersfield, Hants', *Arch.J.*, 66, 33–52.

WILLIAMS, J. 1976: 'Excavations on a Roman site at Overstone near Northamptonshire', *Northants.Arch.*, 11, 100–33.

WILLIAMSON, T.M. 1984: 'The Roman Countryside: Settlement and Agriculture in North West Essex', *Britannia*, 15, 225–230.

WILMOTT, A.R. 1980: 'Kenchester (Magnis): A Reconsideration', *Trans.Wool. Nat.Field Club*, 43, 117–34.

WILSON, D.R. 1974: 'Romano-British Villas from the Air', *Britannia*, 5, 251–60.

WILSON, D.R. 1975: 'The "Small Towns" of Roman Britain from the Air', in Rodwell, W. and Rowley, T. (eds.) 1975, 9–49.

WILSON, D.R. 1982: *Air Photo Interpretation for Archaeologists* (London).

WINBOLT, S.E. 1926: 'The Roman Villa at Folkestone', *Arch.Cant.*, 38, 45–50.

WINDELL, D. 1983: 'Clay Lane 1980. Interim report', *Northants.Arch.*, 18, 33–42.

WOLSELEY, G.R. and SMITH, R.A. 1926–7: 'Prehistoric and Roman Settlements on Park Brow', *Archaeologia*, 76, 1–40.

YOUNG, C. 1986: 'The Upper Thames Valley in the Roman Period', in Briggs, G., Cooke, J. and Rowley, T. (eds.) 1986, 58–63.

Index

Abingdon 115, 137
administration 2, 11, 25–6, 88, 90, 94, 114, 128, 133, 145
aerial photography 14, 56, 57, 75, 88, 97, 99, 100, 124, 139, 145
Africa 115
aisled houses 39–45, 48, 67–71, 80, 84, 136, 149–50, 152, 153, 154, 155
Alcester 81, 93
Alchester 74, 87, 115
ancestors 7–9
annona 26
Applebaum, S 39, 41, 43, 102, 106, 107, 155
Appleford 160–1
army 21, 114, 120, 127, 133, 139, 144, 145, 160
Ashton 57, 71, 73, 74
Atrebates 136–7

Baldock 82, 89, 115
Bancroft 40, 66
Barnsley Park 48
Barton Court 66, 76
Bath 90, 136
bath-house 21, 31, 41, 45, 55, 64, 65, 67, 69, 84, 153, 154, 159
Beadlam 68
Belgae 136–7
Belgium 71, 105, 106
Bignor 52, 85, 107
Bodeni 43
Boxmoor 47, 49
Brading 86
Bradley Hill 36, 37, 48, 55, 58, 59–60, 76, 150–1
Brampton 93
Branigan, K 107, 136
Braughing 71, 73, 74, 81, 117
Brigantes 139–40
Brixworth 45, 46
Bronze Age 129
Bryngwyn Caerwys 98–9
Bullock Down 161

Callow Hill 109
Camerton 87
Cantiaci 134–6
Carn Euny 147

Carsington 38
Carvetii 139–40
Catsgore 13, 30, 35, 36, 56, 58, 59, 60, 67, 77, 78, 80, 81, 89, 97
Catuvellauni 137
Cefn Graeanog 62
Celtic 5, 7–8, 9, 41, 116, 150, 159, 161
Chalton 77
Charterhouse-on-Mendip 82
Chedworth 52, 54, 67, 85
Chelmsford 36
Chesterton-on-Fosse 115, 117
Chew Stoke 127
Chignall St James 15, 16
Chiragan 105
Chisenbury Warren 77, 89
Churchover 115
Chysauster 23, 55, 60, 63, 77, 78, 143
Cirencester 137
civitas 10, 25, 133
civitas capitals 2, 4, 10, 47, 57, 88, 90, 118, 133
Claydon Pike 40, 56, 80, 83, 84, 154, 155, 160
Clay Lane 46, 58
Clear Cupboard 36, 49
clients 146
climate 12, 124, 146, 148
Collingwood, R 2, 11, 122, 124, 128–9
coloni 117
colonia 2, 90, 118
Columella 22
Combe Down 127
Combley 40, 66
community 5, 6, 8–9, 75, 97, 100, 109, 127, 131, 144, 149, 152–6, 157, 158
compound 6, 8, 55–73, 75, 76, 80, 82–6, 87, 89, 93, 97, 100, 147–8, 149, 150–2, 153, 155, 160
  agricultural 83–6, 153, 154, 155
  villa 8, 64–71, 83, 151, 153, 154
Corbridge 90
Coritani 137, 138–9, 142
Cornovii 138–9, 142
corridor house 37, 45–6, 65, 67–71, 83, 117
Cotswold 112, 137, 157
'cottage house' 37–9, 46, 48, 50, 51, 155
courtyard house 41, 51–4, 57, 76, 83, 107, 136, 138, 155, 159

Index

Cox Green 49
Cranborne Chase 122, 124, 128, 129, 131, 136, 159
Crosby Garrett 15
Crosby Ravensworth 77, 140
Cuniffe, B 129, 135
Cwmbrwyn 36, 62

Dartmoor 76
Davies, J 116
Demetae 141–2
Detsicas, A 136
Din Lligwy 62
Dinorben 34–5, 82–3, 84, 147, 154
Ditchley 51, 57, 109
Dobunni 28, 112–3, 114, 119, 136, 137, 138, 139
Dorchester-on-Thames 91, 136
Downton 46
Dragonby 72, 73
Dumnoni 142
Dunston's Clump 36, 96
Durotriges 136–7

Egypt 131
élite 2, 4, 22, 53, 100, 121, 122, 123
Emperor 24, 97, 124, 127, 128, 132, 153, 156
enclosure 55–9, 139, 140, 142, 143, 144, 147–8
estate 11, 12, 21–2, 24, 41, 47, 53, 67, 71, 87, 95, 100–9, 110, 117, 118, 120, 121, 124, 127, 134, 146, 147, 151, 152, 154, 155, 156, 158
Ewell 122, 123
excavation 13–4, 55, 57, 71, 74, 75, 76, 78, 86, 87, 97, 100, 111, 124, 126, 139, 150, 152
exchange 10–11

fair 115–6
familia 7, 154
family 5, 6–8, 64, 65, 67, 78, 97, 100, 119, 122, 124, 147, 149–52, 153–6, 157, 159
    extended 6–8, 39, 41–5, 55, 59, 60, 64, 71, 149–52, 155, 158
    nuclear 6–8, 37, 39, 42, 55, 59, 60, 64, 149, 150, 151, 152, 158
Feltwell 38
Fenland 12, 15, 16–7, 56, 75, 76, 95, 97, 99–100, 101, 114, 124, 125, 128, 131, 137, 153, 157, 158, 159, 160, 161
festival 146
field survey 14–9, 75, 76, 97, 99, 124
Fishbourne 51, 53
Folkestone 51
Forcegarth Pasture 61, 96
fort 3, 26, 115, 144, 145
Fotheringhay 102, 103, 137

France 48, 105
Frere, SS 88
Frilford 82, 92, 102, 103, 104, 105, 116, 117, 118, 120, 137
Frocester Court 38, 66

Gadebridge 50
Gardner, W 147
Garnsey, P 151
Gatcombe 71, 72, 87, 107, 108, 153
Gaul 6, 8, 21, 48, 71, 83, 106
Gayton Thorpe 65, 68, 151
Germany 6, 41, 48, 71, 83, 106
girdle-pattern 95–100, 131, 152–3, 158
Glastonbury 8, 44–5, 55, 60, 150
Godmanchester 80, 91, 118
Goldherring 63
Gorhambury 32, 39, 84, 86, 154, 155
Grambla 33, 63
granary 44
Grandford 17, 160
Great Chesterford 117
Gwithian 144

Hadrian's Wall 139
Hallam, S 16, 75, 76, 97, 100
hall villa 48, 50
Halstock 68
Hambleden 49
hamlet 75, 76–7, 153
Haverfield, F 2, 3, 133
headman 42–3, 152
Hibaldstow 49, 73, 74, 87, 88
Hodder, I 118
Hogg, A 141
Holcombe 40
Holme House 34, 38, 66
Hopkins, K 9–11
house 8, 30–54, 59, 149
household 6–8, 30, 67, 151, 152
Huntsham 46
hypocaust 21, 41, 42, 43, 45, 69, 71, 153

Iceni 137
Ilchester 87, 136
Imperial estate 95, 127–8, 129, 131, 156, 157, 159
Imperial Post 26, 28
India 1
industry 9–11, 31, 39, 93, 94, 114, 133, 145
inscription 2, 127
Irchester 137
Ireland 7, 9
Iron Age 8, 10, 31, 33, 35, 39, 45, 55, 56, 59, 80, 84, 97, 100, 122, 145, 146, 148, 154, 155
Islip 65
Italy 7

Jones, GR 98

Kelvedon 45
Kenchester 79, 87, 115
Kineton 102

Langton 46
Lands End 143
lease 97, 128, 131, 153
Leech, R 30, 35, 37, 59
Littlebury Green 18–9
Llantwit Major 52, 68
local centre 11, 25–9, 33, 35, 37, 39, 47, 57, 71–4, 78–80, 86–93, 111–20, 121, 123, 128, 133, 134–9, 141, 142, 150, 152, 156
Lockington 17–8, 102, 103
Lockleys 45, 46
Lydia 131
Lye Hole 104

Maddle Farm 17
Mancetter 93
Mansfield Woodhouse 69, 70
mansio 26, 90
market 9, 10–1, 25–9, 111–20, 124, 133, 144, 156, 158
market-hall 90, 91
Marshfield 46, 65
medieval 1, 37, 39, 42, 102–3, 105, 112–3, 114, 115, 151
Middle Gunnar Peak 61, 96
Miles, D 160
Military 2, 25, 80, 111, 114, 133, 142, 143, 144, 157, 160
Millett, M 118
monogamy 150
Montmaurin 105
mosaic 2, 21, 31, 41, 42, 43, 69, 71, 153, 159
municipium 118

Natalinus 43
Nene Valley 39
Neatham 74, 78, 80, 81, 88
non-villa settlement 3, 4, 8, 9, 11, 23–5, 28, 31, 33–4, 35, 37, 39, 56, 59–64, 75–8, 80, 82–3, 95–105, 106, 107, 108, 111, 117–22, 123–7, 131, 134–44, 144–8, 149, 151–7, 159, 160, 161
Norfolk Street 85, 86
North Leigh 52, 109
North Oxfordshire Grim's Ditch 107–8, 109, 122
North Warnborough 40, 43–5, 149, 150, 151, 155, 158
North Wraxhall 15
Norton Disney 67, 69, 70

Odell 33, 55, 56

one-roomed rectangular house 35
Overstone 33
Overton Down 36, 58, 161
ownership 6, 9, 11, 41, 47, 69, 102, 106, 108, 110, 124, 131, 147, 151, 153, 158

Parisi 138–9
Park Brow 58, 129, 130
Park Street 38
peasant 1, 114, 127, 128, 134, 159, 160
Penrith 32, 61
Penwith Uplands 144
Percival, J 105
peripheral holdings 102, 106–8
planning 87–93
polyandry 6–7
polygamy 6–7, 148, 150
population 3–4, 9, 78, 95, 113
Potter, T 159, 160
poverty 5, 9–12, 89, 144–7, 157, 160

Regnenses 134–6
Richmond, I 30, 37, 38, 41, 45, 48, 67, 69
Rivet, A 11, 22, 118, 121, 145
road 26–8, 71, 74, 87, 116, 144
Rochester 136
Rock 46
Rockbourne 38, 52, 65, 67, 68
romanization 2, 23, 34, 133, 141, 142, 147, 153
'round' 143
round house 31–5, 147
Roystone Grange 40

St Enoder 143
Salisbury Plain 124, 127, 131, 136, 157, 159
Saller, R 151
Salway, P 144
Savory, H 147
Scars Farm 104
Scole 57, 73, 82
servant 39, 42, 69, 100, 152
Shakenoak 109
Silloth Farm 61, 96
Silures 138, 139, 141–2
slave 7, 11, 24, 41, 48, 67, 71, 80, 105, 107, 108, 121, 127, 134, 151, 152, 153, 156
small town 3, 4, 25, 93, 124
Smith, J 6, 41, 45, 151
soldiers 26, 160
Sparsholt 69, 70
Spoonley Wood 52
status 11, 31, 45, 65, 69, 80, 83, 131, 148, 153–6, 157, 159
Stonea 17, 90, 91
Stonesfield 104
street 88
Stroud 42, 49, 51, 66, 155

Studland 36, 55, 58, 60, 64
surplus 9, 10, 11, 12, 22, 111, 116, 121, 124, 129, 133, 145, 148, 156
Sussex Coastal Plain 122, 125, 129, 135
Sussex Downs 126, 128, 129, 131
symbol 11, 47, 59, 82, 124, 131, 146, 148, 156, 157, 158, 159

tax 10, 11, 26, 28, 145, 146, 159, 160
temple 31, 90, 92, 116
tenant 11, 24, 35, 41, 48, 67, 82, 83, 100, 105, 107, 108, 121, 128, 131, 134, 156, 159
tenure 9, 87, 97, 102, 105, 106, 124, 131, 144
tessellated floor 21, 31, 69
Thorplands 32
Thruxton 43, 149, 151, 155
Tiddington 40, 87
Todd, M 39, 118, 139, 144
Topsham 45, 46
Towcester 74, 79, 87, 88, 91, 137
Tower Knowe 61
town 2, 3, 9, 78–80, 116, 118–9, 133, 144, 156
trackway 56, 80, 98, 100
trade 9, 146
Tregonning 96
Trelissey 36
Trethurgy 32, 60, 63
tribe 10, 116, 118, 133, 135, 136, 138
Trinovantes 28, 112, 114, 118, 136, 137, 139
two- to three-roomed houses 35–7

'unit system' 8, 50–1, 53–4, 67, 151
Upper Thames Valley 100, 112, 122, 124, 125, 127, 128, 129, 131, 153, 159, 160

Varro 22
Verulamium 137
vicus 2, 25, 88, 111, 139, 143, 144–5

villa 2, 3, 4, 6, 8, 9, 11, 12, 13, 20–3, 31, 33, 35, 37, 39, 43, 45, 47, 55, 57, 64–71, 76–8, 82, 83–6, 95, 100–9, 111, 117–20, 121–3, 124, 127–9, 131–9, 141, 142, 144–50, 153, 155–61
village 23, 75, 76–80, 105, 122, 127, 129, 143, 153
Vinogradoff, P 158
Virgil 22

Wales 26, 30, 31, 33–4, 56, 57, 76, 82, 98–9, 100, 114, 116, 120, 133, 138, 139, 140–2, 144, 145, 146, 151
walls, town 25–6, 90
Wanborough 81, 88
Wasperton 160
Water Newton 79, 87, 90, 93, 115, 117, 118, 137
wealth 2, 3, 5, 7, 9–12, 31, 45, 47, 69, 86–7, 100, 115, 119, 124, 129, 136, 146, 147–8, 158–61
Webster, G 13
Weeting 36
Wessex 15
Wetwang Slack 97, 98, 99, 153
Wharram Grange 18
Whitminster 103
Whitton 32, 33, 62, 64
Whitwell 39
Wiggonholt 107
Winchester 136
winged corridor house 37, 39, 41, 47–51, 57, 67–71, 76, 83, 87, 107, 117, 136, 152, 153, 155, 159
Winterton 32, 70
Witcombe 51, 52, 53
Withington 103
Woodchester 51, 52, 85, 86, 107, 154
Woodcuts 56
Wrington 103, 104
Wymbush 36, 47